D0516167

Second Edition

Active Training

A Handbook of Techniques, Designs, Case Examples, and Tips

Mel Silberman, Ph.D.

assisted by

Carol Auerbach

Jossey-Bass
Pfeiffer

San Francisco

Copyright © 1998 by Jossey-Bass/Pfeiffer

ISBN: 0-7879-3989-7

Library of Congress Cataloging-in-Publication Data

Silberman, Melvin L.
    Active training : a handbook of techniques, designs, case
examples, and tips / Mel Silberman with Carol Auerbach. — 2nd ed.
        p.   cm.
    ISBN 0-7879-3989-7
    1. Employees—Training of—Handbooks, manuals, etc.   I. Auerbach,
Carol.   II. Title.
HF5549.5.T7S555   1998
658.3'124—dc21   98-17420

Printed in the United States of America

Published by

Jossey-Bass
Pfeiffer

350 Sansome Street, 5th Floor
San Francisco, California 94104-1342
(415) 433-1740; Fax (415) 433-0499
(800) 274-4434; Fax (800) 569-0443

Visit our website at: www.pfeiffer.com

Acquiring Editor: Larry Alexander   Marketing Manager: Matt Holt
Director of Development: Kathleen Dolan Davies   Copyeditor: Helen Hyams
Developmental Editor: Susan Rachmeler   Interior Design: Joseph Piliero
Senior Production Editor: Dawn Kilgore   Cover Design: Jennifer Hines

Printing 10 9 8 7 6 5 4 3

 This book is printed on acid-free, recycled stock that meets or exceeds the minimum
GPO and EPA requirements for recycled paper.

To my parents, Elsie and Jules Silberman.
May their memory be for a blessing.

Contents

Figures

Preface

*B*ack in 1990, I set out to write a comprehensive text about training. The first edition of *Active Training* had three goals:

1. To explore all aspects of training.

Training has a front end, a middle, and a back end. The front end involves all the activities involved before the first overhead or exercise is ever developed. Foremost are the assessment of the training need and the establishment of training objectives. The middle contains the detailed planning and delivery of the training program. The back end focuses on the events that encourage back-on-the-job application, ongoing performance support, and the evaluation of training outcomes. The first edition of *Active Training* was committed to examining all three phases of training.

2. To promote an active approach to training.

The active approach to training described in the first edition of *Active Training* involved a commitment to *learning by doing.* Everything we know about adult learners suggests that participants must be actively engaged during a training program for results to occur. If there is little activity, participants will forget or fail to apply what they are taught and will be bored by the material presented.

3. To provide a practical handbook of techniques, designs, case examples, and tips.

As *Active Training* promoted learning by doing, it showed how to acquire these skills through *learning by example.* It not only described several active training techniques but also illustrated how they have been applied in actual training situations. Designs and case examples drawn from private and public sector training professionals were presented to give readers ideas for their own situation. One of the special features of the first edition of *Active Training* was the wide variety of training topics from which its examples were pulled. I did not promise to provide readers with the perfect example for their particular needs at every point. Nonetheless, examples were given that were flexible enough to be customized to the topics and groups any reader might be training.

These three goals continue to be the basis of this second edition of *Active Training*. Since 1990, however, much has happened. Training continues to be delivered in classroom settings but now is also delivered in new ways that all of us only had a glimpse of when I was preparing the first edition. As a matter of fact, the view of training as something that only occurs in classrooms has been broadened to include the concept that training means supporting learning wherever it occurs in the organization—in meetings, on computer screens, through mentors, or during actual work team projects. Also, my techniques have been sharpened by the many interactions I have had over the decade with public and private sector training professionals, most notably at conferences of the American Society for Training and Development, the International Society for Performance Improvement, and the North American Simulation and Gaming Association. Consequently, I have included a discussion of these new realities and the fruits of my dialogue with others in this second edition.

During the 1990s, I also embarked on a collaboration with several gifted training designers that resulted in the publication of *20 Active Training Programs,* Volumes 1, 2, and 3. These loose-leaf binders contained sixty full-day workshops on timely topics, all utilizing the techniques promoted in the first edition of *Active Training.* Many new examples of active training activities and designs from this series are incorporated in this second edition. As a result, you will find case examples from an enlarged and updated list of training topics in *Active Training.* They include

Assertiveness training	Banking
Business writing	Career development
Change management	Child care
Coaching and counseling	Communication skills
Computer training	Conflict management
Creative thinking	Cultural diversity
Customer service	Disabilities
Drug testing	Family education and therapy
Group dynamics	Health care
Insurance	Interviewing skills
Leadership	Management training

Measurement and testing
Performance appraisals
Project management
Real estate
Sexual harassment
Teaching
Time management
Train-the-trainer

Motivation
Problem solving
Purchasing
Sales
Stress management
Team building
Total quality

You will also find a new section entitled "Introducing Active Training" (Part One) that, among other things, examines the case for active training. It contains a discussion of the nature of adult learning, exploring the reasons why adults learn best when they are active in the learning process. It also identifies the frequently asked questions people concerned with the introduction of active training techniques most often query me about. Finally, it examines the contexts in which active training is delivered. While most training takes place in classroom-type settings, an active approach to training can be incorporated in other delivery modes.

As was the case with the first edition, this second edition of *Active Training* emphasizes what you can do to create training designs, not just to deliver them. Some professional trainers are asked to teach a program straight from a published instructor's manual, with no opportunity to modify either the structure or the content of the course. *Active Training* is intended for use by those of you who have some freedom to modify how a course (or seminar, workshop, or program) is taught. Altering the sequence of course modules or changing, however slightly, the format and methods through which the course materials are delivered can often improve the learning experience dramatically for your participants. Further, you may have the opportunity to redesign a previously taught course, adding new approaches and ideas gained through the reading of *Active Training*. And finally, you may find yourself in complete control over a course design. It is in this situation, when trying to make the multiple design decisions that make up a professional training program, that the many tips, designs, and case examples described within *Active Training* become especially useful.

If you are new to the training environment, reading *Active Training* can help you to learn the reasons why trainers make the design choices they do when creating an active training program.* In addition, you will learn a variety

---

*A distinction is often made between a "course designer" and a "trainer" when the assumption is made that they are two separate people. We will use the term "trainer" throughout this book to designate a person who both designs and conducts training programs. This "trainer" will alternately be referred to in the singular as "he" or "she" (except when an actual person is being mentioned), since both sexes are well represented within training ranks.

of facilitation techniques that can help you to conduct any training program professionally. The examples help you to make sense out of the components of a good active training program in a way that straight text never could.

It is my hope that *Active Training* will continually provide you with specific guidance as you reference the text throughout your career, whether you work in a business, governmental, educational, or human service setting.

Princeton, New Jersey   Mel Silberman
March 1998

Acknowledgments

Several training professionals have contributed tips, designs, and case examples for this book. They include Jackie Agostini, Marie Amey-Taylor, Sharon Balaban, Jeff Brown, Marion Burns, Gretchen Castle, Claire Conway, Karen DiNunzio, Germaine Edwards, Kevin Eikenberry, Jody Gandy, Allan Geller, Chris Gillespie, Neal Goodman, Linda Guerra, Dan Harvey, Janis Heil, Ann Houser, Cathleen Hulce, Linda Hyman, Maryann Keenan, Jeff Kindler, Steve Krupp, Kevin Kruse, Karen Lawson, Janice Engler Marks, Monica McGrath, Rick McKnight, Elaine Mendelow, Chrissa Merron, Lee Miller, Leigh Mundhenk, Karla Nurcyzk, D. J. O'Loughlin, Cindy Perkiss, Bill Pinchuk, Whit Raymond, Sandy Saville, Milt Silver, Jane Silverman, Scott Simmerman, George Spence, Bill Stieber, Fay Stokes, Maria Sudeck, Karon West, Susan Wheelan, Vicky Whiteling, Charlotte Zaback, and Ruth Zasloff. I wish to express my appreciation to them.

Three people deserve special acknowledgment. Without Jane Silverman, president of Training Management Corporation, *Active Training* would not have come into existence. Back in 1988, Jane asked me to collaborate with her in developing a train-the-trainer course for J. P. Morgan & Co. that became the basis for the first edition of *Active Training*. At the time, I was an academic with limited experience in the "real world." Her confidence in my ability to create a practical program for real-world trainers will always be remembered. Karen Lawson, president of the Lawson Consulting Group, has been my student, an associate, and now a valued colleague. Karen worked with me in the development of *101 Ways to Make Training Active*, the companion book to *Active Training*, and honed several active training techniques in her own consulting work. I take pride in the fact that she herself has become a prolific author of training books. Carol Auerbach has assisted me in compiling both editions of *Active Training*. Carol is a talented training professional who combines wisdom and warmth. With her thoroughness, decisiveness, and good taste, she has been an ideal writing partner.

During the time I spent on this second edition of *Active Training,* I have been simultaneously occupied with cancer treatments. Throughout this ordeal, my wife, Shoshana, has been my constant support. I know there are blessings at a time like this, and she surely is the greatest blessing of them all. My children, Steven, Lisa, and Gabe, and my son-in-law, Daniel, have also been my tireless cheerleaders. I love you all.

Mel

Part I

Introducing Active Training

*T*raining is a method of enhancing human performance. Whenever a person's ability to perform a job is limited by a lack of knowledge or skill, it makes sense to bridge that gap by providing the required instruction.

Sounds simple, doesn't it? Not really. The problem begins with the notion that learning something you don't already know requires another person (a trainer) or medium (a book, a computer) to provide it. Let me explain.

One of my favorite exercises is to cover a wristwatch with the opposite hand and ask those who are observing, "What am I doing?" Immediately, someone will say, "You're covering your watch." I then request a synonym for the word *cover*. Typically, suggestions such as *hide, obscure,* or *block* are given. With this opening, I quip that the next time *you* have something to cover with a person you are training, you might be hiding the information, obscuring it, or completely blocking it from view. That's because, at that moment, it's *your* information and *your* understanding of it. It does not belong to the *other* person. As you are covering the subject matter, the other person has to "uncover" what you are saying. This "uncovering" process only happens by virtue of the learner's own activity. Ultimately, you—or a book or a computer—cannot do the work for the learner.

Active training occurs when the participants do most of the work. If you neatly package the information or elegantly demonstrate the skills, you, not the participants, are doing "the work" for them. No one is suggesting that well-designed instruction is unnecessary. The key to effective training, however, is how the learning activities are designed so that the participants *acquire* knowledge and skill rather than merely *receive* them.

Yes, there is a whole lot more to training than "show and tell." Learning is not an automatic consequence of pouring information into another person's

1

head. It requires the learner's own mental involvement and doing. Lecturing and demonstrating, by themselves, will never lead to real, lasting learning. Only training that is active will.

Let's consider more fully why training needs to be active.

THE NATURE OF ADULT LEARNING

Over twenty-four hundred years ago, Confucius declared:

*What I **hear**, I forget.*

*What I **see**, I remember.*

*What I **do**, I understand.*

These three simple statements speak volumes about the need for active learning.

I have modified and expanded the wisdom of Confucius into what I call the Active Learning Credo:

*When I **hear**, I forget.*

*When I **hear** and **see**, I remember a little.*

*When I **hear**, **see**, and **ask questions** or **discuss** with someone else, I begin to understand.*

*When I **hear**, **see**, **discuss**, and **do**, I acquire knowledge and skill.*

*When I **teach** to another, I master.*

Why do I make these statements? Popularizers of active learning give the following average retention rates from various instructional modes:

Lecture	5 percent
Reading	10 percent
Audiovisuals	20 percent
Demonstration	30 percent
Discussion	50 percent
Practice by doing	75 percent
Teaching others	90 percent

Such round numbers are hardly evidence of solid research! However, they do suggest a progression worthy of discussion.

There are several reasons why most adults tend to forget what they hear. One of the most interesting has to do with the rate at which a trainer speaks and the rate at which participants listen.

Most trainers speak at about 100 to 200 words per minute. But how many of those words do participants hear? It depends on how they are listening. If

STYLE	FAMOUS EXAMPLES	WHAT TO DO WITH THEM	HOW SWEET IS IT?
• Fortified Wines (*continued*)	Vin Doux Natural Muscat Beaumes- de-Venise Banyuls/Dr. Parcé, Domaine de Coyeaux, Beaumalric	Serve as dessert or with crème brûlée or fruit Serve with chocolate	Dried apricot flavor Very sweet Raisiny flavor Quite sweet
• Dried-grape wines	Italian Vin Santo/ Antinori, Avignonesi	Serve with biscotti	Toffee-almond flavor Usually off-dry
• "Ice Wines"—made from grapes frozen on the vine, but some wineries put the grapes in the freezer	German Eiswein/Dr. Loosen Canadian and American ice wine/Inniskillin, Chateau Ste. Michelle	Serve alone; also good with meringue, pavlova, or baked Alaska	Passionfruit flavor Very sweet

Why Wine and Food?

Isn't this the whole point? Restaurants are by no means the only place to have fun with wine and food, but they are the place where people seem to get the most uptight about having the "right" wine and food match. I have just one thing to say about that: Relax. No one ever ruined an evening by picking the "wrong" wine. (If it's that important, I'd say you should look for more interesting dining partners.)

Now, here are some rules of thumb about wine and food that can help you have more fun experimenting, which is something I do daily. Even if I'm having leftovers, I still taste a couple of wines with dinner—whatever's around or open from the day before. And in restaurants, of course, I always try several different wine and food combinations.

Wine is a love letter to food, largely because of its acidity. Quite simply, acidity is like a turbocharger for flavor. It makes your mouth water, and when your mouth waters, food tastes better. This is because the enzymes in your saliva break down the food and unlock the flavors, so they really explode.

the participants are really concentrating, they might be able to listen attentively to about 50 to 100 words per minute, or half of what a trainer is saying. That's because participants are thinking a lot while they are listening. It's hard to keep up with a talkative trainer. Even if the material is interesting, it's hard to concentrate for a sustained period of time. Studies show that participants hear (without thinking) at the rate of 400 to 500 words per minute. When they are listening for a sustained period of time to a trainer who is talking up to four times more slowly, they are likely to get bored and their minds will wander.

In fact, one study demonstrates that participants in lecture-based college classrooms are inattentive about 40 percent of the time (Pollio, 1984). Moreover, although students retain 70 percent of what is said in the first ten minutes of a lecture, they only retain 20 percent in the last ten minutes (McKeachie, 1986). It's no wonder that participants in a lecture-based introductory psychology course knew only 8 percent more than a control group who had never taken the course at all (Rickard, Rogers, Ellis, and Beidleman, 1988).

David and Roger Johnson, well-known figures in the cooperative education movement, along with Karl Smith, point out several problems with sustained lecturing (Johnson, Johnson, and Smith, 1991):

- Audience attention decreases with each passing minute.
- Sustained lecturing appeals only to auditory learners.
- It tends to promote lower-level learning of factual information.
- It assumes that all learners need the same information and need it at the same pace.
- People tend not to like it.

To alleviate the audio bombardment of lecturing, master trainer Bob Pike recommends that participants should be given a chance *every eight minutes* to internalize what they have been hearing before it's simply supplanted by the next wave of information. Pike also points out that adding visuals to a lesson results in a 14 to 38 percent improvement in retention (Pike, 1994). Studies have also shown an improvement of up to 200 percent when vocabulary is taught using visual aids! Moreover, the time required to present a concept is reduced up to 40 percent when visuals are used to augment a verbal presentation. A picture may not be worth a thousand words, but it is several times more effective than words alone.

When teaching has both an auditory and a visual dimension, the message is reinforced by two systems of delivery. Also, some participants, as I will discuss later, prefer one mode of delivery over the other. By using both, therefore, you have a greater chance of meeting the needs of several types of participants.

But merely hearing something and seeing it is not enough to learn it. Let's explore the reasons why.

How the Brain Works

The adult brain does not function like an audiotape or videotape recorder. Because of our vast storehouse of old information, incoming information is continually being questioned. Our brain asks questions such as

Have I heard or seen this information before? What does it remind me of?

Where does this information fit? What can I do with it?

Can I assume that this is the same idea I had yesterday, or last month, or last year?

The brain doesn't just receive information; it *processes* it. To process information effectively, it helps to carry out such reflection externally as well as internally. If adults discuss information with others and if they are invited to ask questions about it, their brains can do a better job of learning. For example, Ruhl, Hughes, and Schloss (1987) asked students to discuss with a partner, at frequent intervals during the class, what the instructor had presented. Compared to participants in a control class in which there were no pauses for discussion, these participants received up to two letter grades higher.

Better yet, if we can "do" something with the information, we can obtain feedback about how well we understand. Learning is enhanced if people are asked to do the following:

1. State the information in their own words

2. Give examples of it

3. Recognize it in various guises and circumstances

4. See connections between it and other facts or ideas

5. Make use of it in various ways

6. Foresee some of its consequences

7. State its opposite or converse

In many ways, our brain is like a computer and we are its users. A computer needs to be "on" in order to work. Our brain needs to be on as well. When learning is passive, the brain isn't on. A computer needs the right software to interpret the data that are entered. Our brain needs to link what we are being taught with what we already know and how we think. When learning is passive, the brain doesn't make these linkages to the software of our mind. Finally, a computer cannot retain information that it has processed without "saving it." Our brain needs to test the information, recapitulate it, or explain it to someone else in order to store it in its memory banks. When learning is passive, the brain doesn't save what has been presented.

What occurs when trainers flood participants with their own thoughts (however insightful and well organized they may be) or when they rely too often on "let me show you how" demonstrations and explanations? Pouring facts and concepts into participants' heads and masterfully performing skills and procedures actually interfere with learning. The presentation may make an immediate impression on the brain, but without a photographic memory, participants simply cannot retain very much for any period of time, even though they think they will never forget it.

In any case, real learning is not memorization. Most of what we memorize is lost in hours. In order to retain what has been taught, participants must chew on it. Learning can't be swallowed whole. A trainer can't do the mental work for participants because they must put together what they hear and see to form a meaningful whole. Without the opportunity to discuss, ask questions, do, and perhaps even teach someone else, real learning will not occur.

Further, learning is not a one-shot event; it comes in waves. It takes several exposures to material to chew long enough to understand. It also takes different kinds of exposures, not just a repetition of input. For example, a software application can be taught with manuals, through classroom exercises, and through individual work assignments. Each way shapes the participants' understanding. Even more important is the way in which the exposure happens. If it happens *to* the learner, there will be little mental engagement *by* the learner. When learning is passive, the learner comes to the encounter without curiosity, without questions, and without interest in the outcome. When learning is active, the learner is *seeking* something. He or she wants an answer to a question, needs information to solve a problem, or is searching for a way to do a job.

Learning Styles

Adult learners come in different styles. For example, some adults learn best by seeing information as well as hearing it. When learning skills, they like to watch someone else demonstrate them before they try them on their own. Usually, these "visual" learners like carefully sequenced presentations of information. They prefer to write down what a trainer tells them. During class, they are generally quiet. High on their preference list are videos, slides, and demonstrations. These adults contrast with "auditory" learners, who often don't bother to look at what a trainer does or to take notes. They rely on their ability to listen and remember what was said. During class, they may be quite talkative. High on their preference list are lectures, discussions, and question-and-answer sessions. "Kinesthetic" learners learn mainly by direct involvement in activity. They tend to be impulsive learners, with little patience. During class, they may be fidgety unless they can move about and "do." Their approach to learning can appear haphazard and random. High on their preference list are experiential activities such as role plays, games, and group exercises.

Of course, most participants are not exclusively one kind of learner. In fact, Grinder (1991) notes that in every group of thirty people, an average of twenty-two are able to learn effectively as long as an instructor provides a blend of visual, auditory, and kinesthetic activity. The remaining eight people, however, prefer one of the modalities over the other two so strongly that they struggle to understand the subject matter unless special care is taken to present it in their preferred mode. In order to meet these needs, instruction has to be multisensory and filled with variety.

One of the things that adult educators have been noticing is that the learning styles among their students have been changing. For the past fifteen years, Schroeder and his colleagues (Schroeder, 1993) have been giving the Myers-Briggs Type Indicator® (MBTI) to incoming college students. The MBTI is one of the most widely used instruments in the world of education and business today. It has been an especially useful tool toward understanding the role of individual differences in the learning process. Their results indicate that approximately 60 percent of entering students have a *practical* rather than a *theoretical* orientation to learning and the percentage grows year by year. These students prefer to be involved with immediate, direct, and concrete experiences rather than learning basic concepts first and applying them later. Other MBTI research, Schroeder points out, shows that high school students prefer learning activities that are "concrete and active" to activities that are "abstract and reflective" by a ratio of five to one. From all this, he concludes that active modes of teaching and learning create the best match for today's young adults. To be effective, trainers should use all the following: small-group discussions and projects, in-class presentations and debates, experiential exercises, field experiences, simulations, and case studies. In particular, Schroeder stresses that young adults "adapt quite well to group activities and collaborative learning" (1993, p. 25).

These findings come as no surprise if we consider the active pace of modern life. Young people (the so-called Generation X) today grow up in a world where things happen quickly and where many choices are presented. Sounds come in clever "bites," and the colors are vibrant and compelling. Objects, both real and virtual, move quickly. The opportunity to change things from one state to another is everywhere. Generation Xers are especially receptive to active, experiential learning.

The Social Side of Learning

All adults, young or old, now face a world of exploding knowledge, rapid change, and uncertainty. As a result, they can be anxious and defensive. Abraham Maslow taught us that human beings have within them two sets of forces or needs—one that strives for growth and one that clings to safety. A person who must choose between these two needs will choose safety over growth. The need to feel secure has to be met before the need to reach out, take risks, and explore the new can be entertained. Growth forward takes place in little steps, according to Maslow, and "each step forward is made possible by the feeling of being safe, of operating out into the unknown from a safe home port" (Maslow, 1968, p. 45).

One of the key ways for people to attain a feeling of safety and security is to be connected to other people and to feel that they are included in a group. This feeling of belonging enables participants to face the challenges set before them. When they are learning with others rather than alone, they have available the emotional and intellectual support that allows them to go beyond their present level of knowledge and skill.

The social side of learning is recognized by Jerome Bruner in his classic book, *Toward a Theory of Instruction* (1966). He describes a "deep human need to respond to others and to operate jointly with them toward an objective," which he calls "reciprocity" (p. 67). Bruner maintains that reciprocity is a source of motivation that any educator or trainer can tap to stimulate learning. He writes: "Where joint action is needed, where reciprocity is required for the group to attain an objective, then there seem to be processes that carry the individual along into learning, sweep him into a competence that is required in the setting of the group."

These concepts of Maslow and Bruner underlie the development of the small-group learning methods that are so popular in training circles. Placing participants in teams and giving them tasks in which they depend upon each other to complete the work is a wonderful way to capitalize on their social needs. They tend to get more engaged in learning because they are doing it with their peers. Once they have become involved, they also have a need to talk with others about what they are experiencing, which leads to further connections.

Collaborative learning activities help to drive active training. Although independent study and full-class instruction also stimulate active learning, the ability to teach through small-group cooperative activities will enable you to promote active learning in a special way. Remember that what a participant discusses with others and what a participant teaches others enable him or her to acquire understanding and master learning. The best collaborative learning methods (see, for example, "Jigsaw Learning" in Chapter Five) meet these requirements. Giving different assignments to different participants prompts them not only to learn together but also to teach each other.

In summary, three factors about adult learning form the basis for active training: (1) how the adult mind works in the learning process, (2) the variety of learning styles adults exhibit, and (3) the need for a social component in the learning environment.

CONCERNS ABOUT ACTIVE TRAINING

Despite the arguments I have used to support an active approach to training, many people are still apprehensive about it. If you share any of these frequently expressed concerns, I hope my responses are helpful.

Is active training just a bunch of "fun and games"? No, it's not just fun, although learning can be fun and still be worthwhile. Actually, many active training techniques present participants with unusual challenges that require much hard work.

Does active training focus so much on activity for its own sake that participants don't reflect on what they are learning? This is a real concern. Much of the value of active training activities comes from thinking about them when they are over and discussing their meaning with others. Don't overlook this fact. You will find many suggestions in *Active Training* to help participants reflect on what they have experienced. In addition, it is often valuable to give a short lesson after an active training activity to connect what the participants experienced to the concepts you want to get across.

Doesn't active training require a lot of time? How can you cover course material using active training methods? Isn't lecturing more efficient? There is no question that active training takes more time than straight lecturing, but there are many ways to avoid a needless waste of time. Furthermore, even though a lecture can cover considerable ground, we have to question how much is really learned. Also, remember the "coverage" trap. The more you try to cover, the more you may be hiding.

Can active training methods spice up dry, uninteresting information? Absolutely! When the subject is interesting, it's easy to train. When it is dry, often the mere excitement of active training methods catches up with the participants and they become motivated to master even boring material.

When you use groups in active training, how do you prevent them from wasting time and being unproductive? Groups can be unproductive when little team building is done in the beginning of the class and group work is not carefully structured from the outset. Participants become confused about what to do, organize themselves poorly, and easily get off task. Or they may do the work as quickly as possible, skimming the surface rather than digging into the material. There are several ways to teach participants how to learn in groups, such as assigning roles to group members, establishing group ground rules, and practicing group skills. Many tips and techniques in *Active Training* are geared to this problem.

Can you "group participants to death" using active training? Yes, it can happen. Some trainers overuse groups. They don't give participants enough chance to learn things individually and they don't bring the entire class together enough for teaching and discussion. The key is variety. A variety of learning modalities is the spice of good training. Several techniques in *Active Training* will give you alternatives to small-group learning.

Is there a danger that participants will misinform each other in group-based active training methods? I suppose there is some danger of that, but the advantages of giving learning a social side far outweigh the disadvantages. Anyway, a trainer can always review material with the entire class after participants try to learn it on their own and teach it to each other.

Doesn't it require more preparation and creativity to teach using active training methods? Yes and no. Once you get the hang of it, the extra preparation and creativity will not feel like a burden. You will feel excited about your training and this energy will transfer to your participants' learning. Until then, you should find that creating ideas for active training can be challenging. At first, you will wonder how in the world you can teach certain topics actively. This is where *Active Training* comes in. It is intended to ease the transition by providing you with several concrete ways to build activity, variety, and participation into your training. I believe that these techniques are useful for virtually any subject matter.

I'm sold on active training, but I wonder if my participants will be. Generation Xers will enthusiastically buy active training. Because many of them were "latchkey kids," they have learned to be self-reliant. As a result, they are quite good at learning by doing. They also don't mind the fast pace of activity, having grown up in an MTV world. Of course, the less accustomed to active training participants are, the more uneasy they will be initially. They may be used to trainers who do all the work and to sitting back and believing that they have learned something and will retain it. Some participants will also complain that active training is a "waste of time." Older workers, in particular, may prefer well-organized, efficient delivery of information or may be anxious about learning by discovery and self-exploration. In the long run, they will benefit from active training as much as anyone else. In the short run, they will be less anxious if you introduce active training gradually. If you don't, you may get considerable resistance.

Your participants will need to know what to expect if your approach is new to them. Following is a statement I have used to convey how the training will be conducted.

Welcome to Active Training!

This training class is based on the principles of active learning. The methods we will use are designed to

- Increase Participation
- Enliven Learning
- Deepen Retention
- Encourage Application

You will be asked lots of questions, urged to take a stab at an answer, explore, and try things out. You will also work, at times, with others and will be asked to test yourself periodically to see for yourself what you have learned and what skills you possess.

At all times, this class will be guided by the idea that it's not what **I tell you** that counts; it's what **you take away**.

In addition, I will not cover everything about our topic. I want you to feel that you have **really learned something** rather than having been **exposed to everything**. If I do a good job focusing on the most important topics, you will be able to learn the rest of what you need on your own.

So rev your engines, fasten your seat belts, and get ready for some active learning.

THE DELIVERY OF ACTIVE TRAINING

Active Training is based on the assumption that you are training a group of participants at one site in a classroom setting. An active approach to training, however, is not limited to this delivery mode but can be incorporated into other modes. Since the instructional design principles are essentially the same regardless of how training is delivered, the ideas in *Active Training* can be easily applied to a wide range of training approaches.

As we enter the twenty-first century, the use of computer-delivered instruction is revolutionizing the way people obtain training. Multimedia training programs are now increasingly available on CD-ROMs or can be obtained through the Internet or company-sponsored intranets (internal Web sites). The advantage of computer technology is its ability to provide more training, delivered sooner, in more places, and potentially at a lower cost, than traditional classroom-based instruction. The value of computer-based instruction is enhanced when it is designed for maximum interactivity. Straightforward presentation of information, even when it is in "hypertext" format and replete with visual graphics, limits the learning experience. The use of questions, case problems, and simulations and the inclusion of interactive exercises alter the quality of learning that will be obtained. Such activities can be built into individuals' interactions with computer-based instruction through user input options that enable them to "talk" to the material. To add the social side of learning, it is also possible to bring together, both face-to-face and virtually, people who have experienced the same computer-based instruction and give them group activities to reinforce what they have learned individually.

What can make computer-based training (CBT) and the Internet a truly active learning experience is the fact that the learner can make his or her decisions about how to learn the material. Classroom-based instruction is linear. A participant learns point A before point B. Nonlinear learning is the hallmark of CBT and the Internet. A participant can repeat material, skip material, and, in fact, begin and end whenever she or he wants. Simply creating a technological version of a linear lecture would be a waste of the learner's time.

Currently, the issue of computer-based "skills" training is being hotly debated. How well can an interactive CD-ROM, for instance, teach and allow the learner to practice interpersonal behaviors used in areas such as presentations, coaching sessions, and sales calls? Such skill-based learning includes input of the knowledge necessary to perform the skill, demonstration, preparation, practice application, feedback, and reapplication. The most critical of these steps are the quality and delivery of coaching and feedback and the reapplication. Some say that it's tough for technology to deliver these steps as well as good old-fashioned human beings can—at least for now.

Distance learning is a way to provide training when the trainer and participants are not at the same site or cannot interact at the same time. It can be accomplished through both videoconferencing and computer conferencing. Once again, the value of distance learning is diminished when the learning process is one-way, with a "talking head" lecturing on TV or an on-line instructor filling computer screens with endless information. Fortunately, distance educators are becoming mindful of this. For example, the 12th Annual Conference on Distance Teaching & Learning was devoted to "Designing for Active Learning" (University of Wisconsin, 1996). Much research was presented that tested the hypothesis: "Whatever can be done in a classroom can be done in a distance learning classroom." Experimentation in fostering active learning on-line, creation of team learning experiences for remote students, electronic journaling, and collaborative computer-mediated conferencing were among the topics exchanged.

Moreover, Piskurich (1997) has suggested the practice of "interactive distance learning" (IDL) and describes several innovative ideas on how to design and implement it. One suggestion, for instance, is to use a broadcast format involving a moderated process interspersed with prerecorded video segments and panel discussions. Activities are given to learners at each site and the products of their work are reported back to the studio. Synchronous IDL is a viable medium for training. The program is live, with a live trainer delivering the material, using, at a minimum, one-way video and two-way live audio. Participants can ask questions, talk with other people at different sites, and interact with the trainer, live in real time. With two-way video, participants can also practice skills and receive coaching and feedback.

Another delivery mode for active training is the use of "self-directed learning teams." In this approach, small groups of learners meet face-to-face at their convenience and experience training that has been designed by an "absent" trainer. Guided by materials that do not require a "live" trainer or outside facilitator, teams learn by themselves. The self-directed learning team has the following benefits:

- It promotes high levels of active learning.
- It develops a sense of "ownership" of training.
- It provides built-in social support for learning.
- It allows for different perspectives.
- It is based on a common language of understanding.
- It minimizes training costs and maximizes convenience.

In order for learning teams to be self-directing, well-organized learning packages are needed. Learning team participants require professionally designed training program materials that not only have clear, useful content but also contain directions for active learning activities that promote involvement, retention, and application.

Of course, despite the premature obituaries, classroom training is alive and well. According to the 1997 industry report of *Training* magazine, 94 percent of the organizations surveyed report that they still use classroom training. Further, 81 percent of all courses are classroom-based, with a live trainer.

When classroom training is active, the participants use their brains, studying ideas, solving problems, and applying what they learn. The training is fast-paced, fun, supportive, and personally engaging. Often, participants leave their seats, moving about and thinking aloud.

Active training is a way to enliven classroom learning. Some of the techniques are a lot of fun and some are downright serious, but they are all intended to deepen understanding and retention. Active training includes strategies to get participants active from the start through activities that build teamwork and that immediately cause the participants to think about the subject matter. It also has strategies for conducting full-class learning and small-group learning, stimulating discussion and debate, practicing skills, prompting questions, and even getting the participants to teach each other. Finally, it has techniques to help you review what's been learned, assess how participants have changed, and consider the next steps to take so that the training sticks.

♦   ♦   ♦

Part II

Designing an Active Training Program

..........................*M*any training programs seem like an inert, gray mass. Each part of the program blends into the rest. Even when intentions are sincere, the activities seems to progress like an endless freight train of content, going nowhere in particular. By contrast, an active training program is characterized by ***activity, variety,*** and ***participation***. More specifically, eight qualities set it apart from other program designs:

1. **Moderate level of content.**

In designing training programs, too often the tendency is to cover the waterfront by throwing in everything possible about a given subject. After all, you only get one shot at these participants, so you'd better make sure you have covered it all. You may fail to realize, however, that participants will forget far more than they will ever learn. The best approach is to be selective, choosing the "need to know" before the "nice to know." Training programs that promote active learning have a lean curriculum. They concentrate on the critical learning areas—those elements of the subject that provide the essential basis for building later. When the content level is kept moderate, the trainer has the time to design activities that introduce, present, apply, and reflect upon what is being learned.

2. **Balance between affective, behavioral, and cognitive learning.**

Active training involves a three-pronged approach: fostering attitudes, developing and practicing skills, and promoting understanding of the concepts and models behind the subject. Although some training programs tend to focus on one of these areas to the exclusion of the others, you want participants not only to know about something, but also to be able to do it. Furthermore, you want them to look at themselves in relation to what you are teaching and to consider how it works for them.

3. Variety of learning approaches.

Active training employs a wide assortment of training methods. A variety of learning approaches keeps interest alive and can help to minimize the down-times when energy levels are low. Another and even more important argument for variety is that adults learn in different ways. Using different learning approaches is likely to be more effective than a single approach that may work for some but not for others. Time allocations, group formats, and the physical setting can also be varied to heighten the training experience.

4. Opportunities for group participation.

Group participation has advantages in any training program. Involving the group moves training from the passive to the active. Group activity engages participants in the learning process and makes them working partners with the trainer. Lecturing is held to a minimum as highly participatory methods like role playing, simulated exercises, and case discussions are featured.

5. Utilization of participants' expertise.

Each participant in a training program brings relevant experiences to the classroom. Some of these experiences will be directly applicable; others may involve analogies from previous jobs or situations. In either case, much of the active learning in a training program comes from one's peers. You can build into your design many opportunities for participants to learn from each other.

6. Recycling of earlier learned concepts and skills.

Programs that feature active training have designs that are continually referring back to and incorporating earlier skills and concepts. In effect, the curriculum spirals. Participants get the chance to review what they have already learned and apply it to more challenging tasks. What has previously been taught is rarely passed over, never to appear again. Instead, key concepts and skills get reintroduced as the program becomes more advanced.

7. Real-life problem solving.

Active training designs emphasize the real world. Opportunities are set up for the participants to utilize course content to address and help solve actual problems they are currently experiencing. Application is not only something that happens after training; it is a major focus during training. Participants learn best when they get to work on their own material, cases, and examples. This gives the information immediacy and enables participants to assess its utility on the spot.

8. **Allowance for future planning.**

At the conclusion of any training program, participants will naturally ask, "Now what?" The success of an active training program is really measured by how that question is answered—that is, how what has been learned in the course is transferred to the job. An active training design ends with consideration of the next steps participants will take and the obstacles they will face as they implement new ideas and skills.

When you go about the task of designing a training program that reflects these eight qualities, you face a creative challenge not unlike an artist's. Many decisions are ahead, and there is no right way to make them all. There are also different ways to create the same effect. Consequently, there is no orderly way to proceed. Many instructional designers, in fact, don't always function their best by proceeding in a step-by-step progression. The following sequence of steps, however, should serve as a general guide to designing an active training program.

1. **Assess the need for training and the participants.**

The first step in designing an active training program is to determine what, if any, training need exists and to find out as much as possible about the participants who will be affected. If this information cannot be collected prior to training, assessment activities should be incorporated into the beginning of the program. The more assessment data you can obtain, the better it is for planning, customizing, and modifying a design.

2. **Set general learning goals.**

With the assessment data in mind, identify potential learning goals for participants. In general terms, describe their needs in the areas of affective awareness, cognitive understanding, behavioral skill building, real-life problem solving, and on-the-job application.

3. **Specify objectives.**

Get specific about the kinds of learning you want the participants to experience and the results you want to achieve. Each general learning goal will have one or more objectives that, when met, will signal accomplishment of that goal. State these objectives in a form that will make them effective tools for managing, monitoring, and evaluating the training.

4. **Design training activities.**

Now that the objectives have been clearly and explicitly stated, you must design training activities to achieve them. At this stage, it's sufficient to generate the broad outline (method and format) of all the activities you think will be necessary for each objective in your program. List the possibilities in pencil, on index cards, on a personal computer, or in any other medium that is erasable or rearrangeable.

5. Sequence training activities.

Play with the order of activities until you obtain a sequence that has a good mixture. Consider which designs are needed for the beginning, middle, and end of your program. Adjust activities to improve the flow.

6. Start detailed planning.

Now begin working on the details, specifying how to conduct each activity in your overall design. Decide on timing, introductory remarks, key points and instructions, materials, setting, and ways to end.

7. Revise design details.

Mentally walk through the overall design, visualizing the participants' experience. Revise any details (particularly timing and instructions) so that each activity complements the ones that precede and/or follow it. Delete any designs that now seem unnecessary, impractical, or ill conceived. Develop contingency plans in case time runs short or the group is more or less skilled than you thought, as well as for any other turn of events you can imagine.

8. Evaluate the total result.

Examine the program to see if it has the eight characteristics of an active training program. If you see flaws at this point, redesign to achieve a better result.

Designing is never static. It's an ongoing process in which you try things out, perhaps making revisions even as the program is being implemented; obtain feedback from participants; evaluate participant performance; and then modify the design for the next time around. The continuing challenges you'll face in designing an active training program are their own reward. The process is creative, exhilarating, and reinforcing, and the outcome is not only something in which you can take pride but also a real benefit to the people you are training.

The ten chapters that comprise Part Two have been sequenced in order to assist you, step by step, in the process of designing an active training program. As promised, the chapters will be filled with examples drawn from real-life training situations to illustrate every point made. Here is an overview of their contents.

Chapter One explains and illustrates how to assess a training group prior to the start of a program in order to help determine course content, obtain case material, and establish an early relationship with participants.

Chapter Two tells how the development of training objectives drives the design of a training program and illustrates how objectives are specified, expressed, and presented to participants.

Chapter Three shows how to create opening exercises that promote team building, on-the-spot assessment, and immediate learning involvement. It also suggests ten ways to obtain participation in the opening phase of a training program.

Chapter Four describes ways to gain interest in a lecture, maximize understanding and retention, invite audience participation, and reinforce what has been presented.

Chapter Five discusses and illustrates strategies to avoid or reinforce a lecture presentation.

Chapter Six shows how role playing, games and simulations, observation, mental imagery, writing tasks, and projects can be utilized to achieve affective and behavioral learning.

Chapter Seven demonstrates how training activities are formed around a purpose, method, and format. It further provides guidelines for detailed construction of active training activities and criteria for including those activities in an overall design.

Chapter Eight suggests ways to sequence training activities in order to achieve an effective mix and flow.

Chapter Nine identifies strategies that can be employed prior to, during, and at the end of a training program to promote the transfer of learning.

Chapter Ten illustrates the overall structure and flavor of an active training program and outlines the steps you should take to plan one of your own.

As you navigate each chapter, avoid being a passive reader. Identify a design problem you are currently facing or anticipate facing in the future and keep it in mind as you read. By maintaining a problem-solving mindset rather than an information-receiving one, you will be an active reader.

To further encourage your participation, I have provided a worksheet at the end of each chapter in Part Two that will give you an opportunity to apply what you have learned. From time to time, I will also surprise you with questions and brief exercises. That way, I know I'm doing *my* job as an active trainer.

◆   ◆   ◆

Chapter One

Assessing the Need for Training and the Participants

.... All too often, the training needs in an organization are viewed in isolation from the bottom-line results that the organization is seeking. As a result, training courses are not part of an overall strategy for performance improvement. When this occurs, the design of a training program is often approached on a hit-or-miss basis. Many trainers decide what they want to teach (or receive orders from management) without sufficient regard for what the participants need to learn so that the organization can succeed. All this can be avoided by making an effort to assess the need for training and the training participants prior to training. Gathering information about the training need and the actual or potential participants is the first step in designing an active training program from scratch or tailoring an existing one for a specific group.

Unfortunately, the opportunity to assess the training situation is often limited by time constraints and a lack of availability of data. Even in less than ideal circumstances, however, some assessment is necessary before finalizing the design. At the very least, it is helpful to obtain whatever information you can to answer the following questions:

1. What is the nature of the roles and tasks performed by the intended participants? What competencies do these roles and tasks require?

2. How many participants will there be?

3. How familiar are the participants with the subject matter of the training program?

4. What are the ages, sexes, or other important descriptive factors of the participants?

5. What are their attitudes and beliefs relevant to the training topic?

6. What successes and problems have the participants encountered?

7. What is the competence level of the participants?

8. Is the training voluntary or mandatory?

9. How well do the participants know one another?

10. What, if any, expectations do the participants' supervisors have with regard to the training program?

WHY DO ASSESSMENT?

When a problem exists within an organization, the first impulse is often to solve it with a training program. But training is not always the right solution, because the root cause of the problem is not always a lack of knowledge or skill. Instead, according to Gilbert (1996), it might also be any of the following:

- Unclear performance expectations and poor performance feedback
- Lack of tools, resources, and materials to do the job
- Inadequate financial and other rewards
- A poor match between employees' skills and the requirements of the job
- Lack of assurance of job security

Consequently, before even thinking about developing a training program, you need to determine whether training is the answer to the concerns being addressed. This requires an assessment process that, at its minimum, involves three steps (Gupta, 1996):

1. **Pinpoint the problem** by interviewing the client, uncovering underlying issues, and identifying key stakeholders.

2. **Confirm the problem** by interviewing stakeholders, assessing the effect of the problem on the organization.

3. **Seek solutions** by identifying possible actions and gaining consensus on an action plan.

If the problem can be solved with training, some form of assessment is needed to *help determine the training content.* For instance, your group may need certain information or skills more than others. Perhaps the group has some prior exposure to the training topic and now requires more advanced knowledge and skills. Or possibly the group faces certain problems that will affect how much they can apply what you are going to teach them. Without such assessment information, it will be difficult to gear your program to the participants' needs.

Here are some examples of how assessment work completed prior to the training program paid off.

EXAMPLE: A bank manager felt that his platform service personnel needed further product knowledge training. An assessment survey revealed that what they needed more than additional product knowledge was training on how to sell the bank products to potential customers. The subsequent training was well received by the participants and led to increased sales figures for the branches.

EXAMPLE: A trainer was designing a course on assertive communication for battered women. She consulted with experts in the field and learned that batterers often beg for forgiveness between episodes. She decided to include in the course a discussion of why these pleas occur and when they may be misleading.

There are other good reasons to do assessment prior to the training program. When designing training activities, it is extremely helpful to **obtain case material** directly from the workplace or personal situation of the participants. If you do this, your designs can be based on real issues participants actually face rather than on simulated or "canned" material. Here are two examples.

EXAMPLE: For a sales training course in the office automation field, a trainer obtained examples of how area sales managers failed to collect ongoing feedback from accounts who had made recent purchases. The examples were woven into role-playing exercises that successfully engaged participants who previously had disliked the "artificiality" of role playing.

EXAMPLE: Prior to a training program, Head Start teachers were asked to list the most common problem behaviors they faced in their classrooms. The list was utilized in a course worksheet in which participants were asked to evaluate their consistency as classroom managers. The teachers reported that their evaluations were highly revealing because their own list had been used.

One further reason to conduct assessments is the opportunity it affords to **develop a relationship with participants** prior to meeting them at the training site. Sending a questionnaire to participants, for instance, can be an occasion for writing about yourself and your plans for the upcoming program or for learning about their expectations. Phoning or visiting some or all of the participants for an assessment interview can represent a chance to get acquainted face-to-face. Having some prior contact with participants reduces the feeling of awkwardness when you meet in the classroom at the start of the program. Here are two examples.

EXAMPLE: A training consultant was asked to conduct a course on organizational change for a management team in an insurance company. When he learned that some members strongly opposed the course, he arranged a meeting prior to the start-up date to gain their trust and willingness to participate. The consultant clarified the agenda of the course and responded to the concerns of the group. At the conclusion of the meeting, he obtained not only their agreement to participate but also their commitment to play an active role in planning the course.

EXAMPLE: A trainer decided to interview some of the participants who would attend her course on performance appraisals. Knowing that management had been unhappy about the quality level of performance appraisals in the organization, the trainer began each interview with both frankness and reassurance by saying, "I have been asked by management to develop a training program to improve the ways performance appraisals are conducted here. I said I wanted to talk to some of the participants first before I planned the program. I'd like to learn straight from the source what actually happens in conducting performance appraisals as they are set up now. That way I might learn more about the problems that are occurring." Word circulated about the interviews and helped to establish greater acceptance of the training program that followed.

_____

To summarize, three major reasons exist for assessing participants prior to the beginning of a training program:

1. It helps to determine the training content.
2. It allows you to obtain case material.
3. It permits you to develop a relationship with participants.

WHAT INFORMATION SHOULD BE COLLECTED?

As you think about the kinds of information that would be useful to you, consider first asking participants directly *what are their training needs.* Going straight to the participants for their input gives them a hand in helping to design their own program. Moreover, involving them in this manner is usually well appreciated.

One simple way to do this for a public workshop is to send out a brief questionnaire similar to the one shown in Figure 1–1. You can attach it to a course registration or confirmation form.

For an in-house program, consider sending a precourse questionnaire similar to the one described in the following case example.

EXAMPLE: A training department instituted the practice of sending a precourse participant feedback form to all participants of upcoming courses. It asked three basic questions:

1. What are your expectations of the course you are about to take?
2. Based on the course description outlined in the catalog, how do you perceive this program helping you in your current position?
3. What additional objectives or needs would you like the course to address?

_____

Such a form usually gains widespread acceptance because it is perceived as a positive desire to meet the needs of company employees.

Besides participants' wishes, many other areas are worth exploring, both with the participants and with others who know them. First and foremost is information concerning the *nature of the participants' work situations:*

FIGURE 1–1. STRESS MANAGEMENT
WORKSHOP PARTICIPANT QUESTIONNAIRE

In order to make your stress management workshop productive for you, please take a few minutes to respond to the following:

1. My current job position is:

2. I have been to a stress management workshop before.

   ____ never   ____ once before   ____ twice or more before

3. I would benefit by a general overview of stress management strategies.
   (no need)   1   2   3   4   5   (strong need)

4. I need to learn more about physical health and stress.
   (no need)   1   2   3   4   5   (strong need)

5. I need to know what stress management resources are available.
   (no need)   1   2   3   4   5   (strong need)

6. I need to know how to manage my emotions more productively.
   (no need)   1   2   3   4   5   (strong need)

7. I need to know how to use relaxation techniques.
   (no need)   1   2   3   4   5   (strong need)

8. I need to learn more about developing myself spiritually.
   (no need)   1   2   3   4   5   (strong need)

9. What other needs or areas of interest do you have?

10. List three specific questions that you hope this workshop will be able to answer for you:
    a._____
    b._____
    c._____

Please mail this questionnaire in the enclosed envelope before September 25. Thank you.

- What are the participants' responsibilities? What does their job entail?
- Whom do they report to or relate to?
- In what aspects of their work will the skills and knowledge you will teach be employed?

If you were asked to conduct a program on meeting management, for example, you would want to know to what extent the participants' work involved team meetings and what those meetings were like. If you were conducting a public workshop on conflict resolution, knowing whether or not most of your participants are usually the victims in conflict situations would make a big difference in your design.

Next in importance is information about the ***knowledge, skills, and attitudes of the participants:***

- How familiar are participants with the content of your training program?
- How much opportunity have they had to practice or utilize skills that have been demonstrated to them previously?
- What are their feelings about the training topic? Do they value its importance?

Suppose you were designing a program on coaching and counseling skills for managers. It would be useful to assess what skills they already have acquired about coaching new employees or what attitudes they have held about the value of counseling troubled employees. Likewise, you would benefit from knowing how many participants in a weight control program have ever seriously exercised or what they fear about being thin.

Finally, it is helpful to find out any ***conditions that will affect participant involvement*** in the training program:

- What kind of support are participants likely to receive in implementing the training they are given?
- Are participants worried about their level of competence relative to that of other participants?
- Do participants feel they have been sent to the program because someone thinks they need to be "fixed"?
- Are participants unaccustomed to the active learning methods you hope to employ?

Assume, for example, that you have been asked to conduct a program for employees with writing deficiencies. Naturally, it would be useful to know if these employees have merely been sent to the program as opposed to having been positively encouraged by their supervisors to improve their skills.

Notice in the two questionnaires shown in Figures 1–2 and 1–3 how several areas of assessment information are tapped.

FIGURE 1–2. USING THE INTERNET PARTICIPANT QUESTIONNAIRE

Please take a few moments to answer the questions below. Your response will be helpful in planning this course. Your participation is voluntary and your answers are confidential.

1. Rate your interest in using the Internet for

    a. Shopping   (low)   1   2   3   4   5   (high)

    b. Business and investments   (low)   1   2   3   4   5   (high)

    c. Communication   (low)   1   2   3   4   5   (high)

    d. Entertainment   (low)   1   2   3   4   5   (high)

    e. General research   (low)   1   2   3   4   5   (high)

2. Do you send e-mail   _____ almost every day?

                          _____ once or twice a week?

                          _____ rarely?

                          _____ never?

3. Have you ever seen a site (home page) on the World Wide Web?

    _____ a. Yes, I have seen many sites on the World Wide Web and feel very familiar with the Web.

    _____ b. Yes, I have seen sites on the World Wide Web on a few occasions but I am not that familiar with the Web.

    _____ c. No, I have never seen a site on the World Wide Web but I understand some of the Web's basic capabilities.

    _____ d. No, I have never seen a site on the World Wide Web and I am not familiar with the Web.

4. Circle any of the following terms that you already know:

a flame	search engine	file transfer protocol
hypertext	URL	download
upload	listserv	usenet newsgroups
MUD	modem	HTML

5. Are you connected to the Internet

    at work?   _____ yes   _____ no

    at home?   _____ yes   _____ no

6. Describe one skill that you would really like to learn during this class:

7. I learn new skills best by: (select one in each column)

    _____ step-by-step instruction   _____ a quickly paced course

    _____ some guidance and some   _____ a leisurely paced course
          of my own trial and error

FIGURE 1–3. ASSERTIVENESS TRAINING PARTICIPANT QUESTIONNAIRE

Please take a few minutes to answer this brief questionnaire. The information we get from participants will help to determine the direction of our assertiveness training program. Your answers will not be revealed to anyone besides the program leaders.

1. Sex: M ___   F ___   Age: ___   Occupation: _____

2. The people with whom I feel I need to increase my level of assertiveness are (check as many as apply)

   ___ Coworkers   ___ Peers

   ___ Immediate family   ___ Extended family

   ___ Supervisors   ___ Subordinates

   ___ Close friends   ___ Strangers

   ___ Other _____

3. Please rank the following skills in order of importance to you, with "1" indicating the most important and "5" the least important:

   ___ Saying no without apologizing

   ___ Initiating a conversation

   ___ Stating my feelings honestly

   ___ Being persuasive

   ___ Handling very difficult people

4. Indicate the degree of difficulty you have in the following situations:

	Easy	Somewhat Difficult	Very Difficult
Talking with the opposite sex	_____	_____	_____
Disciplining children	_____	_____	_____
Talking on the telephone	_____	_____	_____
Asking for a raise	_____	_____	_____
Talking in a group	_____	_____	_____
Resisting salespeople	_____	_____	_____
Returning food in a restaurant	_____	_____	_____

5. Briefly describe a recent situation in which you acted assertively:

FIGURE 1–3. continued

---

6. Describe a recent situation in which you did not act assertively and regretted it:

7. Who are the people in your life who will support you in becoming more assertive?

8. Who are the people in your life who will resist your newfound assertiveness?

9. Complete the following two sentences:
   a. One reason I sometimes don't like to assert myself is

   _____ .

   b. Sometimes, I feel I have the right to

   _____ .

10. Please circle any of the following techniques with which you are familiar:

    fogging   the broken-record technique

    free information   empathic assertion

    "I" messages   negative inquiry

HOW CAN INFORMATION BE COLLECTED?

If you had unlimited time and resources, how would you ideally collect information for a training program you were designing? Would you only utilize a questionnaire? Give this question some thought and then compare your ideas to the chart in Figure 1–4.

As Figure 1–4 indicates, you can choose among a wide variety of techniques to gather assessment information. In addition, you can easily combine some of them. Here is a case example.

EXAMPLE: The president of a credit union contracted out for a team-building program for his senior management team. In preparation for the program, the trainer requested a copy of the new business plan that the team had recently submitted to its board of directors and a copy of the minutes of the team's weekly meetings in the last two months. He also interviewed the president and the three vice presidents of the credit union. These interviews

FIGURE 1–4. ADVANTAGES AND DISADVANTAGES OF NINE BASIC NEEDS ASSESSMENT TECHNIQUES

	Advantages	Disadvantages

Observation

- Can be as technical as time-motion studies or as functionally or behaviorally specific as observing a new board member interacting during a meeting.
- May be as unstructured as walking through an agency's offices on the lookout for evidence of communication barriers.
- Can be used normatively to distinguish between effective and ineffective behaviors, organizational structures, and/or process.

- Minimizes the interruption of routine work flow or group activity.
- Generates in situ data, highly relevant to the situation where response to identified training needs/interests will impact.
- (When combined with a feedback step) provides for important comparison checks between inferences of the observer and the respondent.

- Requires a highly skilled observer with both process and content knowledge (unlike an interviewer who needs, for the most part, only process skill).
- Carries limitations that derive from being able to collect data only within the work setting (the other side of the first advantage listed in the preceding column).
- Holds potential for respondents to perceive the observation activity as "spying."

Questionnaires

- May be in the form of surveys or polls of a random or stratified sample of respondents, or an enumeration of an entire "population."
- Can use a variety of question formats: open-ended, projective, forced-choice, priority-ranking.
- Can take alternative forms such as Q-sorts, slip-sorts, or rating scales, either pre-designed or self-generated by respondent(s).
- May be self-administered (by mail) under controlled or uncontrolled conditions, or may require the presence of an interpreter or assistant.

- Can reach a large number of people in a short time.
- Are relatively inexpensive.
- Give opportunity of expression without fear of embarrassment.
- Yield data easily summarized and reported.

- Make little provision for free expression of unanticipated responses.
- Require substantial time (and technical skills, especially in survey model) for development of effective instruments.
- Are of limited utility in getting at causes of problems or possible solutions.
- Suffer low return rates (mailed), grudging responses, or unintended and/or inappropriate respondents.

Key Consultation

- Secures information from those persons who, by virtue of their formal or informal standing, are in a good position to know what the training needs of a particular group are:
  a. board chairman
  b. related service providers
  c. members of professional associations

- Is relatively simple and inexpensive to conduct.
- Permits input and interaction of a number of individuals, each with his or her own perspectives of the needs of the area, discipline, group, etc.
- Establishes and strengthens lines of communication between participants in the process.

- Carries a built-in bias, since it is based on views of those who tend to see training needs from their own individual or organizational perspective.
- May result in only a partial picture of training needs due to the typically non-representative nature (in a statistical sense) of a key informant group.

FIGURE 1–4. continued

	Advantages	Disadvantages

d. individuals from the service population

- Once identified, data can be gathered from these consultants by using techniques such as interviews, group discussions, questionnaires.

Print Media

- Can include professional journals, legislative news/notes, industry "rags," trade magazines, in-house publications.

Advantages:
- Is an excellent source of information for uncovering and clarifying normative needs.
- Provides information that is current, if not forward-looking.
- Is readily available and is apt to have already been reviewed by the client group.

Disadvantages:
- Can be a problem when it comes to the data analysis and synthesis into a useable form (use of clipping service of key consultants can make this type of data more useable).

Interviews

- Can be formal or casual, structured or unstructured, or somewhere in between.
- May be used with a sample of a particular group (board, staff, committee) or conducted with everyone concerned.
- Can be done in person, by phone, at the work site, or away from it.

Advantages:
- Are adept at revealing feelings, causes of and possible solutions to problems which the client is facing (or anticipates); provide maximum opportunity for the client to represent himself spontaneouly on his own terms (especially when conducted in an open-ended, non-directive manner).

Disadvantages:
- Are usually time consuming.
- Can be difficult to analyze and quantify results (especially from unstructured formats).
- Unless the interviewer is skilled, the client(s) can easily be made to feel self-conscious.
- Rely for success on a skillful interviewer who can generate data without making client(s) feel self-conscious, suspicious, etc.

Group Discussion

- Resembles face-to-face interview technique, e.g., structured or unstructured, formal or informal, or somewhere in between.
- Can be focused on job (role) analysis, group problem analysis, group goal setting, or any number of group tasks or themes, e.g., "leadership training needs of the board."
- Uses one or several of the familiar group facilitating techniques: brainstorming, nominal group process, force-fields, consensus rankings, organizational mirroring, simulation, and sculpting.

Advantages:
- Permits on-the-spot synthesis of different viewpoints.
- Builds support for the particular service response that is ultimately decided on.
- Decreased client's "dependence response" toward the service provider since data analysis is (or can be) a shared function.
- Helps participants to become better problem analysts, better listeners, etc.

Disadvantages:
- Is time consuming (therefore initially expensive) both for the consultant and the agency.
- Can produce data that are difficult to synthesize and quantify (more a problem with the less structured techniques).

FIGURE 1–4. continued

	Advantages	Disadvantages

Tests

- Are a hybridized form of questionnaire.
- Can be very functionally oriented (like observations) to test a board, staff, or committee member's proficiency.
- May be used to sample learned ideas and facts.
- Can be administered with or without the presence of an assistant.

• Can be especially helpful in determining whether the cause of a recognized problem is a deficiency in knowledge or skill or, by elimination, attitude. • Results are easily quantifiable and comparable.	• The availability of a relatively small number of tests that are validated for a specific situation. • Do not indicate if measured knowledge and skills are actually being used in the on-the-job or "back home group" situation.

Records, Reports

- Can consist of organizational charts, planning documents, policy manuals, audits and budget reports.
- Employee records (grievance, turnover, accidents, etc.)
- Includes minutes of meetings, weekly, monthly program reports, memoranda, agency service records, program evaluation studies.

• Provide excellent clues to trouble spots. • Provide objective evidence of the results of problems within the agency or group. • Can be collected with a minimum of effort and interruption of work flow since it already exists at the work site.	• Causes of problems or possible solutions often do not show up. • Carries perspective that generally reflects the past situation rather than the current one (or recent changes). • Need a skilled data analyst if clear patterns and trends are to emerge from such technical and diffuse raw data.

Work Samples

- Are similar to observation but in written form.
- Can be products generated in the course of the organization's work, e.g., ad layouts, program proposals, market analyses, letters, training designs.
- Written responses to a hypothetical but relevant case study provided by the consultant.

• Carry most of the advantages of records and reports data. • Are the organization's data (its own output).	• Case study method will take time away from actual work of the organization. • Need specialized content analysts • Analyst's assessment of strengths/weaknesses disclosed by samples can be challenged as "too subjective."

Source: Steadham, 1980, pp. 56–61. Copyright 1980 by the American Society for Training and Development, Inc. Reprinted with permission. All rights reserved.

focused on the problems facing the entire twelve-member team. On the basis of the interviews, the trainer designed a questionnaire. Before all the team members were sent the questionnaire, the interviewees were asked to evaluate and approve the first draft. Several items were reworded to use language that was friendly to the group. Figure 1–5 reproduces the final questionnaire, preceded by the cover letter that accompanied it.

As a result of the data obtained from the reports, interviews, and questionnaire, the trainer discovered that two problems significantly affected the effectiveness of this team: (1) a lack of understanding of the needs of each work unit in the credit union and (2) poor team meetings. The standard course on team building offered by the trainer was redesigned in order to give significant attention to these two problem areas.

FIGURE 1–5. SENIOR MANAGEMENT QUESTIONNAIRE, WITH COVER LETTER

Dear (Team Member):

I am a team-building consultant who has been asked to conduct a special two-day course with the senior management staff of your credit union.

As your organization is making a clear commitment to its own professional growth and development, I hope that you will see these two days as a valuable opportunity to communicate with each other without the constraints of daily deadlines and to build relationships with each other that will make you feel cohesive and united in purpose.

We will begin with some activities designed to "warm us up" and help us feel good about working together as a group. Following this, there will be some skill-building exercises to increase your group's effectiveness as a problem-solving team. The third phase of the course (and the longest) will be focused on identifying issues that need to be worked through in order to maximize your future effectiveness as a group.

An excellent way to begin doing some of this work is to collect information through a questionnaire and to feed back that information for group discussion during the course. I would like you to join with your colleagues in filling out the attached questionnaire. Your honest responses will enable the group to have a clear view of itself.

Your participation will be totally anonymous. My job will be to *summarize* the results and report them to you for your reactions.

Thank you in advance for your cooperation and support. I look forward to working with you.

1. To what extent do you agree or disagree with the following statements?

   a. We avoid conflict among ourselves to keep things peaceful.

      (strongly disagree) 1 2 3 4 5 6 7 (strongly agree)

FIGURE 1–5. continued

b. We are dedicated to the credit union movement.

   (strongly disagree) 1 2 3 4 5 6 7 (strongly agree)

c. We speak up when we need to; there can be healthy disagreements among us.

   (strongly disagree) 1 2 3 4 5 6 7 (strongly agree)

d. We don't communicate with each other frequently enough.

   (strongly disagree) 1 2 3 4 5 6 7 (strongly agree)

e. It's not always clear who's responsible for a certain assignment or problem ("I thought you were going to do it").

   (strongly disagree) 1 2 3 4 5 6 7 (strongly agree)

f. Others don't understand my operation and its needs.

   (strongly disagree) 1 2 3 4 5 6 7 (strongly agree)

g. There's little backbiting around here.

   (strongly disagree) 1 2 3 4 5 6 7 (strongly agree)

h. We have a tendency to be unrealistic.

   (strongly disagree) 1 2 3 4 5 6 7 (strongly agree)

i. There are different beliefs among us about the way the credit union should conduct its business and relate to members.

   (strongly disagree) 1 2 3 4 5 6 7 (strongly agree)

j. Men and women in our group can work comfortably together.

   (strongly disagree) 1 2 3 4 5 6 7 (strongly agree)

k. We give each other recognition and words of appreciation.

   (strongly disagree) 1 2 3 4 5 6 7 (strongly agree)

l. It's hard to know what others think about the issues and problems around here.

   (strongly disagree) 1 2 3 4 5 6 7 (strongly agree)

m. We are well organized, with clearly defined procedures. Things run smoothly here.

   (strongly disagree) 1 2 3 4 5 6 7 (strongly agree)

n. Decisions are controlled from the top.

   (strongly disagree) 1 2 3 4 5 6 7 (strongly agree)

FIGURE 1–5. continued

---

2. Because the president holds the key leadership role in this credit union, it would be helpful to provide him with some feedback. Please comment about the following:

What are some things you would like the president to

a. Continue doing?

b. Stop doing?

c. Start doing?

3. What suggestions do you have to maximize your teamwork and team effectiveness in the future?

One additional technique for assessing participants should be considered in addition to those already discussed. If conditions warrant, a trainer can give a ***precourse assignment*** to participants both to learn about their skills and to obtain case material for the course, as shown in the following example.

EXAMPLE: A precourse assignment was used in a train-the-trainer program. The memorandum reproduced in Figure 1–6 was sent to participants. When Part I of the assignment was returned, it was possible to assess how well the participants were able to specify training objectives. Part I was also used as an exercise in the training program: when the portion of the program devoted to the skill of specifying objectives had been completed, participants were asked to rewrite their own statement of objectives. Part II of the assignment also served to provide course material for the program.

FIGURE 1–6. TRAIN-THE-TRAINER PRECOURSE ASSIGNMENT

TO: Participant
FROM: Human Resources Department
SUBJECT: Administrative Information and Precourse Assignment

We are pleased to confirm your enrollment in the Active Training program that is being conducted at the Federal Plaza Building on June 30 through July 2.

As our organization changes, the ability to train and develop people on the job has become increasingly critical. Our main purpose in this seminar is to help managers and professional staff to effectively and efficiently share their expertise with others.

This seminar is designed to help you improve your effectiveness in any training you may be asked to do. Our goal is to help you with your specific training needs. To ensure that we can accomplish this, please complete Part I of the precourse assignment by Monday, June 22.

Part I

COMPLETE AND RETURN TO (*trainer*)
AT (*place*) BY (*date*)

Select a topic that you might be asked to teach over a two- to three-hour period. This topic could be something that you've already taught in a training program or a topic that you can imagine teaching in the future.

What are your objectives for this session? Outline them below.

Part II

COMPLETE AND BRING TO CLASS ON (*date*)

Choose a fifteen-minute segment from the training topic you described in Part I and follow the directions below.

- Specify your objectives for this fifteen-minute segment.
- Think about how you would present this fifteen-minute segment.
- Identify the instructional materials, if any, you would use. *Please bring an example of these materials to class.*
- Develop an outline of your presentation.

NOTE: *On the second day of the program, you will be asked to present this material to four or five other participants. In this way, you will get some useful feedback on your presentation style.*

WHAT IF THERE IS NO TIME TO DO A PROPER ASSESSMENT?

The last question to be considered is a practical one. Not all situations are ideal; obstacles to undertaking assessment data collection do arise. With significant lead time, you can utilize many of the techniques that I have just outlined. But you may easily face a situation in which a training program has to be designed and implemented hastily and/or the identity of the participants is largely unknown (this is particularly true for public workshops).

When these problems occur, try not to be discouraged. You will, of necessity, have to design the program by making your best guesses about the nature of the participants and their needs. However, you will still have some ability to obtain quick information and adjust the design accordingly. Here are some recommendations:

1. Phone a contact person who may have some familiarity with the participants and ask that person the basic questions listed at the beginning of this chapter.

2. Phone a few known participants, introduce yourself, and ask them some key questions. Hope that their responses are representative and treat them as a sample of the larger group. Or ask a contact person to set up a phone interview schedule for you.

3. Have any relevant materials (surveys, meeting notes, or records) express mailed, faxed, or e-mailed to you.

4. Contact other trainers who have worked with your training group to get their opinions and impressions.

5. Talk to participants who arrive early on the day of the program and obtain whatever information you can.

6. Design some activities at the beginning of the program that will enable you to make some assessments of the group. (More information about this is given in Chapter Three.)

If you have done some contingent planning in your overall design, it still should be possible to make final adjustments before your class begins.

WORKSHEET

ASSESSING THE NEED FOR TRAINING AND THE PARTICIPANTS

Before going on to the next chapter, try your hand at applying the ideas in this chapter. Use this worksheet to outline how you might assess participants for your next training program.

Information Desired: (*check as many as desired*)

___ Participants' stated needs

___ The nature of the participants' work

___ Participants' knowledge

___ Participants' skills

___ Participants' attitudes

___ Conditions affecting participant involvement

Methods Desired: (*check as many as desired*)

___ Observation	___ Print media	___ Tests
___ Questionnaire	___ Interview	___ Records, reports
___ Key consultation	___ Group discussion	___ Work samples

Assessment Outline:

_____

_____

_____

_____

_____

_____

_____

_____

_____

_____

_____

_____

_____

_____

_____

_____

◆ ◆ ◆

Chapter Two

Developing Active Training Objectives

After assessing participants, you are in a position to start planning your training program. At this stage, it is not enough to simply list the topics you intend to cover. An active training program is constructed in terms of the achievement of objectives. *The critical question, therefore, is not what topics to cover but what you want participants to value, understand, or do with those topics.* A clear sense of where you want to go and what you are trying to accomplish is the single most important ingredient for designing active training programs.

Determining training objectives may take long-term thinking up front, but it is worth it. Objectives are the pillars of your program, not straitjackets. The single best reason to work hard on developing training objectives is that objectives drive your training design. When you are designing a training program, you are figuring out what steps will lead to the accomplishment of your objectives. If you are not clear about your objectives, you might overlook some of the learning experiences that your participants require. Here is a case in point.

EXAMPLE: A trainer's assessment revealed that a group of real estate sales trainees knew little about the closing process in the sale of properties. Consequently, the trainer decided to cover this topic in his real estate course. He did a good job of explaining how a closing is done, but afterward participants still seemed hazy about how to conduct a closing themselves. Wanting to improve the situation, he decided to ask experienced sales personnel to identify the specific on-the-job skills the trainees would need to possess when dealing with closings. Their responses enabled him to develop a clear set of objectives for the next time he taught the course. Specifically, he concluded that trainees needed to be able to

- Describe the closing cost payments for which the buyer would be responsible
- Clearly and concisely answer typical customer questions about closing costs
- Estimate closing cost payments for different types of properties

With these objectives in mind, the program was redesigned to include experiences that not only taught the closing process but also tested the group's understanding of the process and allowed ample opportunities to practice situations in which this knowledge would be applied on the job.

————————

When you set training objectives, you also wind up setting appropriate limits on how much material you will cover. Active trainers keep their content level moderate because they are serious about achieving their objectives. They realize that covering too much material is a sure way to prevent real learning from taking place.

Clearly stated objectives also provide participants with a list of what is expected of them. Knowing what they are being held accountable for gives participants direction and responsibility. They can then be active partners in your program rather than mere attendees.

SETTING LEARNING GOALS

Once you have decided on the basic subject matter for a training program, begin your planning by setting general learning goals. Learning-goal statements articulate the basic purpose and outcomes you want to achieve. As you develop learning goals for your training program, keep in mind that some types of learning differ from others.

Three major types of learning are easily remembered as "ABC":

1. Affective learning
2. Behavioral learning
3. Cognitive learning

Affective learning includes the fostering of attitudes, feelings, and preferences. For example, you may want participants to value a certain situation, procedure, or product. Or you may wish them to become more aware of their feelings and reactions to certain issues and new ideas. Here are some examples of affective learning:

- First-line supervisors in an engineering company explore their feelings about managing the work of employees who were previously their coworkers.

- Bank managers examine the extent to which their orientation was inward-looking or customer-focused.

- New hires share reactions to their first weeks on the job, including feelings about corporate culture, new procedures, and relations with coworkers.

Behavioral learning includes the development of competence in the actual performance of procedures, operations, methods, and techniques. For example, you may want participants to practice skills you have demonstrated and receive feedback on their performance. Here are examples of behavioral learning:

- Participants attending new-employee orientation learned how to complete payroll time cards.

- Research and development personnel practiced creative thinking techniques by applying them to problems back on the job.

- Staff nurses at a hospital practiced ways to effectively prepare preoperative patients who were about to undergo surgery.

Cognitive learning includes the acquisition of information and concepts related to course content. You may want participants not only to comprehend the subject matter but also to analyze it and apply it to new situations. Here are some examples of cognitive learning.

- Participants in a training program called "The Law and the Workplace" learned the legal definition of sexual harassment and applied it to issues in their jobs.

- Spouses of alcoholics learned to identify common characteristics of co-dependency, such as people pleasing, workaholism, and perfectionism.

- Managers with responsibility for hiring learned to identify unlawful questions that should not be asked in an interview.

Although it is possible to design your training program with only one of these types of learning in mind, a design that incorporates all three is more likely to result in lasting change. Even a relatively short program can include affective, behavioral, and cognitive learning goals, as represented in these two examples.

EXAMPLE: A trainer accepted an assignment to teach managers how to use a new purchasing system. She decided that her overall learning goals were to have participants

- Value the benefits of the new system (affective learning)

- Complete and process the forms (behavioral learning)

- Determine the correct forms to use (cognitive learning)

EXAMPLE: For a course on understanding team dynamics, the trainer chose to devote one session to the task and maintenance roles members need to play in teams. He designed the session so that participants would be able to

- Identify people's current and future preferences for task or maintenance roles in a team (affective learning)
- Utilize new task and maintenance behaviors when facilitating a team meeting (behavioral learning)
- Differentiate between task and maintenance behaviors when they are exhibited by colleagues at a team meeting (cognitive learning)

Of course, your training program may be a response to a specific organizational problem. In this instance, you can focus on the kind of learning goal that is dictated by the problem it is addressing:

1. **Cognitive** goals are the priority when there is a **lack of knowledge.** This is often referred to as a "don't know" situation.
2. **Behavioral** goals are the priority when there is a **lack of skill.** This is often referred to as a "can't do" situation.
3. **Affective** goals are the priority when there is a **lack of desire** or **fear** about using new knowledge or skills. This is often referred to as a "won't do" situation.

SELECTING OBJECTIVES

Once you have established a set of learning goals, the next step is to break those goals down into specific training objectives (or outcomes). These should represent the concrete accomplishments to be attained in the training. Each learning goal will have one or more objectives that, when met, will identify accomplishment of that goal. Here is a case example.

EXAMPLE: A trainer in a term lending seminar for bankers set for himself the **cognitive** learning goal that participants would become familiar with the key business and legal considerations in structuring a term lending agreement that would meet both the bank's and the customers' needs. The results he wanted to achieve included the ability to analyze complex corporate organizations and financial statements and to understand how complex credit facilities are structured. The training objectives he selected were that, at the completion of the seminar, participants would be able to

- Identify the key credit risks in a range of complex lending situations
- Analyze the corporate structure of an organization with multiple subsidiaries, with emphasis on the appropriate lending entity
- Identify key management issues for at least three companies seeking term lending facilities

For the **behavioral** learning goal of applying term lending strategies on the job, the results he wanted to achieve included the drafting of a term lending agreement for review by a more experienced bank officer. The objectives he developed were that, at the completion of the seminar, participants would be able to

- Draft a proposed structure for term credits for the three companies previously analyzed

- Draft terms for each of the credits and discuss them with the appropriate bank attorneys

- Monitor at least two ongoing term credit facilities and write waivers and amendments as appropriate

Finally, the trainer wanted to include the **affective** learning goal that participants would value the interests of both the borrower and the lender in a term loan. The objectives developed were that, at the completion of the seminar, participants would be able to

- Identify their own feelings about business risk and protection

- Support the goals of each party for a term lending agreement, unless the goals were mutually exclusive

Sometimes trainers have too many objectives crammed into one program. To avoid this, be careful to distinguish between objectives that are nice to obtain and those that are necessary. For example, it may be critical for insurance claims adjusters to know how to access medical reference books in their office when evaluating injury claims. It would be "nice" but not critical, however, to teach them common prefixes and suffixes in medical terminology. Likewise, there is little point in setting objectives that can be achieved before participants ever come to the training program. For example, the learning of factual information such as the features and benefits of new products and services can be accomplished by having participants undertake precourse reading or computer-based instruction. By expecting them to acquire *knowledge* before a training program, you can then select higher-order objectives that involve *application* (using information), *analysis* (dissembling information), *synthesis* (putting information together), and *evaluation* (judging the value of information).

Whether something is required training or not can depend on a thorough analysis of the tasks involved in a job. Mayo and DuBois (1987) cite eight criteria for including a task in a training course (see Figure 2–1). Think about how you would apply these criteria to a task area you teach, such as performance appraisals or project management.

FIGURE 2–1. CRITERIA FOR SELECTING A JOB TASK FOR TRAINING

1. The percentage of job incumbents who actually perform the task
2. The percentage of total work time that job incumbents spend on the task
3. How critical the task is
4. The amount of delay that can be tolerated between the time when the need for performance of the task becomes evident and the time when actual performance must begin
5. The frequency with which the task is performed
6. The difficulty or complexity of the task
7. The probability of deficient performance of the task by job incumbents
8. How soon the task must be performed after a person is assigned to a job that involves it

---

Finally, the selection of training objectives may also hinge on one's understanding of adult learning needs. For example, adult learners tend to be less enthralled by survey courses. They prefer single-concept or single-theory courses (Zemke and Zemke, 1981). Adult learners also want to see the immediate value of the skills and knowledge they are taught. They require information on the significance and application of the training topic (Vella, 1994). Furthermore, adult learners like to build on prior experience. They expect the opportunity to relate what you teach them to what they already know or have thought about (Knowles, 1990).

SPECIFYING OBJECTIVES

When you have selected your objectives, state them in a form that will make them effective tools for managing, monitoring, and evaluating the training. Typically, training objectives use a format such as "By the completion of the program, participants will be able to . . ." (the specific objectives would then be listed).

This written format will give you specific criteria for determining whether the course design is appropriate. For example, if your objective is that participants will be able to utilize a skill in a job-related situation, you might ask if sufficient time to practice that skill has been built into the course.

When training objectives are more technical in nature, some trainers make it a practice to state not only what participants should be able to do after training but also under what **conditions** and according to what **standards** this will happen. Conditions include such things as the availability of informational aids or an allowance for performance simplifications. Standards consist of the level of performance being sought in terms of perfection, time utilization, output, and so forth. Here are two examples.

EXAMPLE: At the end of this training session, employees will be able to process lockbox items at a rate of 500 per hour with no more than two errors per 1,000 items.

EXAMPLE: When practicing in skits on telephone interruptions, participants will deal with five phone call interruptions in ten minutes with no quantitative decrease in work completed.

If objectives are in the right format, the development of training evaluations can be very straightforward. In fact, evaluations can relate specifically to previously stated objectives. A comparison of the written objectives to the participants' experiences provides a direct means of evaluating the success of your training program.

You should be careful, however, to avoid overspecifying your training objectives, particularly in nontechnical training programs. When teaching management skills, for instance, being overly precise about objectives can lead to mechanistic training. No one wants managers to do everything precisely "by the book," with little room to exercise their personal style and their own sense of the right way to do things. Often, your job is not to train but to educate—to expose participants to new ways of thinking, feeling, and acting and allow them to integrate these ways into their being. You may be advocating a five-step procedure for counseling troubled employees but your participants may willingly accept and adopt only some of the steps. Or they may decide that they need to figure out an entirely different first step to make the procedure work for them. The better you educate participants concerning your subject matter, the less likely they are to leave the program as mindless clones.

EXPRESSING OBJECTIVES

With the above caution in mind, it is still important for the training objectives you do specify to be written in a style that is easy to understand and to the point. Avoid commonly misinterpreted terms such as those in Figure 2–2. Additionally, use specific action verbs to assist both the group members and the sponsor of your training program to evaluate your program. Figure 2–3 lists action verbs that are frequently used when writing training objectives.

FIGURE 2–2. TIPS IN WRITING OBJECTIVES

Skill	Commonly Misinterpreted Terms	Behavior Terms
Knowledge	To know, learn	To write, define, repeat, name, list
Comprehension	To understand, appreciate	To restate, discuss, describe, explain, review, translate, locate
Application	To show, apply a thorough knowledge of	To operate, illustrate, use, employ, sketch
Analysis	To analyze	To differentiate between, appraise, calculate, test, compare, contrast, solve, criticize
Synthesis	To establish creativity	To compose, propose, plan, design, manage, collect, construct, organize, prepare
Evaluation	To show good judgment	To evaluate, rate, select, estimate, measure

FIGURE 2–3. EXAMPLES OF ACTION VERBS FREQUENTLY USED IN WRITING TRAINING OBJECTIVES

Administer	Consolidate	Expedite	Proceed
Adopt	Consult	Formulate	Process
Advise	Control	Furnish	Promote
Analyze	Coordinate	Implement	Propose
Anticipate	Correlate	Improve	Provide
Appraise	Correspond	Initiate	Recommend
Approve	Delegate	Inspect	Report
Arrange	Design	Instruct	Represent
Assemble	Determine	Interpret	Research
Assign	Develop	Investigate	Resolve
Assist	Devise	Issue	Review
Assume	Direct	Maintain	Revise
Assure	Discuss	Monitor	Schedule
Authorize	Dispose	Negotiate	Secure
Calculate	Disseminate	Notify	Select
Circulate	Distribute	Obtain	Sign
Clear	Draft	Operate	Specify
Collaborate	Endorse	Participate	Stimulate
Collect	Establish	Perform	Submit
Compile	Estimate	Place	Supervise
Concur	Evaluate	Plan	Train
Conduct	Execute	Practice	Transcribe
Confer	Exercise	Prepare	Verify

COMMUNICATING TRAINING OBJECTIVES TO OTHERS

Communicating your objectives effectively to others is an important skill to develop. You may submit your training plans to management for approval only to discover that they are confused by your language or put off by the format of your objectives. In addition, participants can feel overwhelmed by a laundry list of objectives like those sometimes presented in course catalogs or by language that is laden with jargon. Figure 2–4 contains such an example. Organize objectives into a clearer, easier-to-read list such as the example in Figure 2–5.

FIGURE 2–4. MANAGEMENT SKILLS: TRAINING OBJECTIVES

When you complete this course, you will be able to

- Define and identify what affects motivation
- Discuss the impact of leadership style on motivation
- Identify your leadership style
- Identify and determine different leadership strategies
- Explain the impact of effective communication on motivation and leadership
- Demonstrate effective verbal and nonverbal communication skills
- Use positive reinforcement and coaching skills
- Give corrective or negative feedback to keep motivation intact and maximize workers' productivity
- Use the performance appraisal process effectively
- Recognize the benefits of teamwork and win-win situations
- Describe the difference between compromise and collaboration
- Assess the impact of your style on team development
- Remove barriers to teamwork and overcome resistance to change
- Develop a strategy to promote and build teams
- Discuss ways to maximize individual workers' learning
- Identify common pitfalls made in on-the-job training and ways to avoid them
- Systematically plan, implement, and follow up with on-the-job training skills
- Explain your role in customer service and the overall company image
- Use effective communication skills with customers to build relationships and establish a rapport
- Demonstrate effective conflict resolution techniques
- Develop personal action plans for improvement

FIGURE 2–5. SHELTER PRODUCTS: TRAINING OBJECTIVES

At the end of this course, you will be able to

A. Define the following mortgage terms:
    1. Mortgage
    2. Condominium
    3. Co-op and co-op loan
    4. Second mortgage
    5. Equity source account
    6. Refinancing
    7. Bridge loan
    8. Real estate loan

B. Perform calculations
    1. Demonstrate use of an amortization table
    2. Show how you determine monthly payments of principal and interest for fixed- and adjustable-rate mortgage loans
    3. Explain origination fees and the annual percentage rate

C. Mortgage finance
    1. Explain the role of the secondary market for mortgage funds
    2. Identify FNMA requirements and their relationship to the NYBD RAAC

WORKSHEET

DEVELOPING ACTIVE TRAINING OBJECTIVES

Try your hand at specifying objectives. Take the content of a program you are presently conducting or hope to teach in the near future and state the objectives you have for the program on the worksheet below.

Upon completion of this [module/course], participants will be able to:

_____

◆   ◆   ◆

Chapter Three

Creating Opening Exercises

Once you have gathered information about the needs of your intended participants and selected your training objectives, you can start planning your program. Opening exercises are an important element in the beginning of an active training program. They can sometimes be considered as the "appetizers" to the full meal: they allow participants to get a taste of what is to follow. Although some trainers choose to begin a course with only a short introduction, including at least one opening exercise in your design is a first step that has many benefits.

WHAT OPENING EXERCISES ACCOMPLISH

Many people assume that opening activities are only social in nature. If participants are strangers to each other, something has to be done to allow them to introduce themselves to each other. For this reason, probably the most popular icebreaker in the training world is to pair up participants, have them interview each other, and then have them introduce their partner to the large group. Imagine how many times people have experienced this ritual! There are many more creative and compelling icebreakers and a much wider view of their function.

In the first moments of an active training program, three goals are equally important, even if the program is short or an assessment has preceded the course:

1. *Team building*—helping participants to become acquainted with each other and creating a spirit of cooperation and interdependence

2. *On-the-spot assessment*—learning about the attitudes, knowledge, and experience of the participants

3. *Immediate learning involvement*—creating initial interest in the training topic

49

All three of these goals, accomplished singly or in combination, help to develop a training environment that engages the participants, promotes their willingness to take part in some active learning, and creates positive training norms. You can take as little as five minutes or as much as two hours on opening activities (depending on the overall length of your program); it will be time well spent.

Team Building

Team-building exercises foster positive group attitudes by asking participants to learn each other's names and to get to know each other. If the members have already met, opening exercises can help them to become reacquainted after a period of separation. Either way, an opening design that stresses team building can develop a feeling of spirit and pride among the members of your program.

There are numerous getting-acquainted exercises that give participants an opportunity to introduce themselves to the other members of the group in an interesting and nonthreatening manner. An excellent example is Name Bingo, the instructions for which appear in Figure 3–1.

Almost all opening exercises can be varied to produce different effects. For example, Name Bingo can be modified to increase self-disclosure. Besides names, participants can be asked to obtain and record on the Bingo form one fact about each person they meet. *Each time participants are asked for a fact about themselves, they are required to share one that is different from those given to other participants.* In step 7, all the participants share the many facts they have learned about the person whose name is picked. This change lengthens the exercise, however, so it's best to use it only when the group is small.

FIGURE 3–1. NAME BINGO

---

1. Participants mill around the room and meet each other.

2. Each time a participant exchanges names with someone, she or he writes the new name anywhere on a Bingo form.

3. After all participants have met, each one places an *O* in any unused box.

4. The trainer then places a copy of everyone's name in a hat.

5. The hat is passed around the group, one participant at a time. Each participant picks a name out of the hat. Everyone places an *X* on the box containing the name picked.

6. Whenever any player obtains 5 *X*s in a row (horizontally, vertically, or diagonally), he or she yells "Bingo!" (Eventually, everyone will get Bingo several times.)

7. As their names are picked, participants should introduce themselves to the group and share three facts about themselves.

FIGURE 3–1. continued

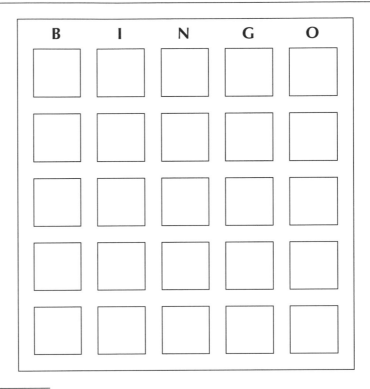

Note: Use a three-by-three format if the group includes fewer than ten people or a four-by-four format if the group numbers between ten and sixteen.

A fun way to do group building once participants have become acquainted is a takeoff on the game show "To Tell the Truth" (see Figure 3–2 for instructions).

FIGURE 3–2. TO TELL THE TRUTH

1. Ask each participant to write down (legibly!) on a card three personal facts not previously shared with the group.

2. Mix up the cards and distribute a card to each participant. (Be sure no one receives his or her own card.)

3. Have each participant read the card she or he has been dealt, then ask for three guesses as to whose card was read. Prior to the guesses, request that participants not reveal their identity even if it is guessed.

4. Ask, "Will the real bearer of this card please stand up?"

5. Allow for surprise or self-congratulatory applause.

A more self-disclosing yet fun-filled way to accomplish the same purpose is Predictions, a guessing game based on first impressions. Participants are formed into small groups to do the activity, which is described in Figure 3–3.

FIGURE 3–3. PREDICTIONS

Your job is to predict how each person in your group would answer the following questions. (Try to be as specific as possible. Don't be afraid of bold guesses!) When you have finished your predictions, the participants should respond to the questions themselves.

1. Where did you grow up?
2. What were you like as a child? A student?
3. Were your parents strict or lenient?
4. What type of music do you enjoy?
5. What are some of your favorite leisure activities?
6. How many hours do you usually sleep nightly?

Note: Other questions can be added or substituted.

Other team-building activities are especially appropriate for a group where members already know each other well. Often, they involve some way for the group to produce something they can take pride in. One example that can be used in a longer training program is called TV Commercial (see Figure 3–4).

FIGURE 3–4. TV COMMERCIAL

---

1. Divide participants into teams of no more than six members.
2. Ask teams to create a thirty-second TV commercial that advertises their team, their organization, their common job, or the importance of the training topic.
3. The commercial should contain a slogan (for example, "Just Do It") and visuals.
4. Explain that the general concept and an outline of the commercial are sufficient. However, if teams want to act out their commercial, let them.
5. Before each team begins planning its commercial, discuss the characteristics of currently well-known commercials to stimulate creativity (for example, the use of a well-known personality, humor, or a comparison to the competition).
6. Ask each team to present its ideas. Praise everyone's creativity.

A second example is called Group Résumé (see Figure 3–5).

FIGURE 3–5. GROUP RÉSUMÉ

1. Divide participants into groups of at least six members.

2. Tell the group that within it is an incredible array of talents and experiences.

3. Suggest that one way to identify and brag about the group's resources is to compose a group résumé. (You may want to suggest a job or contract the group could be bidding for.)

4. Give the groups newsprint and markers to display their résumé. It should include any data that sell the group as a whole, such as information about

   Educational background and schools attended

   Total years of professional experience

   Positions held

   Professional skills

   Hobbies, talents, travel, and family

   Major accomplishments

   Publications

5. Invite each group to present its résumé and celebrate the total resources contained within the entire group.

Yet another way to promote group cohesion is to invite participants to set ground rules that provide agreements about how they will interact and work with each other. One way to accomplish this is to provide a list of several possible ground rules. Ask participants to select three from the list. Tabulate the results and take note of the rules most often selected.

The following items might be suitable for your list:

- Respect confidentiality
- Have everyone participate when working in small groups or teams
- Observe the starting time of the class
- Get to know others who are different from you
- Let others finish what they are saying without being interrupted
- Allow no put-downs or cheap shots
- Speak for yourself
- Be brief and to the point when speaking

- Use gender-sensitive language
- Be prepared for class
- Don't sit in the same seat for every session of the class
- Agree to disagree
- Give everyone a chance to speak
- Build on each other's ideas before criticizing them

On-the-Spot Assessment

On-the-spot assessment exercises ask participants to do such things as

- Share their learning goals or expectations
- Raise questions or concerns they may have about the course
- Relate their knowledge and experience to the course topics
- List the successes and problems they have experienced that are relevant to the course
- Explore their opinions and attitudes about the course topic

Such exercises elicit information that will help you to gauge the expertise of the group while giving participants a sense of immediate participation. Often, you can request the information you want in a spontaneous manner by asking **general questions** in the opening minutes of the training program—for example, "What motivated you to come here today?" or "Do you have any concerns about today's session or what you may be asked to do?" Or you can ask **training-specific questions** such as these used in a time management seminar: "Who uses a 'to-do' list on a daily basis?" "How does it help you to organize your day?"

Structured exercises can also be used to gain on-the-spot assessment information, as the following examples illustrate.

EXAMPLE: Managers participating in a mandatory workshop on new corrective action policies were asked to discuss the following questions with their seat partner:

1. From your experience, what constitutes a "problem behavior"?

2. How do you feel when you have to confront a problem employee?

3. What actions have you taken in the past to discipline employees?

After each question, the trainer asked two or three participants to share their answers with the whole group. As group members had an opportunity to explore their own perspectives on handling problem situations before learning new corrective action procedures, the trainer gained valuable information about the training group.

EXAMPLE: Child care workers in group homes were formed into a rotating group of panelists. Each "panel" was asked to discuss its responses to one of the following questions:

1. What do you like about the kids you work with?
2. What turns you off about the kids you work with?
3. What do the kids do to "push your buttons"?
4. What advice do you think you will get in this training program?

As panelists responded in front of their coworkers, the trainer learned about their willingness to self-disclose, their feelings about the children they cared for, and their understanding of the course content.

EXAMPLE: Family therapy trainees were asked to form trios. Each trio was asked to generate two questions, one concerning the theory of family therapy and the other concerning the practice of family therapy. The questions had to relate to topics the participants hoped to learn about during the training program. Some of the questions that emerged were these:

- (Theoretical) What is the role of interpretation in family therapy?
- (Practical) Do you have to see the entire family to do family therapy properly?
- (Theoretical) Are the various models of family therapy really different from each other?
- (Practical) Is a "fifty-minute" hour enough for most family sessions?

The trainer gained in two ways from hearing these questions. She not only learned some of the issues that participants wanted to discuss but also found out about their knowledge regarding program content and their expectations regarding its level of sophistication.

An interesting way to gather on-the-spot assessment information is recommended by Thiagarajan (1989). He suggests letting the participants collect the data as a kind of icebreaker. Here are six design steps he offers:

1. Figure out the assessment questions you want to ask.
2. Divide the participants into as many teams as you have questions.
3. Ask the teams to spend a few minutes devising a strategy for efficiently collecting information about their assigned question.
4. Ask the teams to collect the data simultaneously, using whatever strategies they devised earlier.

5. Call time and ask the teams to meet in the corners of the training room and prepare a summary of their data.

6. Have each team make a presentation.

Another design to consider, outlined in Figure 3–6, focuses on the concerns participants might bring to a training session.

FIGURE 3–6. CONCERNS OF A TRAINING GROUP

1. Hand out a blank index card to each participant.

2. Ask the participants to write down any concerns they have about the nature of the present training program (names should be withheld). These concerns might include the following:
   - How difficult or time-consuming the training may be
   - How they can participate freely and comfortably
   - How they will function in small learning groups
   - How available the trainer will be
   - What access there will be to reading materials
   - What the time schedule for the course will be

3. Request participants to pass the card clockwise around the group. Each time a participant receives a card, she or he should read it and place a checkmark on the card if it contains a statement that is also of concern to the reader.

4. By the time all of the participants have gotten back their own cards, each person will have reviewed the concerns of the entire group. At this point, hold an open discussion of the concerns that have emerged.

Variation: Instead of holding a discussion, identify the top four concerns in the group by establishing which cards contain the most checks. Break the class into four groups and invite each group to elaborate on the concern written on one of the four index cards. Ask each group to summarize its discussions for the whole class.

Immediate Learning Involvement

Immediate learning involvement exercises ask participants to respond to initial questions about the course content, to try out learning activities related to the course content without previous instruction, or to view presentations or demonstrations that give an initial description of skills to be learned within the program. These activities help to introduce the course in a dramatic, active manner that draws the participants into the training program right from the beginning of the session.

One of the simplest ways to involve participants for this purpose is to display an interesting proverb or slogan related to the training topic and then ask each participant to introduce herself or himself and share reactions to the statement. (Divide into small groups if the total group size is too large.) Here is a sample of sayings that could be used for well-known topics:

- Why put off until tomorrow what you can do today? (time management)
- It's not what you say but how you say it. (communication)
- You can't sell a product until you understand how it works. (sales)
- We cannot fully understand the beginning of anything until we understand the end. (planning)
- Nobody washes a rented car. (employee empowerment)
- A company is known by the people it keeps. (customer service)
- There is no "I" in TEAM. (team building)
- Yesterday's home runs don't win tomorrow's ball games. (product improvement)
- Managers do things right; leaders do the right things. (leadership)
- The only person who likes change is a wet baby. (organizational change)

Another simple immediate involvement technique is called Active Knowledge Sharing (see Figure 3–7). This is a great way to draw participants immediately into the subject matter of your course. It would work with any group and with any topic.

FIGURE 3–7. ACTIVE KNOWLEDGE SHARING

1. Provide a list of questions pertaining to the subject matter you will be teaching. You could include some or all of the following categories:
   - Terms to define (for example, "What does TQM mean?")
   - Multiple-choice questions concerning facts, concepts, procedures, policies, and so on (for example, "A psychological test is valid if it [a] measures an attribute consistently over time or [b] measures what it purports to measure")
   - People to identify who are important to the subject matter (for example, "Who is Kurt Lewin?")
   - Questions concerning actions one could take in certain situations (for example, "How would you deal with an employee who is persistently late?")

FIGURE 3–7. continued

- Incomplete sentences (for example, "A _____ identifies the basic categories of tasks you can perform with a computer program")

2. Ask participants to answer the questions as well as they can.

3. Then invite them to mill around the room, finding others who can answer questions they do not know how to answer. Encourage participants to help each other. Or invite participants to compare answers with a partner or small team.

4. Reconvene the full group and review the answers. Fill in answers unknown to any of the participants.

Finally, you can create an immediate learning-involvement exercise that is tailored to introduce your particular training topic. Naturally, the development of a customized exercise requires greater effort than the simpler techniques described above, but the return on your investment of time will be rewarded many times over. Here are some examples.

EXAMPLE: A trainer introduced the topic of organizational change by projecting a cartoon depicting a wagon with square wheels, carrying a load of round tires, that was being pulled by a single person and pushed from the rear by two other people. Participants were asked to generate as many associations to this illustration as they could and to share their reactions with others. This metaphorical tool is a proven and engaging approach to identifying alternatives to the ways things are done in organizations. The illustration links neatly to issues of organizational change. Over two hundred points about the illustration have been accumulated, such as "Square wheels are better for going downhill" and "We also don't use the round wheels we already have" (Simmerman, 1998).

EXAMPLE: A trainer began a program on effective communication by asking participants to mingle and introduce themselves to one another. After meeting five different partners, participants were asked, "What communication behaviors did others display that formed positive first impressions?" Responses were captured on newsprint and used to link to skills that were to be taught in the training session.

EXAMPLE: Participants in a course on conflict resolution were given a sheet that listed, in scrambled fashion, fourteen methods of handling conflict, ten of which might be considered "negative" methods and four of which might be considered "positive." They were asked to circle the five methods they personally used most often and underline the five methods used most often by other people in their personal and/or professional lives. The selections were then tabulated across the full group and significant discrepancies were observed. Typically, the participants saw themselves as users of positive methods more often than they perceived others doing so. The trainer then pointed out the human tendency to project negative attitudes on others and asked participants to discuss how this tendency affects people's behaviors in conflict situations.

Multipurpose Exercises

While it is possible to design one of each kind of exercise as part of your course introduction, too much time spent on opening exercises may require you to skimp on the meat of the training program. Another approach is to design one opening exercise that simultaneously accomplishes ***team building, on-the-spot assessment,*** and ***immediate learning involvement.*** An example is an opening exercise called Rotating Trio Exchange, described in Figure 3–8. This is an in-depth way for participants to get acquainted and become immediately involved in the course topic. At the same time, valuable assessment information is obtained.

FIGURE 3–8. ROTATING TRIO EXCHANGE

Participants are asked to discuss within trios a variety of questions that help them to get to know each other; learn about their attitudes, knowledge, and experience; and begin discussion of the course content. For example, a group of managers could be divided into groups of three and asked such questions as "How have you been managed by others?" "What advice would you give yourself to be more effective as a manager?" and "What do you want to learn from this training program?" Similar questions could be developed for other subject matter areas. In a course on stress management, participants could be asked questions such as "What are some of the causes of stress in your job? At home?" or "How do you currently try to deal with stress in your life?" With each question posed by the trainer, new groups are formed by rotating two members, thereby increasing the number of participants who become acquainted with each other.

Another opening exercise that both fosters group building and provides assessment information is based upon a scavenger hunt. Participants receive a set of questions that must be answered with the names of other group members. Use a wide variety of questions that touch upon both personal information and course content. (This activity is extremely flexible, because you can easily adapt the questions to fit any type of group.) You might want to offer a token prize to the participant who finishes the scavenger hunt first. When a winner has been declared, reassemble the participants and survey the entire group about each of the items. Promote short discussions of some items. A sample human scavenger hunt for a team-building workshop is given in Figure 3–9.

FIGURE 3–9. HUMAN SCAVENGER HUNT

Read the following items. Then, for each item, find someone in the group who fits the description. Write his or her first name in the space under the item. You may not use any person's name more than once.

Find someone . . .

1. Who has the same first initial as you

2. Who thinks that teams often waste time

3. Who meets in teams more than three hours a week

4. Who was born in the same month as you

5. Who likes to do things alone

6. Who has had prior training in team problem-solving tools

7. Who thinks that an effective team usually has a fair amount of conflict

---

If you have time, it is also possible to sequence together opening exercises that flow well with each other and promote team building, on-the-spot assessment, and immediate learning involvement. Figure 3–10 contains the opening sequence of a training program on coaching and counseling skills. Notice how all three goals are accomplished.

**FIGURE 3–10. OPENING SEQUENCE FOR
COACHING AND COUNSELING TRAINING PROGRAM**

1. Overview of the Program
   a. Welcome participants and briefly explain the distinction between coaching and counseling. (As a coach, the manager identifies a need among employees for instruction and direction, usually directly related to their current work assignments. A coaching relationship is indicated when employees are open to advice and show little defensiveness. As a counselor, the manager identifies a problem that is interfering with the work performance of her or his employees. A manager needs to switch from a coaching to a counseling mode when employees are not as open to her or his input.)

FIGURE 3–10. continued

---

    b. Indicate the importance both coaching and counseling play in a manager's work and the sensitivity a manager must have in knowing when to use each.

    c. Share these objectives:

- To understand the value of coaching and counseling in a manager's work

- To know when to coach and when to counsel

- To examine how one's personality affects the coaching or counseling role

- To develop basic competence in applying coaching and counseling skills

2. Quartet Exchange

    a. Form quartets and ask them to discuss the following question: "How have you been coached and counseled by managers in your career? Which approaches were effective and which were ineffective?"

    b. Invite four participants to share with the full group a personal example of a manager, two sharing examples of an effective manager and two sharing examples of an ineffective one.

    c. Form new quartets and ask them to identify specific examples in which coaching and counseling have taken place or might take place in their work as managers.

    d. Obtain one example from each participant and record it on newsprint. Retain the list as a data bank of examples that can be used in later designs.

    e. Form new quartets one more time and ask them to respond to the following question: "What are some of your strengths and weaknesses when coaching and counseling employees?" Suggest that each person in the group take a turn sharing his or her response.

3. The Difference Between a Coach and a Counselor

    a. Refer to the newsprint list that was made previously and identify some situations that clearly call for coaching, some that call for counseling, and some that may involve both.

    b. Give out a handout that defines coaching to half the group and a handout that defines counseling to the other half. Have each participant read over her or his definition. Pair participants with different handouts and ask them to explain their contents to each other.

4. Initial Questions About Coaching and Counseling

    a. Ask participants to state on an index card one question they have about how to be an effective coach and counselor.

    b. Pass the index cards around the group in a clockwise direction so that each person gets to read each index card.

    c. Invite participants to place a check on any card that expresses a question that is important to them.

FIGURE 3–10. continued

---

d. Identify the questions that received the most votes and respond to each by (1) giving an immediate, but brief, answer; (2) postponing the question to a later, more appropriate time in the program; or (3) noting that the program will not be able to address the question (promise a personal response, if possible).

Source: Silberman, 1992a, pp. 21–22.

WHAT TO KEEP IN MIND WHEN CREATING OPENING EXERCISES

As you design your active training program, take the time to consider carefully what initial objectives you wish to accomplish in the opening moments of your session. Your goals might include any combination of team-building, assessment, or involvement exercises. In addition, you should be aware of other considerations as they relate to the particular group you will be training:

1. *Level of threat.* Is the group that you will be training open to new ideas and activities or do you anticipate hesitation and reservations from the group members as you begin your session? Opening with an exercise that exposes participants' lack of knowledge or skill can be risky; group members may not yet be ready to reveal their limitations. Alternatively, an activity that asks participants to comment on something familiar to them eases them into the course content.

2. *Appropriateness to group norms.* A group of executive managers may initially be less accepting of playing games than would a group of students. Health care professionals and therapists might feel more comfortable sharing their feelings in a Rotating Trio Exchange exercise (see Figure 3–8) than would a group of research scientists. You are setting the stage for the entire course as you plan your opening activity; consider your audience and design appropriately.

3. *Relevance to training content.* Unless you are interested in a simple exchange of names, an initial design offers an excellent opportunity for participants to begin learning course material. Adapt one of the icebreakers suggested here to reflect the material you are planning to teach in your course. The closer your exercise ties into the course content, the easier a transition you will be able to make to your next design.

These design considerations have relevance for every aspect of your training program but are especially important in the opening stages. A successful opening exercise sets the stage for a successful program; likewise, one that seems threatening, silly, or unrelated to the rest of your course can create an awkward atmosphere that will be difficult for you to overcome.

TEN WAYS TO OBTAIN PARTICIPATION

No matter how creatively you design your opening exercises, they may still fall flat if the training group is reluctant to participate or if certain participants dominate. A wide range of methods can be used to obtain active participation in the opening phase of a training program. If you use a few of them on a consistent basis, you will avoid the phenomenon of hearing from the same participants all the time. Here are ten possibilities, one or many of which likely will suit the opening exercise you have in mind. You can also use these methods when designing activities for other portions of an active training program.

1. *Open discussion.* Ask a question and open it up to the entire group without any further structuring.

Use open discussion when you are certain that several participants want to participate. Its voluntary quality is also appealing. Don't overuse this method. If you do, you will limit participants to those who are comfortable about raising their hand. If you have a very participative group and are worried that the discussion might be too lengthy, say beforehand, "I'd like to ask four or five participants to share . . ." If you are worried that few people will volunteer, say, "How many of you can tell us . . . ?" rather than "Who can tell us . . . ?"

2. *Response cards.* Pass out index cards and request anonymous answers to your questions.

Use response cards to save time, to provide anonymity for personally threatening self-disclosures, or to make it easier for shy people to contribute. The need to state yourself concisely on a card is another advantage of this method. Say, "For this discussion, I would like you to write down your thoughts first before we talk together any further." Have the index cards passed around the group or have them returned to you to be read at a later point. Be careful to make your questions clear and encourage brief, legible responses.

3. *Polling.* Verbally poll all participants or provide a questionnaire that is filled out and tallied on the spot.

Use polling to obtain data quickly and in a quantifiable form. Pose questions that call for a clear-cut answer such as "I agree" or "That's true." Ask participants to raise their hand when the responses they agree with are given. In place of raising their hand, you can ask them to hold up response cards that represent their choice (for example, a yellow card might indicate "false") or place a color-coded dot on a designated area of a large form such as a chart or newsprint. If you use a questionnaire, make it short and easy to tally immediately.

4. ***Subgroup discussions.*** Form participants into subgroups of three or more to share and record information.

Use subgroup discussions when you have sufficient time to process questions and issues. This is one of the key methods for obtaining everyone's participation. You can assign people to subgroups randomly (for example, by counting off) or purposively (for example, by forming an all-woman group). Pose a question for discussion or give the subgroup a task or assignment to complete. It is often helpful to designate group roles such as facilitator, timekeeper, recorder, or presenter and to obtain volunteers or assign members to fill them. Make sure that participants are in face-to-face contact with each other. Try to separate subgroups so that they do not disturb each other.

5. ***Partners.*** Form participants into pairs and instruct them to work on tasks or discuss key questions.

Use partners when you want to involve everybody but do not have enough time for small-group discussion. A pair is a good group configuration for developing a long-term supportive relationship and/or for working on complex activities that would not lend themselves to larger group configurations. Pair up participants either by physical proximity or by a wish to put certain participants together. Often, it is not necessary to move chairs to create pair activities. You can ask pairs to do many things, such as reading and discussing a short written document together, developing or responding to a question, or comparing their results to those of some activity they performed previously on an independent basis. Give instructions such as "Read this handout together and discuss it. Come up with examples or applications of what you are reading," "Create a question you both have about this topic," "Discuss together your response to the following question," or "Compare your results on this survey. How are you alike or different?"

6. ***Go-arounds.*** Go around the group and obtain short responses to key questions.

Use this method when you want to obtain something quickly from each participant. Sentence stems (for example, "One thing that makes a manager effective is . . .") are useful in conducting go-arounds. Invite participants to "pass" when they wish. Avoid repetition, if you wish, by asking each participant for a new contribution to the process. If the group is large, create a smaller go-around group by obtaining short responses from one side of the room, from people who are wearing glasses, or from some other smaller sample.

7. ***Games.*** Use popular games or quiz game formats to elicit participants' ideas or knowledge.

Use games to stimulate energy and involvement. Virtually any game can be adapted for training purposes, including basketball, Bingo, darts, Jeopardy, poker, Family Feud, Pictionary, Wheel of Fortune, bowling, Scrabble, soccer, and crossword puzzles. Be sure that the game requires everyone's participation and make the instructions crystal clear.

8. *Calling on the next speaker.* Ask participants to raise their hand when they want to share their views and ask the present speaker in the group, not the trainer, to call on the next speaker.

Say, "For this discussion, I would like you to call on each other rather than having me select who is to speak next. When you have finished speaking, look around to see whose hand is raised and call on someone." (Do not allow participants to call on people who have not indicated a desire to participate.) Use calling on the next speaker when you are sure that there is a lot of interest in the discussion or activity and you wish to promote participant interaction. When you wish to resume as moderator, inform the group that you are changing back to the regular format.

9. *Panels.* Invite a small number of participants to present their views in front of the entire group.

Use panels when time permits to have a focused, serious response to your questions. Rotate panelists to increase participation. An informal panel can be created by asking for the views of a designated number of participants who remain in their seats. Serve as panel moderator or invite a participant to perform this role.

10. *Fishbowls.* Ask a portion of the group to form a discussion circle and have the remaining participants form a listening circle around them.

Use a fishbowl to help bring focus to large-group discussions. Although it is time-consuming, this is the best method for combining the virtues of large- and small-group discussion. Bring new groups into the inner circle to continue the discussion. You can do this by obtaining new volunteers or assigning participants to be discussants. As a variation of concentric circles, you can have participants remain seated at a table and invite different tables or parts of a table to be the discussants as the others listen.

Bear in mind that you can combine some of these ten methods of obtaining participation. For example, you might pose a question, form partners to discuss it, and then obtain whole-group reaction through methods such as open discussion, calling on the next speaker, and panels. By inserting the partner exchange first, you will have more people ready to participate in the whole-group setting. Or begin with response cards, followed by a go-around or subgroups.

WORKSHEET

CREATING OPENING EXERCISES

This worksheet can help you to plan an opening exercise for your next training program. Modify one of the sample exercises from this chapter or go ahead and create your own.

Goals Desired: (*check as many as desired*)

____ Team building

____ On-the-spot assessment

____ Immediate learning involvement

Method Selected: (*check as many as desired*)

____ Open discussion	____ Go-arounds
____ Response cards	____ Games
____ Polling	____ Calling on the next speaker
____ Subgroup discussions	____ Panels
____ Partners	____ Fishbowls

Activity Outline:

_____

_____

_____

_____

_____

_____

_____

_____

_____

_____

_____

_____

_____

_____

_____

_____

◆ ◆ ◆

Chapter Four

Preparing Effective Lectures

As you move from designing the opening exercises to the more central portion of your training program, you will almost certainly decide to present some of the information you wish to cover in a lecture-type format. Lecturing is the most efficient and lowest-cost method of transmitting information in a classroom setting and is useful for conveying information to a large group, especially when you need to get across general knowledge. It is a standard tool that remains in use in most training environments.

If you are committed to active training, however, you face a potential problem: *lectures put participants in a position of sustained, passive listening*. This is even true when tools such as PowerPoint presentations or videos are used to visually highlight key points. As I have already noted in Part One of this book, learning cannot occur simply by listening and seeing. It requires the person's own mental processing to take place. Therefore, lecturing by itself will never lead to real learning.

Nonetheless, a lecture still can hold an important place in an active training program if you work to involve participants and maximize understanding and retention through participative techniques. To accomplish these ends, a lecture has to be as carefully designed as any other training activity.

FIVE WAYS TO GAIN YOUR AUDIENCE'S INTEREST

The first design element you should consider if you want a lecture to be effective is a method to grab hold of your listeners' attention. Instead of diving right into your course content, try building your participants' interest and involvement in the subject matter. Here are five techniques (with examples) to help you to do just that.

Introductory Exercise

Begin with a game or fun-filled activity that dramatically introduces the main points of the lecture.

EXAMPLE: A lecture on the merits of one-way versus two-way communication was about to begin. Before plunging in, the trainer utilized the short activity in Figure 4–1 to build interest in the lecture.

FIGURE 4–1. PAPER-TEARING EXERCISE

Time Allocation: 5 minutes

Materials: Blank 8½-by-11-inch sheets of paper for each participant

Instructions:

1. Tell the participants the following: "We are going to play a game that will show us some important things about communication. Pick up your sheet of paper and hold it in front of you. Now close your eyes and follow the directions I will give you—*and no peeking!*

2. Give the following directions, carrying them out yourself with your own sheet of paper and pausing after each instruction to give the group time to comply:

   "The first thing I want you to do is to fold your sheet of paper in half."

   "Now tear off the upper right-hand corner."

   "Fold it in half again and tear off the upper left-hand corner of the sheet."

   "Fold it in half again. Now tear off the lower right-hand corner of the sheet."

3. After the tearing is complete, say something like "Now you can open your eyes, and let's see what you have. If I did a good job of communicating and you did a good job of listening, all of our sheets should look the same!" Hold your sheet up for them to see. It is highly unlikely that any sheet will match yours exactly. There will also be a variety of shapes among the participants.

4. Observe the different shapes. There will probably be much laughter.

5. Ask the group why no one's paper matched yours. You will probably get responses like "You didn't let us ask questions!" or "Your directions could be interpreted in different ways." Then lead into a presentation on the need for two-way communication in the workplace.

EXAMPLE: A trainer was about to give a presentation about the ways in which people in organizations feel stuck because they believe they lack the resources to obtain the results expected of them. Before the presentation, the trainer gave participants six toothpicks each and challenged them to create four triangles with the toothpicks. After several frustrating minutes, the participants complained that the result couldn't be obtained because there weren't enough toothpicks. The trainer then showed the participants that they did indeed have "enough resources." The solution lies in making a three-dimensional pyramid with the six toothpicks, thereby creating three standing triangles and one base triangle. After the exercise, the trainer began his presentation about the importance of creative problem solving in organizations.

Leadoff Story or Interesting Visual

Begin with a work-related anecdote, fictional story, cartoon, or graphic that focuses the audience's attention on the subject matter of your lecture.

EXAMPLE: A trainer accepted an assignment to deliver time management training to a group of hospital administrators. Instead of jumping into a lecture on organization and time wasters, she began her presentation with the well-known leadoff story recounted in Figure 4–2.

FIGURE 4–2. A STORY ABOUT TIME MANAGEMENT

The utility of planning the day's work is seen clearly in a well-known story concerning Charles Schwab. When he was president of Bethlehem Steel, he presented Ivy Lee, a consultant, with an unusual challenge. "Show me a way to get more things done with my time," he said, "and I'll pay you any fee within reason."

Handing Schwab a sheet of paper, Lee said, "Write down the most important tasks you have to do tomorrow and number them in order of importance. When you arrive in the morning, begin at once on No. 1 and stay on it till it's completed. Recheck your priorities; then begin with No. 2. If any task takes all day, never mind. Stick with it as long as it's the most important one. If you don't finish them all, you probably couldn't do so with any other method, and without some system you'd probably not even decide which one was most important. Make this a habit every working day. When it works for you, give it to your team. Try it as long as you like. Then send me your check for what you think it's worth."

Some weeks later Schwab sent Lee a check for $25,000 with a note saying that the lesson was the most profitable he had ever learned. In five years, this plan was largely responsible for turning Bethlehem Steel Corporation into the biggest independent steel producer in the world.

Schwab's friends asked him later about the payment of so high a fee for such a simple idea. Schwab responded by asking, "What ideas are not basically simple?" He reminded them that, for the first time, not only he but his entire team were getting first things done first. On reflection Schwab allowed that perhaps the expenditure was the most valuable investment Bethlehem Steel had made all year.

Source: Excerpted by permission of the publisher, from THE TIME TRAP © 1990 Alec MacKenzie. Published by AMACOM, a division of American Management Association. http:www.amanet.org. All rights reserved.

EXAMPLE: During a course on measurement and testing, a trainer was about to lecture on four ways that psychological tests are validated (predictive validity, concurrent validity, construct validity, and content validity). Before the start of his presentation, he displayed a list of the vocabulary words on the Wechsler Adult Intelligence Scale. He then asked participants if they thought that the use of such vocabulary words was a valid way to test intelligence. After receiving a variety of opinions (mostly dissenting), he proceeded to explain how test developers make positive claims about the validity of using vocabulary words to test intelligence and how these procedures can be used for all psychological tests.

Initial Case Problem

Present a short problem around which the lecture will be structured.

EXAMPLE: Figure 4–3 outlines a brief case problem that was used to introduce a lecture given to claims adjusters on what constitutes a work-related injury.

FIGURE 4–3. CASE PROBLEM 1: CLAIMS ADJUSTMENT

Sarah Secretary drives to work each day. Her route takes her past the post office. Each day she stops and picks up the mail for the office, and on her way home each afternoon she drops off the outgoing mail. One day, on her way home, she is involved in a two-car accident and is injured.

Is it compensable? As I discuss the factors defining a work-related injury, try to answer this question for yourself.

EXAMPLE: The case problem in Figure 4–4 was used to introduce a lecture on résumé writing.

FIGURE 4–4. CASE PROBLEM 2: RÉSUMÉ WRITING

Joan has been an employee of a national pharmaceutical company for the last seven years. She began her work at the company as a secretary in the human resources department and after four years moved into an entry-level position as a benefits administrator. Her job responsibilities included answering employees' benefit questions, handling the enrollment of new employees into one of the company's medical plans, and researching any problems that employees had as they filed insurance claims with the medical plan providers.

FIGURE 4–4. continued

Yesterday Joan found out that her job had been eliminated. All responsibility for benefits administration will be handled out of corporate headquarters in New York. Joan and three other coworkers have been told that they will be let go at the end of the month. Once they have left the company, they will each receive three months of job severance pay.

Joan is terrified of looking for a new job. She enjoyed working at the company very much and hates to think of starting all over again somewhere else. Moreover, she has not written a résumé since the last time she had to look for a new job. The old résumé identified only her skills as a secretary, yet Joan is certain that she would like to continue her career in benefits and not return to a secretarial position.

What advice could you give Joan as she writes her new résumé? As I present some tips on résumé writing, think through how Joan can best present her last seven years of work at the pharmaceutical company.

Test Questions

Ask participants a question related to the lecture topic (even if they have little prior knowledge) so that they will be motivated to listen to your lecture for the answers.

EXAMPLE: Most people might think that the purchase of a co-op is financed by a mortgage; in fact, co-ops are financed with loans, because co-op owners do not actually own their apartments but, rather, own shares in a corporation. Thus, the lender does not hold title to the property and cannot repossess an apartment in the event of foreclosure. A one-dollar mortgage is a way for a bank to establish title when a home equity loan is taken on a co-op. Such a loan is generally a second mortgage, so this device gives the lender some security.

Before presenting this information in a lecture on the nature of co-op loans in a course for loan officers, the trainer asked this simple question: "Why would anyone want a one-dollar mortgage?" He invited several responses by urging participants to speculate. During this time, he did not convey the correct answer. Then he proceeded with his lecture, explaining to participants that at the end of the presentation the answer to the question would be clear.

EXAMPLE: A trainer was preparing a lecture presentation on techniques for managing meetings effectively. Concerned that participants would find the lecture boring, she decided to introduce it with a true-false test (see Figure 4–5). Instead of going over the answers immediately, she promised participants that the correct answers would become evident during her presentation. The group was all ears.

FIGURE 4–5. MEETINGS! (QUESTIONNAIRE)

True or false?

_____ 1. Preparing an agenda in advance tends to promote meeting efficiency.

_____ 2. Distributing an agenda to members in advance generally does not affect the efficiency of meetings.

_____ 3. Starting meetings on time is inconsiderate to latecomers; wait until everyone is present before starting the meeting.

_____ 4. Begin to wind meetings down five to ten minutes before the meeting is scheduled to end.

_____ 5. Brief meetings (ten minutes or shorter) can be efficiently held standing.

_____ 6. Experts consider the ideal meeting length to be two to two-and-a-half hours.

_____ 7. Most experts advise holding meetings even if the agenda does not justify the expenditure of time and money.

_____ 8. Reading something out loud at a meeting when a printed version has been distributed is generally considered to be a waste of time.

_____ 9. Meetings are the most efficient forums for making general announcements.

_____ 10. Don't hold a large meeting to deal with a problem that affects only a few people.

Preview of Content

Give highlights or "coming attractions" of the lecture in an enthusiastic manner to entice interest and involvement.

EXAMPLE: A trainer was about to give a lengthy presentation on a new automated purchasing system. To build interest in the lecture, he stated: "You have been asked to come here today for an explanation of our company's new automated purchasing system. Before I get into details about how the system operates, I want each one of you to realize that, when you leave this room today, you will know how to spend approximately two hours a week less on ordering forms and supplies than you currently do. You will also know how to use the system effectively to monitor items that are on back order and to anticipate when items will arrive. Finally, by the end of this session, you will know how to receive your purchased items two weeks sooner than you did with the old paper-based system of ordering supplies."

EXAMPLE: A trainer introduced a lecture on the history of leadership theory with the following remarks: "For the next twenty minutes, we are going to explore how our thinking about the nature of leadership has changed dramatically over the last thirty-five years. In that span of time, we have gone from rather simple notions of what makes a good leader to highly complicated models of leadership behavior. You be the judge! Are we any better off today than we were back in the fifties? My opinion is that we are better off but I don't know if you'll be convinced."

These few remarks immediately hooked the group's active attention to what might have been a presentation that met with resistance because of its theoretical nature.

FIVE WAYS TO MAXIMIZE UNDERSTANDING AND RETENTION

After engaging the interest of your audience with one or more of these five interest-building techniques, it is time to begin the actual lecture. As you design your presentation, remember that your instructional goal is to maximize the participants' understanding and retention of the subject matter. Ultimately, the participants will learn more if they can focus their attention on the subject matter and make the ideas relevant to them. Five ways to maximize understanding and retention follow; try to use some or all of them as you present your lecture.

Opening Summary

At the beginning of the lecture, state (or summarize in writing) the lecture's major points and conclusions to help participants organize their listening.

EXAMPLE: A trainer was about to give a lengthy presentation on business writing styles. He asked participants to read the handout reproduced in Figure 4–6 to give them an overview of the presentation before he began.

FIGURE 4–6. OPENING SUMMARY

To achieve an appropriate style for a specific writing occasion in business, you must speak to the reader in an effective way. It is particularly important to sequence the information in a way that helps the reader to more readily understand what you have to say.

The "most important to least important" order is preferred by most business readers and writers because it is easy to read. The most important points are clearly stated at the beginning and less important evidence or arguments are relegated to minor positions in the body.

FIGURE 4–6. continued

The "most important to least important" order is generally used for

- Summaries
- Memoranda
- Letters requesting information
- Letters replying to requests for information

Another pattern of organization that is commonly used requires the reader to follow a trail of logic and analysis laid out by the writer before receiving the bottom-line message at the end of the report. This inductive pattern is most often used for

- Research reports
- Letters or reports that must say no or that contain a message the reader will perceive as negative
- Reports written to a *hostile audience,* where the writer must explain his or her reasoning process first to enable the reader to understand the bottom-line message and accept an unwelcome idea.

EXAMPLE: A trainer began a lecture on the Project Evaluation and Review Technique (PERT) with the following opening summary: "I'm going to give you a thumbnail sketch of PERT before we look at it in detail. PERT was developed by the Department of the Navy for the Polaris missile. It is useful in the *planning, scheduling,* and *monitoring and control* aspects of project management. In the planning phase, it requires you to list the tasks entailed by the project, calculate the gross requirements for resources, and make time and cost estimates. In the scheduling phase, it involves laying out the tasks in a time sequence and detailing scheduling or resource requirements. In the monitoring and control phase, it entails reviewing the schedule and actual performance; revising the schedule, if necessary; and assessing the likelihood of jeopardy and cost escalation. PERT can be employed in such applications as building construction, installation of a computer system, or end-of-month closing of accounting records. Now let's take a closer look at the process and examine when and how it works."

Headlines

Reduce the major points in the lecture to headlines that act as verbal subheadings or memory aids.

EXAMPLE: A trainer was giving a presentation on supervisory styles. She decided to use these three catchy terms to describe the alternatives that are open to supervisors:

Tell & Sell. In this mode, the supervisor explains to employees what is expected of them and why their cooperation is needed.

Tell & Listen. In this mode, the supervisor also initially explains to employees what is expected and then asks for (and listens to) their feedback to her or his requests.

Listen & Tell. In this mode, the supervisor asks the employees to comment on the work they are doing, listens to their responses, and then tells them his or her reactions to their work performance.

EXAMPLE: To become a better active listener, a trainer asked participants to consider the acronym PROPOSAL found in Figure 4–7.

FIGURE 4–7. AN ACTIVE LISTENING PROPOSAL

P *Probe for understanding.* As a listener, your role is to understand what the speaker is saying and meaning. This may require you to ask questions, dig for deeper understanding.

R *Reflect.* One of the best ways to make sure you are understanding the speaker is to reflect back to that person what you have heard. Opening phrases like "So what I'm hearing is . . ." or "Is this what you mean?" are only two of many ways to begin reflective statements.

O *One thing at a time.* When you are listening, LISTEN. Ignore distractions around you. Don't shuffle papers or mentally plan your response. You have plenty to do just listening.

P *Pause.* You do not have to respond to the speaker's comments immediately. When you allow yourself a momentary silence, you free your mind to form your response during that silence.

O *Observe nonverbal behavior.* Much of what's being said is not being "said." To truly understand, you must pay attention to body language, gestures, facial expressions, vocal inflections, and so on. These clues will really help you understand the speaker's message.

S *Summarize.* To make sure you are comprehending the speaker's message, summarize his or her comments. It ensures that you do understand the speaker; and the speaker will appreciate that you are checking your understanding!

A *Acknowledge.* Acknowledge the message. This doesn't mean you must agree. It simply means that they know you are really hearing the message. Acknowledging the sender is just as important as acknowledging the message.

L *Let the speaker finish.* Interrupting is a waste of time! You frustrate the speaker and sacrifice a complete understanding of the message. Let the speaker finish; then pause to reflect and respond as appropriate.

Source: Eikenberry, 1997, p. 269. Used with permission.

Examples

As much as possible, provide real-life illustrations of the ideas in the lecture.

EXAMPLE: In a course on alcoholism and the family, the trainer explained that family members may not be the cause of a parent's alcoholism but may play a role in keeping the problem alive. He then gave the following example of enabling an alcoholic.

"Consider the family of George, a retired mechanical engineer and an alcoholic. George began as a social drinker and eventually stepped over the invisible line into alcoholism. His wife, Joann, a registered nurse, played a key role in enabling George to remain an alcoholic. By taking on many of George's responsibilities, including budgeting, providing additional income, and handling the physical maintenance of the home, Joann was able to ensure that the household ran smoothly. By doing this, of course, she kept George from having to confront his alcoholism. George's eldest children, Bill and Cathy, also contributed to the enabling process. Successes outside the family, both of them projected the appearance of "having it together," but in truth they were often depressed. A younger sister, Laura, did her share by becoming a difficult teenager, refocusing family anger away from her father to her. All the members of the family adopted three rules that helped to maintain the status quo: (1) keep negative feelings to yourself, (2) don't talk about Dad's drinking with other family members, and (3) don't let outsiders know what happens in the family."

EXAMPLE: In a course called "Selling to Your Client's Style," the trainer was teaching the personality types described in the Myers-Briggs Type Indicator (MBTI), a widely used instrument to help people understand their personal style and the style of others with whom they work. She was discussing the differences between a "Thinker" (T) type and a "Feeler" (F) type and illustrated the distinction by the following example: "A prospect you are selling to who is a T will probably speak in a concise fashion, will appear to be firm and tough-minded, likes to argue, and is focused on the bottom line. To be effective with a T, don't ramble, be logical, and address objections head-on. A prospect who is an F, on the other hand, will appear personable and friendly, takes time to get to know you, seems to like harmony, and is more interested in process than outcome. It's best to spend time getting to know such a person, to be friendly and warm, to be affirming, and to understand that the prospect may have difficulty being critical and may not reveal her or his true feelings about your product or service."

Analogies

If possible, create a comparison between your material and the knowledge or experience the participants already have.

EXAMPLE: A trainer is discussing adult learning needs. She likens the human mind to a computer and points out that people can not acquire knowledge if

Their *computers* are turned off

They don't have the right applications on their *desktops*

They are not allowed to *process* the information

They don't have a chance to *save* the information

Many well-known concepts are effectively explained by way of analogy. Here are a few:

- Another person cannot adjust his or her behavior to meet your needs unless you provide sufficient feedback. You are like a *thermostat* and the other person is like a *heating or cooling unit.* A thermostat reflects the temperature in a room for the heating or cooling unit. When the temperature is too hot or too cold, the heating or cooling unit can adjust its behavior by relying upon the thermostat for feedback that indicates when to do so.
- A database will hold and organize information for you like an *office file cabinet.* Your information is stored in files like the *folders* in your office file cabinet.
- When your selling style is very different from your client's, think of your client as *an AM transmitter* sending out radio waves and you have only *an FM receiver.*
- A body's ability to contain stress is much like a *rain barrel* that overflows when the water reaches the top. We all have rain barrels to contain our stress. As they begin to fill, we start to experience stress-related symptoms. When they reach the point of overflowing, we may have serious illnesses.

Visual Backup

Use flip charts, transparencies, brief handouts, and desktop presentation tools so that participants can see as well as hear what you are saying.

EXAMPLE: To explain how the Internet works, a training program used two visual illustrations (see Figure 4–8). In the first illustration, the squares represent computers and the lines represent the cables that connect the computers together to form a network. If computer #1 wants to send a message to computer #5, the message will have to pass through several cables. The Internet is a network of computers around the world that are connected in a "web" similar to the one in the second illustration.

An effective way to conceptualize the control of upper levels of management in some organizations is to compare their decision-making power to a window shade. Initiative at lower levels of management is often inhibited when the shade is drawn too far down. It is even worse when the window shade is

FIGURE 4–8. HOW THE INTERNET WORKS

Illustration #1

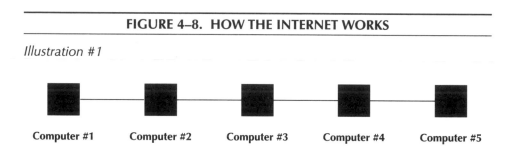

| Computer #1 | Computer #2 | Computer #3 | Computer #4 | Computer #5 |

Illustration #2

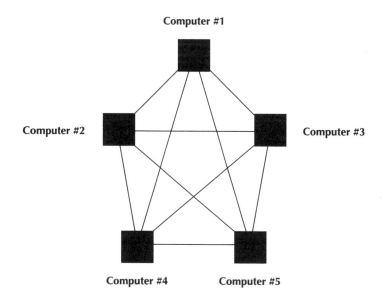

Source: Kruse, 1997, p. 180. Used by permission.

drawn differently every day. In this instance, initiative is further inhibited because middle managers and supervisors are continually confused about where their areas of responsibility lie. This model is illustrated in Figure 4–9.

FIGURE 4–9. THE WINDOW SHADE MODEL OF POWER

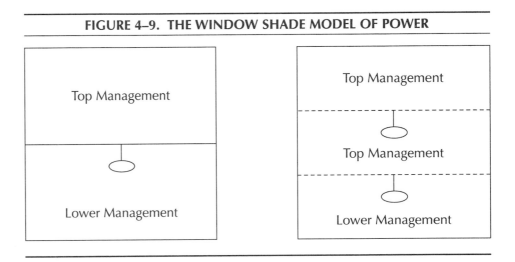

FIVE WAYS TO INVOLVE PARTICIPANTS DURING A LECTURE

No matter how scintillating your presentation is, the participants are still placed in a passive role as they listen to a lecture. Fortunately, steps can be taken to enlist group participation right during the lecture. Following are five suggestions.

Listening Role

Assign participants the responsibility of actively listening to the lecture.

At the end, they should be able to produce points they agree or disagree with, questions to clarify the lecture, a summary of its contents, or quiz questions for other participants. Assignments can be given to the group as a whole, to teams, or to specific individuals.

EXAMPLE: A business writing trainer was about to give a lecturette on six strategies for organizing and communicating information (definition, classification, example, process analysis, comparison and contrast, and cause and effect). The participants were asked to listen carefully to the description of each strategy so that at the end of the lecturette they would be able to provide a summary to their seat partners.

EXAMPLE: A trainer was about to give what might ordinarily be a boring presentation on statistics concerning the current job market, turnover rates, and the cost of replacing an employee. She instead distributed a list of questions for participants to answer as she lectured on the changing job market. By directing participants to search for information covered in the lecture, the trainer was able to actively capture her audience's attention.

Guided Note Taking

Provide instructions or a form indicating how participants should take notes during the lecture.

Stop at intervals for the participants to write reactions or ideas that go beyond what you have presented.

EXAMPLE: In a project management seminar, the trainer was lecturing about the cost management process, including the financial planning of the project and the subsequent collection, organization, and analysis of actual cost data to attain the project's cost objective. Participants had a worksheet in their seminar binder with the following terms: *input, process, output,* and *feedback.* After the trainer discussed each element in the process, participants were asked to recall his remarks in the appropriate section of the worksheet and write down any questions they had.

EXAMPLE: For a training session on delegation, the instructor distributed a handout entitled "The Dos and Don'ts of Delegation." The handout format was a T-chart, with two columns labeled "Do Delegate" and "Don't Delegate."

As the lecture was given, participants could make notes on the chart. When completed by the participants, it would look like this:

Do Delegate	*Don't Delegate*
All routine or sporadic clerical duties	An emergency or short-term task where there is no time to explain or train
Minor decisions	Morale problems
Routine questions	Assignments from your boss that he or she expects you to do personally
Minor staffing problems	A job no one else in the unit is qualified to do
Anything your subordinates are expected to do when you're not there	Hiring, firing, or disciplinary matters

Spot Challenge

Interrupt the lecture periodically and challenge participants to give examples of the concepts presented thus far or answer spot-quiz questions.

EXAMPLE: Before a lecture on hiring interviews, a trainer explained to her audience that she would stop periodically to obtain audience responses. She proceeded to discuss criteria that determine questions that are *clearly legal, not illegal but ill advised,* and *clearly illegal.* The trainer utilized a transcript of a hiring interview that contained all three types of questions. Participants were challenged to identify which questions belonged in each category.

EXAMPLE: A trainer was lecturing on the rights of developmentally disabled adults living in community living arrangements. After each section of the lecture, he gave a multiple-choice quiz to participants to test their understanding of the lecture material. Before continuing the lecture, he reviewed the answers to each quiz question.

Synergetic Learning

Provide different information to different participants.

Allow them to compare notes and briefly teach each other.

EXAMPLE: In a course on group process, the trainer divided the training group in half. One group was sent to another room to read information about the *maintenance* roles performed in effective groups. During this time, the other group heard a lecture on the *task* roles performed in effective groups. Then the "maintenance" group returned to hear a lecturette designed to reinforce what they had read. At the same time, the "task" group was sent out to read information that reinforced the lecturette they had just heard. Members from each group were then paired up to teach each other the material they had just learned.

EXAMPLE: In a course on business insurance, accountants were learning about "loss exposures" and their impact on business assets and income and capital. One-half of the class was given the following chart and was asked to study it with a learning partner so that each of them could share the examples it contains with a participant in the other half of the class.

Types of Loss Exposure

1. Sudden, often violent occurrences that all businesses are exposed to daily, such as fire, flood, wind, vandalism, weight of snow or ice, or frozen pipes

2. Exposure of premises, operations, product liability, directors' and officers' losses, professional liability loss, and so on

3. Employee dishonesty, injury of employees, and computer losses

4. Fines, closures, prosecution, added costs in construction, and taxes

Meanwhile, the trainer gave the other half of the class a brief lecture on the four categories of loss exposures (without examples):

1. External

2. Legal

3. Internal

4. Governmental

Participants from each half of the class were paired up. They told each other what they had learned and, together, attempted to sort the examples into the four categories. The full class was then reconvened and reviewed what they had learned synergetically.

Illuminating Exercise

During the presentation, intersperse a brief activity that illuminates the information, ideas, and skills being presented.

EXAMPLE: A trainer gave a brief lecture summarizing the problems managers face today, including low productivity, poor quality of service, high stress, and low morale. The trainer also noted that traditional management solutions tend to use an approach that, like the mythological Hydra, often generates two new heads for every one solved. A different approach is needed, which she called "creating the ideal." At this point, the trainer interrupted the lecture with an exercise. She asked each participant to find a partner of approximately equal weight and strength. One of the pair was asked to hold out his or her arm horizontally and to resist the partner's attempts to bend it. Most arms were easily bent. The trainer then requested the individual to imagine his or her arm as a steel rod before the partner attempted to bend it and to sustain the vision in the process. In most pairs, arms remained straight despite increased effort from the partners. The lecturer then continued: "Better results are obtained with less effort. The key is what one focuses on. In the first case, the individual tried to achieve contradictory results: keeping his or her arm straight and resisting having it bent. In the second case, he or she focused solely on the desired result." The trainer then presented four key elements that go into making a visionary approach to problem solving work.

EXAMPLE: A team-building instructor utilized an exercise called the "team machine" to help participants understand several points about teamwork. His instructions to participants are reproduced in Figure 4–10.

FIGURE 4–10. THE TEAM MACHINE INSTRUCTIONS

- Lift your right hand and move it as if you are clapping. Listen to the sound of one hand clapping.
- Raise your left hand and clap with both hands. If your task is to clap, wouldn't you want to use all of your available resources?
- This is an example of how the human system operates on an individual level. Each person has several parts and the parts work together to get things done.
- There are other types of systems. Imagine a six-cylinder car—a well-timed, synchronized machine. Each cylinder fires in sequence so the system can function.
- Imagine this automobile running on only four or five cylinders. What would happen to the power? Or what if you put the plug wires on haphazardly?
- Organizational teams are just like individuals and automobiles. The teams work best when they use all of their resources, when there is a plan and they have a coordinated system for getting things done.
- Let's experiment. Watch me as I stand here making a motion and a sound with my voice. Let's pretend we're making a human machine, a well-timed machine. (*The facilitator chooses the first participant.*)
- Please come up here. (*The facilitator points to a place with a large space.*)
- Now I would like you to make a unique sound with your voice, place one hand out in front of you, and make a motion with your body. Good. (*The facilitator asks the remaining individuals to come up one at a time and arrange themselves in a circle.*)

(*To each member say:*)

- Make a different sound, a different motion, and use one hand to connect to the person in front of you.

(*After completing the circle, say:*)

- Continue making your interesting sounds and motions. Notice how you take turns, how you bob and weave or wax and wane.
- Here are some things to think about:

    Have we somehow woven ourselves into a pattern in which we all contribute our vocal and motor skills?

    Is the sum more than the parts?

    Are we synchronized?

    Is there a group system here, something bigger and more complex than each individual?

- Now we have a system for doing things. This is the hallmark of an effective team.

Source: This exercise was developed by Jeffrey D. Kindler. Used with permission.

FIVE WAYS TO REINFORCE LECTURES

When a lecture is completed, the conventional behavior is to wrap it up with a recap of the major points and a question-and-answer period. Although these conventions have merit and should not be overlooked in your planning, there are some more exciting and active ways to debrief and reinforce what has been presented. Consider these five methods.

Press Conference

Invite participants to prepare questions that are submitted to the trainer for her or his response.

Or provide a list of questions from which participants select.

EXAMPLE: At the conclusion of a lecture on "reserving factors" in an accident claim, participants were formed into quartets. Each quartet was asked to pose a question to the trainer that would help to clarify the lecture presentation. Participants were urged to bring up hypothetical cases to incorporate into their questions.

EXAMPLE: During a seminar on a new statistical software package, the trainer gave participants three questions that emerged from the material she had just covered. Participants were asked to vote for one question to be answered by the trainer before she continued with the seminar. By doing this, the trainer helped the participants to review what they had learned throughout the day.

Participant Review

Ask participants to review the contents of the lecture with each other (in any group configuration) and commit the major points to memory, or give them a self-scoring review test.

EXAMPLE: A trainer gave a presentation on six "job-centered motivators," which Herzberg believes have long-term effects on employees' attitudes:

1. Achievement
2. Recognition for achievement
3. The work itself
4. Responsibility
5. Growth
6. Advancement

When he finished, he asked participants to put away their notes and write down the six motivators from memory, providing an example of each. He then allowed participants to check their answers against their notes.

EXAMPLE: After a lecture on total quality tools, the trainer gave eighteen participants one card each that contained either the name of one of these tools or its description. Each participant had to find the mate to his or her card. Figure 4–11 provides a list of these tools and their descriptions.

FIGURE 4–11. TOTAL QUALITY TOOL MATCH

- *Affinity diagram:* Organizes ideas into natural groupings; categories and new ideas are generated by team members working silently

- *Cause-and-effect diagram:* Identifies root causes of the effect being analyzed

- *Pareto diagram:* Organizes causes by frequency; also known as 80–20 rule

- *Histogram:* Shows frequency of occurrence of different measurements for a given quality attribute; used to depict variation in an observed measurement

- *Scatter diagram:* Depicts the relationship between variables, thereby helping to substantiate whether root cause is related to effect

- *Control diagram:* Used to determine whether or not variation is due to common or special causes

- *Flow diagram:* Used to understand a process by depicting its various activities and decision points

- *Relations diagram:* Displays the cause-and-effect relationship between factors in a complex situation

- *Tree diagram:* Displays range of subtasks needed to achieve objective

---

Group Processing

Ask participants to reflect on the lecture's implications for them.

Utilize any group format you feel will maximize the quality of the processing.

EXAMPLE: A training group had just heard a lecture on five steps to effective team facilitation. They were asked to break into small groups to discuss the following two questions:

1. "Which ideas were new for you and which were not?"

2. "Which ideas do you think apply to your team?"

EXAMPLE: A trainer completed a lecture on ten key points to remember when conducting a hiring interview:

1. Build rapport
2. Describe job and organization to candidate
3. Be aware of your body language
4. Review candidate's résumé
5. Ask as much as possible about candidate's past behavior
6. Allow for silence
7. Maintain control
8. Seek contrary evidence
9. Answer candidate's questions
10. Make important notes during the interview

She then asked participants to discuss the following questions with a seat partner:

- Which of these behaviors come easily to you? Which are difficult?
- Which do you want to practice more?
- What would help you to remember these key points the next time you conduct an interview?

Postlecture Case Problem

Pose a case problem for participants to solve based on the information given in the lecture.

EXAMPLE: In a training program on mortgage product sales, the trainer gave a lecture on the ingredients of a mortgage commitment. When the presentation was completed, the following short case problem was presented to participants:

> A customer has received a good-faith estimate but is not sure that this represents a mortgage commitment. The customer is confused and makes an appointment with you for an explanation.

In trios, participants were asked what they would explain to the customer.

EXAMPLE: At the conclusion of a presentation on bank products, the participants were formed into two groups and given the following case problem:

> A customer's daughter was just accepted at a college with very high tuition. Unfortunately, she does not qualify for a federally guaranteed loan. She has come to you for alternatives. What would you recommend?

After small-group discussion, individuals from each group were matched with each other to compare notes on the case problem.

Experiential Activity

Design an activity that dramatically summarizes or illustrates the lecture you have given.

Utilize any of the experiential learning approaches that are presented in Chapter Six (role playing, games and simulations, observation, mental imagery, writing tasks, and action learning projects).

EXAMPLE: A trainer gave a lecture on family systems to drug and alcohol counselors who were learning to use a family treatment approach in their work. In particular, the lecture examined issues of proximity in families: how some family members are closely connected and how others become disengaged. At the conclusion, he asked participants to join him in forming a circle and holding hands. He then released himself from the hand of the person to his right and began to lead the person to his left (and consequently all the other participants who were connected to her) over and under the clasped hands of the other participants. The net result was a human knot, with some participants facing others and some facing no one. In addition, some participants emerged in comfortable body positions while others were in awkward positions. With the knot of participants entangled, the trainer (who managed to end up in a comfortable position facing several other participants) began a discussion of a recent controversial film. The discussion ensued for several minutes, with some participants contributing easily and others with little desire to become involved. The knot was then untangled and participants returned to their seats. The trainer asked the group to discuss their experiences in the knot and to relate them to the lecture he had just presented. This is a dramatic demonstration of the varied degrees of involvement and detachment within a group or human system.

EXAMPLE: A trainer had just finished a lecture entitled "How Brain Dominance Affects Teaching and Learning Style." She wanted to reinforce the lecture with a demonstration showing that if we only teach from our preferred mode, frustration will result for both teacher and student. She asked participants to pair off and asked each pair to decide who would be the student and who would be the teacher. "Students" then were asked to write out their responses to this question: "What are the first two steps you would like your teacher to take in order to help you learn how to drive a car most effectively?" "Teachers" were asked to respond in writing to a comparable question: "What are the first two steps you would take in order to teach someone how to drive a car most effectively?" Each pair was then asked to compare responses and discuss any discrepancies and/or similarities between the steps proposed by the "teacher" and the steps desired by the "student." Pairs were also asked to compare their scores on the Hermann Brain Dominance Inventory (Hermann, 1995), which had been previously completed and profiled for each participant, and to try to draw some conclusions about the impact of their learning style on their approach to teaching.

AN EXAMPLE OF A WELL-DESIGNED LECTURE

When putting together a well-designed lecture, respect the four-part sequence that has been described in this chapter. Always begin with a strategy to build interest. Once the audience is mentally involved, provide the information you wish to impart, using the ways described here to maximize understanding. During this period of time, stop once or several times and obtain audience participation. When the lecture has been completed, reinforce what you have taught with the strategies just discussed. Here is an example of this flow.

EXAMPLE: You are going to lecture on situational leadership styles, a model developed by Ken Blanchard (1997). According to this leadership model, the preferred style of a leader is dependent on the characteristics of the people she or he is leading. The styles are referred to as *directing, coaching, supporting,* and *delegating.*

1. To build interest in the lecture, you might use the following test question:

   What characteristics of the people you lead might determine when you could adopt one of the following styles: *directing, coaching, supporting*, and *delegating?*

   Obtain several responses and remain accepting of participants' answers. Do not reveal the "correct" answers.

2. Provide a handout that contains the following:

Style	Situation	Description
Directing		
Coaching		
Supporting		
Delegating		

Explain the situation factors and general description of each style. For example, you would tell the audience that "low-maturity" people (those who are unable and unwilling to take responsibility and are lacking in competence or confidence) function best with directive leaders who provide clear supervision: defining roles, setting goals, and organizing work assignments. As you discuss each style, invite participants to take notes on the handout. Be sure to provide good examples for each style and use the analogy of parenting children as they grow into adolescence. Use a graphic icon to accompany the presentation of each style, such as a whistle for a coach or a bridge for a supportive leader.

3. Divide the audience into four groups and give each group one of the following assignments after you have presented each style:

   Questioners: Ask a question about this style.

   Agreers: Explain why you agree that this is the best style in this situation.

   Naysayers: Explain why you disagree that this is the best style in this situation.

   Example givers: Give a work-related situation in which this style makes sense.

   Call on each team to question, agree, and so forth.

4. Give participants several case situations. Ask them to identify which style fits each situation. Follow this activity with a role-playing activity in which the participants are asked to portray each style. Discuss their reactions to the role play, exploring their comfort in being able to shift gears in each situation. Hold a press conference in which you are asked final questions about the model.

WORKSHEET

PREPARING EFFECTIVE LECTURES

Use this worksheet to assist you in the design of a well-organized lecture that will initiate participants' interest in your subject matter, retain that interest throughout the presentation, enlist direct participation, and reinforce what has been presented.

Interest-Building Strategies:
(*check as many as desired*)

___ Introductory exercise

___ Leadoff story or interesting visual

___ Initial case problem

___ Test question

___ Preview of content

Notes on techniques:

_____

_____

_____

_____

_____

_____

Understanding- and Retention-Maximizing Techniques:
(*check as many as desired*)

___ Opening summary

___ Headlines

___ Examples

___ Analogies

___ Visual backup

Notes on techniques:

_____

_____

_____

_____

_____

_____

WORKSHEET continued

Participant Involvement:
(*check as many as desired*)

___ Listening role

___ Guided note taking

___ Spot challenge

___ Synergetic learning

___ Illuminating exercise

Notes on techniques:

_____

_____

_____

_____

_____

_____

Lecture Reinforcing:
(*check as many as desired*)

___ Press conference

___ Group processing

___ Postlecture case problem

___ Participant review

___ Experiential activity

Notes on techniques:

_____

_____

_____

_____

_____

_____

♦   ♦   ♦

Chapter Five

Finding Alternative Methods to Lecturing

W hile a well-designed lecture can be an effective training method, overreliance on lecturing usually leads to boredom, lack of involvement, or limited learning for the participants. A different method can often take the place of a particular lecture entirely. A lecture can also be reinforced by utilizing another method. In this chapter, I will examine eight alternatives to lecturing that you can use even if your participants have little prior knowledge of the subject being taught. These methods are

1. **Demonstration**
2. **Case study**
3. **Guided teaching**
4. **Group inquiry**
5. **Information search**
6. **Study group**
7. **Jigsaw learning**
8. **Learning tournament**

DEMONSTRATION

Instead of talking about a concept, procedure, or set of facts, you may be able to walk through a demonstration of the information in action. Involving participants in the demonstration, if possible, is important so that they can actually hear, see, and touch the relevant learning materials. The advantage of a demonstration is that it adds showing to merely telling. Here are two examples.

EXAMPLE: On the third afternoon of a five-day course on family process, a trainer began a module on family permeability—how a family relates to the

93

outside world. He began by explaining that no family is self-sufficient; all need the stimulation and support of others. However, a family needs to rely on itself as well, since always turning to outsiders, he suggested, robs a family of its integrity. At this point, the trainer thought about continuing his presentation, raising specific issues families face in considering how open they want to be. Fearing that he had already lectured too much in the afternoon session, he decided instead to invite one of the participants to be interviewed about her family. By discussing a number of specific questions with the participant (for example, "How much time do you spend with family and with friends?" "Are the religious and sex education of your children left up to professionals?" "Do you tell others about any problems occurring in the family?" "How much contact does the family have with people of other races, religions, or cultures?"), the trainer provided a stunning demonstration of how a family negotiates issues of permeability.

EXAMPLE: In a course on communication, a trainer was about to present a model by group psychologist Jack Gibb on defensive versus nondefensive communication. According to Gibb, people become defensive when others are evaluative, controlling, strategizing, neutral, superior, and overly certain. They become less defensive when others are descriptive, problem-oriented, spontaneous, empathetic, egalitarian, and provisional. Rather than defining and illustrating each of these twelve qualities, the trainer chose instead to create a live demonstration. She enlisted four participants to hold a discussion on the rights of smokers and nonsmokers in the workplace. The twelve categories were prominently displayed on newsprint off to the side of the discussion group. As the trainer heard an example of one of the communication categories emerging from the group discussion, she pointed to the category being demonstrated. In ten minutes, all the defensive communication categories had been illustrated, but few of the nondefensive ones. To demonstrate the remaining nondefensive behaviors, the trainer joined the discussion group and showed how the communication of one member could induce lowered defensiveness in others. She then encouraged others to try out the newly demonstrated behaviors.

Here are some procedural guidelines for conducting creative demonstrations:

1. Choose a concept (or a set of related concepts) or a procedure that can be illustrated by demonstration. Some examples include

   - An office requisition procedure
   - A project management planning tool
   - A feedback loop
   - A hidden agenda in a team meeting

2. Use any of the following methods:

- Have some participants come to the front of the room and ask them to physically simulate aspects of the concept or procedure.

- Create large cards that name the parts of a procedure or concept. Give out cards to some participants. Place the participants with cards in such a way that they are correctly sequenced.

- Develop a role play in which the participants dramatize the material you are teaching.

- Using volunteer participants, walk though a procedure that involves several people.

3. Discuss the learning drama that you have created. Make whatever teaching points you want.

CASE STUDY

A case study can be likened to a written demonstration. You are providing an account of a real or fictitious situation, including sufficient detail to make it possible for groups to analyze the problems involved. You can also embed information in a case study that is normally given in lecture format. The major benefit of a case study is that abstract information is presented concretely. Notice in the two case examples that follow how participants learn what the trainers want to teach without the trainers having to give it to them in a lecture.

EXAMPLE: In a course on counseling employees, the trainer normally used a lecture format to present five steps when confronting a employee who was performing poorly. He decided instead to give out the case example in Figure 5–1 and to ask the participants, working in trios, to identify the five steps that the supervisor took in counseling the employee. The answers were combined across the trios and compared to the trainer's lecture notes. To the trainer's delight, the participants hit on every one of the points that he had planned to cover in the lecture.

FIGURE 5–1. COUNSELING AN EMPLOYEE

The following exchange took place between Suzanne Smith, a manager, and her employee, David White, who had been "called on the carpet":

Smith: Come in, David. Have a seat. I suppose you're wondering why I want to talk to you.

White: Yes, I guess I am.

Smith: Well, David, recently a little thing has come up that I want to know your feelings about. Remember the Adamson report?

FIGURE 5–1. continued

White: What about it?

Smith: To be frank with you, there was a lot of disagreement on the figures that were used, and the boss wants the whole thing done over. It wasn't up to the level of the reports you've been turning out in the past. I have to admit that myself. But I want to hear your views about it.

White: Well, there isn't much to say. I sort of figured it would get rejected anyway. I wasn't happy about the damn thing either (*Getting a little emotional*).

Smith: You weren't pleased with it either?

White: Heck, no, I wasn't. Look, it takes about 25 to 30 hours, at least, for me to write up a report like that even when I've already worked up the figures! You know how long I spent on that report? About five hours! And I wasn't as sure on the figures as I should have been either.

Smith: You didn't get to put in much time on the report, is that it?

White: No, I didn't. In fact, I don't blame them for rejecting it at all. Like I said, it was a lousy job. But it won't be the last lousy job they get from me unless I get some help down here. There's no way I can run a research department and do the odds and ends that get sent in my direction. When we were a smaller outfit, it was possible, but not now. What the heck does everybody expect from me anyway?

Smith: You're saying that you have too many assignments, then?

White: Yes, that's exactly what I'm saying! (*Getting more upset*). I'm expected to do everybody's odds and ends. Production wants this, marketing wants that, cost accounting wants something else. Then along comes the Control Committee and their report. They give me a week's notice to get it out. I know I'm running a staff department, but there's no way one person can handle it all. And this was a sloppy report, I know. But it won't be the last.

Smith: David, you know how we've counted on you in the past for these reports. Frankly, they're very important, and you've been doing such a great job on them. Is there any way we might be able to work out this problem?

White: How we might work it out? Yeah, give me three new people (*Only half joking*).

Smith: You think extra help would do it?

White: Oh, I don't know. I guess we could handle it all if production would get off my back. Whenever they want something, they get the VP to call me and tell me how badly they need it in short order. That's what happened on the Adamson report. I had to finish it in three days. Millican [VP for Production] called with a rush job to be done and said that Henderly would be up to see me with the details. I guess I'm too meek to say, "No, I can't do it on such short notice." But what do I say to a VP?

FIGURE 5–1. continued

Smith: It's hard to turn down a VP. Do you feel that I could help in any way?

White: Well, you have a lot more say with Millican than I do. But he's sure a bull-headed type.

Smith: Well, let me worry about that. I'll have a talk with him. And if he comes up with another of these "emergencies" that you honestly can't handle, explain to him as best you can that you can't get it out that fast. But offer to talk with me about it. If he still insists, then let me know and I'll talk with him. David, it is my job to help.

White: Well, I feel a lot better getting this thing out. I was really getting in a rut.

Smith: Well, I'm also glad that we were able to work this out.

Source: Reprinted from *Supervisory Management,* by Mosley et. al, copyright © 1989. By permission of South-Western College Publishing, a division of International Thomson Publishing, Inc., Cincinnati, Ohio 45227.

EXAMPLE: In a workshop for counselors who provide support for parents who have suffered the death of an infant, the trainer provided the participants with the case example presented in Figure 5–2 and asked them to identify (1) the issues faced by the parents and (2) the concepts of death held by their three children. With this case study approach, participants developed a much richer understanding of the issues and concepts than they could have gained from a lecture.

FIGURE 5–2. THE DEATH OF A CHILD

Lisa and Ron had been married for fifteen years when their child Nicole was born prematurely at twenty-eight weeks. They had three older children, Stevie (age eleven), Robbie (age seven), and Jen (age four).

After Lisa was discharged from the hospital, Lisa and Ron ran to the hospital each day to see Nicole. They felt very close to one another and had deep talks during the one-hour trip back and forth from the hospital. They knew that they had developed a lot of strengths together as a couple over the years and that they could cope with any adversity. Twice a week they would bring their three children with them to the hospital to see Nicole. The children would bring toys and drawings to their baby sister. They didn't seem frightened by all the tubes and wires attached to Nicole in the isolette.

Nicole had many ups and downs in the neonatal intensive care unit. Then, at four weeks of age, she faced a serious setback from which she was unable to rally. Despite the intense efforts of the doctors and nurses, at thirty days old she

---

FIGURE 5–2. continued

---

died as a result of complications of prematurity, never having left the hospital. Lisa and Ron held her in their arms as she died.

At a time when they expected to be making plans for a christening, they found themselves planning a funeral. It was the first time they had ever had to do such a thing, since no one really close to them in their families had died.

The first week or so after Nicole died, Lisa and Ron cried together often. Ron stayed out of work for a week. Lisa's mother looked after the other children and took care of the house. Friends and relatives sent cards and flowers and many attended the funeral. Ron and Lisa felt surrounded by love at the funeral. Their three children attended, despite the advice of some friends that it would be too much for Jen, the four-year-old, to handle.

Close friends and relatives said a lot of things that were aimed at comforting them, such as "Well, it's good you never got to bring the baby home from the hospital, because then you would have gotten attached and it would be harder now" and "Now you have an angel in heaven" and "It's best to put it all behind you." They also heard, "You can have another baby," as well as "You're not going to have another baby, are you?"

Lisa and Ron found that the children had many feelings about the death of their sister. Jen would ask her mother question after question: "Is Nicole with God?" "Is she cold under the ground?" "Will I die?" "When is Nicole coming back?" Sometimes she would pretend that her dolly was dead. Lisa would just freeze and try to hold her tears in until Jen left the room.

Robbie, the seven-year-old, talked a lot about the funeral. He wondered if Nicole could see them from heaven. He explained to his parents, as he said his prayers, that her soul was with God on a cloud. If he saw his mother crying, he would say, "Are you crying about Nicole?"

Stevie, age eleven, asked why God had let Nicole die. He expressed a lot of anger. His schoolwork began to suffer, and he started having nightmares.

Lisa and Ron tried to listen to their children and comfort them, but they felt so consumed with their own grief that it was often very difficult for them to do. They felt helpless. When Stevie asked why God had let Nicole die, it keyed into their own frustration and unanswered questions.

Lisa loved her children beyond words, but she was also frightened by some of her feelings. She sometimes wanted to be left alone to cry and think about Nicole, and the children's need to be fed, readied for school, and cared for seemed overwhelming. She hated herself when she found herself resenting them and their intrusions on her grief. Ron found himself short-tempered with them, yelling at things that never would have bothered him before.

Over the following weeks, back at work, Ron found a lot of people asking him, "How's Lisa doing?" Rarely did they ask about his well-being. Lisa found that their friends and family seemed to be avoiding her. Three weeks after Nicole died, her mother said, "You need to get on with your life. You have people who

---

FIGURE 5–2. continued

---

are depending on you." Ron found it harder and harder to cry, and Lisa began to complain that he was withdrawing from her. Ron expressed his concern that she was staying in her bathrobe all day, saying that he was afraid things would never be the same again.

Lisa and Ron realized how their relationship was changing. Lisa resented Ron because his grief seemed to be so much less of a burden to him than hers was to her, as evidenced by his lack of tears and his seeming desire not to talk about Nicole. Ron knew how much he hurt and felt that his pain was not being acknowledged by society, let alone by his wife.

A month after Nicole died, they felt distant from one another and all alone in their grief. Lisa became particularly alarmed when a friend told her that she had read that 90 percent of all couples who lose a child split up. Both Lisa and Ron secretly worried, "Is there any hope that we can survive this together?"

Source: Janis Keyser Heil, Ph.D. Used with permission.

Finding a case study that exactly fits the bill can be a daunting task. Shop around. Or you may decide to write a case that is especially geared to your training program. Here are some suggestions for writing your own cases:

- Identify the issues, concepts, or principles you want to teach.
- Brainstorm situations (real-life or fictional) that illustrate the concepts or principles.
- Choose one situation that seems the most promising and develop the characters, the events, the background data, and the actions taken.
- Write a first draft of the case and ask someone else to read it without any further information from you. Obtain feedback about its clarity and interest level.
- Rewrite the case and develop discussion questions. Think about adding graphic aids such as charts and photographs or including segments on audio- or videotape.

You might also consider the value of having participants create their own case studies. Here is a procedure you can follow to do this:

1. Divide the class into pairs or trios. Invite them to develop a case study that the remainder of the class can analyze and discuss.

2. Indicate that the purpose of a case study is to learn about a topic by examining a concrete situation or example that reflects that topic. Give some of these examples:

- A transcript of a performance review can be analyzed to study how to appraise employees effectively.
- An account of how a company set up a succession-planning program can be used to study promotion policies.
- A dialogue between a manager and an employee can be examined to learn how to provide positive reinforcement.
- The steps taken by management in a company undergoing a merger can be studied to learn about organizational change.

3. Provide adequate time for the pairs or trios to develop a short case situation or example (100 to 200 words long) that poses an issue to be discussed or a problem to be solved that is relevant to the subject matter of the class. Give these suggestions:

- Use either a real situation or example or an invented one for the case study.
- Make the material subtle and challenging; don't be obvious about what's right or wrong.
- Allow for different points of view.

4. When the case studies are complete, have the groups present them to the class. Allow a member of the group to lead the case discussion.

Case studies are even better when they can be simulated. This is a situation for which an interactive CD-ROM is well suited. Take, for example, a simulation where the learner gets to play the role of a sales representative who is consulting with a doctor on the diagnosis and treatment of two different patients. Each case allows the user to make step-by-step decisions in the diagnosis and evaluation of patients. Different case paths can be created with a variety of interactive questions and outcomes. A program can randomly select one of these paths each time the learner selects the case study module from the main menu. Key points and topics can be reinforced with photo visuals and simulated conversations. At the end of each case, a follow-up conversation provides the learner with final feedback for the current patient (Advanced Consulting Inc., 1997).

GUIDED TEACHING

Instead of presenting a lecture, ask a series of questions to tap the knowledge of the group or obtain their hypotheses or conclusions. Record their ideas, if possible, and compare them to the lecture points you have in mind. The guided teaching method is a nice break from straight lecturing and allows you to learn what participants already know and understand before making your own instructional points. Because it utilizes a Socratic teaching technique, this method encourages self-discovery. Here are two examples.

EXAMPLE: In a basic management skills course, the trainer wanted to broaden participants' thinking about motivation. He posted on a flip chart the following question: "Why does an employee quit?" Numerous and varied responses were given: insufficient money, limited opportunity, lack of recognition or appreciation, conflicts with the supervisor, desire for a career change, and so on. Participants were then asked to categorize their answers into like groups. By interspersing his own ideas, probing, and prompting, the trainer guided the group into identifying three categories: employee factors such as career change, management factors such as conflicts and recognition, and organizational or system factors such as reward systems and culture.

EXAMPLE: While training nurses to develop a plan for teaching patients to prepare for surgery, a trainer decided to refrain from lecturing and instead to use a guided teaching approach. She began by asking the participants what they would want to know before they begin guiding the patient (the patient's fears and concerns, understanding of the surgery, and so on). She then led the group into identifying any deviations in anatomy and physiology and the corrective effects of surgery to be addressed in the teaching plan. From issues of anatomy and physiology, the trainer moved to what elements of the preoperative waiting period the group felt were important to include in the plan (for example, diagnostic studies or dietary and activity restrictions). This discussion flowed into an examination of the components of the postoperative period (recovery room, pain management, exercises, and so on) that needed to be presented. Whenever possible, the trainer asked other questions based on participants' responses (for example, "Yes, mentioning the equipment that the patient can expect to see surrounding him or her postoperatively is an important item. What would you say if you were unsure what equipment would be used?").

Here are some procedural guidelines for using a guided teaching approach:

1. Pose a question or a series of questions that stimulate the thinking of participants. Ask questions that have several possible answers, such as "How can you tell how intelligent someone is?"

2. Give participants some time in pairs or subgroups to consider their responses.

3. Record the ideas of participants. If possible, sort their responses into separate lists that correspond to different categories or concepts you are trying to teach. In the sample question in item 1, you might list ideas such as the ability to solve difficult puzzles or rebuild an engine under the category of motoric intelligence.

4. Present the major learning points you want to teach. Have participants figure out how their responses fit into these points. Note ideas that add to the learning points of your lesson.

GROUP INQUIRY

Instead of asking questions, the trainer can challenge participants to devise their own questions to further their understanding of a topic. If participants have little prior knowledge of the material, they should be presented with relevant instructional materials first (for example, work examples or handouts) to arouse their curiosity and interest and to stimulate questions. Posing a problem that the group must solve might also encourage questions. Allow sufficient time for the group to form some questions, then field the questions one at a time or as a whole group. This method allows you to gear teaching to participants' needs.

Notice how participants' questions are sparked in these two examples.

EXAMPLE: For a course entitled "New Drug Development," the trainer handed out a chart that described what occurs during preclinical and clinical testing of a new drug. Participants were placed in small groups and asked to study the chart and circle any terms or symbols they did not understand. Since the chart was somewhat ambiguous, many items were circled. For example, participants wanted to know the difference between a Phase I, Phase II, and Phase III study and what was meant by "long-term" animal testing. After providing answers to these questions, the trainer asked the participants to study the chart further and develop "why" and "how" questions, such as "Why is animal testing continued after human testing begins?" and "How does the Food and Drug Administration monitor a drug after it has been approved?" Because of the lively questioning, participants were highly engaged and left the session with a good understanding of drug-testing procedures.

EXAMPLE: For a course entitled "Cross-Cultural Issues for an International Assignment," the trainer handed out descriptions of a series of interactions between Indonesians and Americans. One such incident is described in Figure 5–3.

FIGURE 5–3. THE QUIET PARTICIPANT

Machmud, a native of Indonesia, had recently been promoted to a position of authority and was asked to represent his company's and Indonesia's needs at the head office in Butte, Montana.

His relationships with his fellow workers seemed cordial but rather formal from his perspective. He was invited to attend many policy and planning sessions with other company officials, where he often sat, rather quietly, as others generated ideas and engaged in conversation.

The time finally came when the direction the company was to take in Indonesia was to be discussed. A meeting was called, which Machmud was invited to attend. As the meeting was drawing to a close after almost two hours of discussion, Machmud, almost apologetically, offered his first contribution to the meeting. Almost immediately, John Stewart, a local vice president, said, "Why did you wait so long to contribute? We needed your comments all along." Machmud felt that John Stewart's reply was harsh.

Source: Brislin, 1986. Reprinted by Permission of Sage Publications.

Rather than explaining the specific cultural differences involved in each incident, the trainer invited the group to ask him questions, based on the descriptions, about Indonesians, their behavior, and their culture. Some of their questions were immediately relevant to understanding the assigned incidents, while other questions were helpful in understanding a wide range of events that the participants might experience when working with Indonesians. It was unlikely that the group would have developed as many insightful questions without the stimulus of the critical incidents.

Here are some procedural guidelines for using group inquiry:

1. Distribute to participants an instructional handout of your own choosing. (You may use an overhead transparency, slide, or page in a text instead of a handout.) Key to your choice of handouts is the need to stimulate readers' questions. A handout that provides broad information but lacks details or explanatory backup is ideal. The goal is to evoke curiosity. An interesting chart or diagram that illustrates some knowledge is a good choice. A text that's open to interpretation is another good choice.

2. Ask participants to study the handout with a partner or small group. Request that each pair or group make as much sense of the handout as possible and

identify what they do not understand by placing questions next to the information they do not understand on the document. Encourage the participants to insert as many question marks as they wish. (Instead of having them mark questions, give them highlighting pens and have them highlight what they question.) If time permits, combine pairs or small groups and allow time for the participants to help one another.

3. Reconvene the class and field participants' questions. In essence, you are teaching through your answers to participants' questions rather than through a preset lesson. Or, if you wish, listen to all the questions together and then teach a preset lesson, making special efforts to respond to the questions the participants posed.

4. If you feel that participants will be lost trying to study the material entirely on their own, provide some information that orients them or gives them the basic knowledge they need to be able to inquire on their own. Then proceed with participant self-study and questioning.

INFORMATION SEARCH

This method can be likened to an open-book test. Hand out worksheets containing questions about the topic. Have the group search for the information, which you would normally cover in a lecture, in source materials such as handouts, documents, a textbook, reference guides, computer-accessed information, artifacts, and work-related equipment. The search can be performed by small teams or individuals. You can even set up a friendly competition to encourage full participation. Notice how an information search method serves to liven up dry material in the following two examples.

EXAMPLE: For a mortgage product sales and marketing program, a trainer devised a worksheet containing fill-in-the-blank items, true-false items, and a matching test. (See Figure 5–4 for some sample questions.) Participants were organized into teams and told to gather information from a variety of sources found in the training room; each team also received a calculator. When a team completed all items to the satisfaction of all team members, it brought the results to the trainer for scoring. Teams were given points on how quickly they finished. A penalty of sixty seconds per incorrect answer was assessed before the final results were tallied.

EXAMPLE: A different information search approach was employed by a trainer in a course on diversity in the workplace. She presented participants with four articles discussing the topic (the articles focused on gender, race, ethnicity, and age). The participants' job was to research the topic as thoroughly as possible in order to participate in a panel discussion on how to best manage a diverse workforce. They were urged to gather whatever facts, concepts, and

---

FIGURE 5–4. INFORMATION SEARCH

Your mortgage applicant has indicated that a deposit of $10,000 has been made. What follow-up steps must be taken to account for this earnest money?

To be eligible for a mortgage from our bank, second homes must be family- and owner-occupied.

   True _____   False _____

In the space to the left of each number, write the letter corresponding to the correct definition.

_____ 1. Principal

_____ 2. Amortization

_____ 3. Mortgage

A. A conveyance of interest in real property as security for payment of a debt

B. The amount of the loan outstanding at a particular point

C. The process of paying down principal through the life of the loan

---

opinions they could to enhance the quality of the discussion. In order to give every participant an opportunity to take part in the discussion, the membership of the panel changed every ten minutes. By the end of the segment, the participants were very well informed about the topic.

Here are some procedural guidelines for using information search:

1. Create a group of questions that can be answered by searching for information that can be found in resource material you have made available for participants. The resource material can include

   • Handouts

   • Documents

   • A textbook

   • Reference guides

   • Computer-accessed information

   • Artifacts

   • Work-related equipment

2. Hand out the questions about the topic.

3. Have participants search for information in small teams. Consider setting up a competition to encourage participation.

4. Review the answers as a class. Expand upon the answers to enlarge the scope of learning.

STUDY GROUP

Ask participants to read a short, well-formatted handout covering lecture material and then place them in small groups to clarify its contents. A study group is an excellent way to cover new material without lecturing. Here are examples.

EXAMPLE: Sales representatives were given a handout explaining a SPIN sales call sequence: *situation* questions, *problem* questions, *implication* questions, and *need-payoff* questions. They were placed in study groups and asked to review the handout found in Figure 5–5. Following this, they were challenged to develop a model sales call that illustrated the use of these four types of questions.

FIGURE 5–5. SPIN QUESTIONS

Successful salespeople ask a lot of questions, but they're definitely not asked at random. A successful sales call follows a distinct pattern that research psychologist Neil Rackham calls the SPIN sequence.

A SPIN sales call follows this sequence:

1. **Situation questions.** At the start of a call, ask data-gathering questions such as "How long have you had your present equipment?" or "Could you tell me about your company's growth plans?"

2. **Problem questions.** After the buyer's situation has been established, ask questions to uncover problems, such as "Is this operation difficult to perform?" or "Are you worried about the quality you get from your old machine?" These questions explore difficulties and dissatisfaction in areas where the seller's product can help. Inexperienced people don't ask enough problem questions.

3. **Implication questions.** These questions take a customer's problem and explore its effects or consequences. This helps the customer understand a problem's seriousness or urgency. For example, you might ask, "How will this problem affect your future profitability?" or "What effect does this reject rate have on customer satisfaction?"

4. **Need-payoff questions.** These questions get the customer to tell you the benefits your solution could offer. Typical questions are "Would it be useful to speed this operation by 10 percent?" or "If we could improve the quality of this operation, how would that help you?"

FIGURE 5–5. continued

Need-payoff questions have a strong relationship to sales success. Rackham has found that top performers ask more than ten times as many of these questions per call as do average performers!

Source: Trifiletti and Alexandri, 1994, p. 130. Used with permission.

EXAMPLE: In a course on team development, a trainer gave participants a handout that charted the differences between effective and ineffective teams along eight dimensions. He then formed study groups, urging them to conduct themselves like Bible study groups, and asked participants to take turns reading aloud each of the eight sets of statements on the chart (for example, "Controversy and conflict are seen as positive keys to members' involvement" versus "Controversy and conflict are ignored, denied, avoided, or suppressed"). After reading the statements, each reader was told to ask other group members the following questions:

"Do you want the statements clarified?"

"How do you interpret the statements?"

"Can you give an example from your experience that is related to the statements?"

"Do you agree with the statements?"

The groups were then reassembled, and participants discussed the chart as a whole using a fishbowl format.

Here are some procedural guidelines for using a study group:

1. Give participants a short, well-formatted handout covering lecture material, a brief text, or an interesting chart or diagram. Ask them to read it silently. A study group works best when the material is moderately challenging or open to widespread interpretation.

2. Form subgroups and give them a quiet space to conduct their study session.

3. Provide clear instructions that guide participants to study and explicate the material carefully. Include directions such as these:

   - Clarify the contents.

   - Create examples, illustrations, or applications of the information or ideas.

   - Identify points that are confusing or that you disagree with.

- Argue with the text; develop an opposing point of view.
- Assess how well you understand the material.

4. Assign jobs to group members such as facilitator, timekeeper, recorder, or spokesperson.

5. Reconvene the total class and do one or more of the following:

- Review the material together.
- Quiz participants.
- Obtain questions.
- Ask participants to assess how well they understand the material.
- Provide an application exercise for participants to solve.

JIGSAW LEARNING

Jigsaw learning is a variation of a study group. Rather than asking each group to study the same information, you can give different information to different groups and then form study groups composed of representatives of each of the initial groups. The beauty of jigsaw learning is that every single participant teaches something or brings his or her newly acquired knowledge to the learning task. It is an exciting alternative whenever the material to be learned can be segmented or "chunked" and when no one segment must be taught before the others. Each participant learns something that, when combined with the material learned by the others, forms a coherent body of knowledge or skill.

Notice how jigsaw learning was employed in the following examples.

EXAMPLE: In a stress management program, a trainer formed five groups, with five members in each group. A member from each group selected a stress management strategy by picking one from a hat. The five strategies focused on *relaxation, nutrition, delegation, assertiveness,* and *exercise.* Each group received handouts on the strategy it had picked; these were read and discussed within the group. Then five new groups were formed, each containing one representative from the initial study groups. In these groups, each member explained her or his strategy to the others. By taking part in this process, every participant was responsible for teaching some of the information to other participants.

EXAMPLE: In a course on sexual harassment, a trainer divided participants into six study groups and gave each group material on one of six legal factors that help to decide what constitutes sexual harassment:

1. Quid pro quo harassment
2. Unwelcome behavior

3. Isolated occurrences

4. Hostile environment

5. Prior romantic involvement

6. Ordinary reasonable person

After studying the material, jigsaw groups were formed and given the following six questions to discuss:

1. If a woman has tolerated repeated requests for a date by her boss, does she still have grounds for claiming sexual harassment?

2. Does there have to be a repetitive series of incidents to claim sexual harassment?

3. Does the fact that the victim suffered no mental anguish affect her claim?

4. Whose standards determine how offensive an act is—men's or women's?

5. What is the clearest violation of the law?

6. Can you allege that someone you previously dated sexually harassed you?

The trainer pointed out that all the required information to answer these questions had been acquired by someone in the jigsaw group. The participants were then instructed to share their knowledge to answer the six questions.

———————

Here are some procedural guidelines for using jigsaw learning:

1. Choose learning material that can be broken into parts. A part segment can be as short as one sentence or as long as several pages. (If the material is lengthy, ask participants to read their assignment before class.) Examples include

   • A multipoint handout (for example, "Ten Strategies for Forming Teams")

   • A text that has different sections or subheadings

   • A list of definitions

   • A group of magazine-length articles or other kinds of short reading material

2. Count the number of learning segments and the number of participants. In an equitable manner, give out different assignments to different groups of participants. For example, imagine a class of twelve participants. Assume that you can divide the learning materials into three segments or "chunks." You might then be able to form quartets, assigning each group either segment 1, 2, or 3. You would then ask each quartet or "study group" to read, discuss, and learn the material assigned to it.

3. After the study period, form jigsaw learning groups. Such groups contain a representative of every study group in the class. In the example just given, the members of each quartet could count off the numbers 1, 2, 3, and 4, then form jigsaw learning groups of participants with the same number. The result would be four trios. Each trio would consist of one person who had studied segment 1, one who had studied segment 2, and one who had studied segment 3. The diagram in Figure 5–6 displays this sequence.

FIGURE 5–6. JIGSAW LEARNING EXAMPLE

Total Group Explanation

Study Group

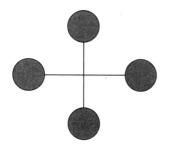 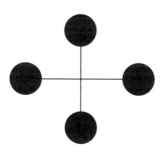 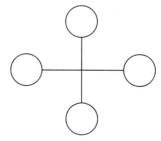

Jigsaw Learning Groups

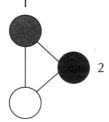 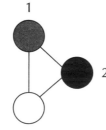 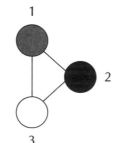 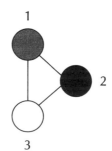

4. Ask the members of the jigsaw groups to teach each other what they have learned or give the groups a set of questions that depend on the varied knowledge of their members.

5. Reconvene the full class for review and any questions remaining to ensure accurate understanding.

In many instances, the number of participants cannot be divided evenly into the number of learning segments and adjustments have to be made (for example, uneven groups). The easiest format for jigsaw learning involves learning partners. Combine the learning material into two segments, assigning one segment to one member of a pair and the other segment to his or her partner. For example, in a seven-point handout, one person can be assigned points 1–4 and the partner can be assigned points 5–7. You can easily create "study buddies" with the same assignment. Then have the original pair teach each other what they have studied.

LEARNING TOURNAMENT

This technique combines a study group and team competition. It can be used to promote the learning of a wide variety of facts and concepts, especially if the information is dry. If you use this approach, provide participants with learning material that you would normally cover in a lecture. Give them time to read and study the material with the knowledge that they will be tested on its contents. Form teams to review the information and test each other. Then give a short quiz on the material to each participant, review (and elaborate on) the answers, and provide instructions on how to score the results and obtain a team average score. To achieve the feeling of a tournament, repeat this process a few times so that teams can rise or fall in their standings relative to each other.

Here are two examples of using learning tournaments.

EXAMPLE: In a class on human resource management, the trainer distributed information about the Americans With Disabilities Act and asked teams to study the facts it contained. In the first round of the learning tournament, every participant took a true-false test. The participants were given five statements:

1. Any new building over two stories high must have an elevator.

2. Organizations with under seventy-five employees are exempt from compliance.

3. Physical requirements for a job may be listed in the job description.

4. The cost of retraining a newly disabled employee is completely assumed by the employer.

5. The term "reasonable accommodations" is clearly defined by government regulations.

After the answers were reviewed by the trainer, the participants totaled their individual scores to obtain a team score. Round 1 was now over and each team returned to study the information further to prepare for round 2 of the tournament. At that time, an additional set of true-false statements was asked of the participants.

EXAMPLE: A trainer decided to use a learning tournament to motivate the learning of "Ten Ways to Obtain Participation," described in Chapter Three. Participants were placed into teams of four members each and given ten minutes to study the material. They were then given the following fill-in-the-blank statements:

- This is a way to obtain participation by asking participants to write instead of speak.

  _____ _____ (response card)

- These are useful in conducting a "go-around."

  _____ _____ (sentence stems)

- This technique is a timesaver when you want small-group discussion but do not have enough time.

  _____ (partners)

- This technique is best when you want to promote participant-to-participant interaction.

  ____ ____ ____ ____ ____ (call on the next speaker)

  _____

Here are some procedural guidelines for using a learning tournament:

1. Divide participants into teams with two to eight members. Make sure the teams have equal numbers. (If this cannot be achieved, you will have to average each team's score.)

2. Provide the teams with material to study together.

3. Develop several questions that test comprehension and/or recall of the learning material. Use formats that make self-scoring easy, such as multiple-choice, fill-in-the-blank, true-false, and terms to define.

4. Give a portion of the questions to participants. Refer to this as "round 1" of the learning tournament. Each participant must answer the questions individually.

5. After the questions have been given, provide the answers and ask the participants to count the number they answered correctly. Then have them pool their score with the scores of every other member of their team to obtain a team score. Announce the score of each team.

6. Ask the teams to study again for the second round of the tournament. Then ask more test questions as part of round 2. Have teams once again pool their scores and add them to their round 1 score.

7. You can have as many rounds as you would like, but be sure to allow the team to have a study session between each one.

APPLYING THE ALTERNATIVES TO A COMMON TOPIC

In order to help you consider how the eight alternatives might be applied to a common topic, take a look at the memo in Figure 5–7. If you received such a memo, how would you respond? Some suggestions follow.

FIGURE 5–7. MEMORANDUM

TO   John Trainer, Assistant Vice President
FROM: Philip Doe, Senior Vice President
RE: Training

I have noticed that some of the people in our current credit training class still have a poor understanding of some basic accounting principles. I think we should start with the difference between a balance sheet and an income statement. Here are some points to stress:

- The balance sheet provides a capsule view of the financial status of an enterprise at a particular date. It helps external users to assess the financial relationship of the assets, liabilities, and owner's equity. Trainees should understand

    The difference between current and long-term assets

    The difference between current and long-term liabilities

    The difference between liabilities and owner's equity as a claim against assets

    The difference between capital stock and retained earnings

    How to use the previous year's financial information for comparison purposes

- The income statement provides a measure of the success of an enterprise over a specific period of time. It shows the major sources of revenues generated and the expenses associated with these revenues. The income statement helps external users to evaluate the earnings potential of the company. Trainees should understand

    What gross margin measures and how it is derived

    How operating income is determined

    How the bottom line is arrived at

    How to compute earnings per share

I know I don't have to tell you how important it is for future credit analysts to have a clear understanding of these two key financial statements. I know that this material is being taught now, but it's not sinking in. Maybe it's the method. Can you think of any better alternatives to just lecturing on this material? Let's brainstorm. I'd like to see your ideas.

---

1. ***Demonstration.*** Illustrate the preparation of both an income statement and a balance sheet by walking through the process in a hypothetical situation. Involve participants in some of the steps, such as separating the income statement accounts from the balance sheet accounts and performing the basic calculations.

2. ***Case study.*** Prepare a written case description of an owner of a business who is seeking help in preparing an income statement and a balance sheet for the year ending December 31. Describe in detail the data provided by the owner and how this information was organized by the accountant in order to prepare the two statements. Have the participants complete the income statement and balance sheet; then hold a discussion to review the two processes and how they differ.

3. ***Guided teaching.*** Provide the participants with a list of account balances of a real or fictitious company. Ask them to select accounts that should be reported on the income statement and accounts that would appear on the balance sheet. If no one in the group knows the answers, encourage speculation. Present the correct lists. Ask the participants if they can figure out the basis for the two lists (for example, revenue and expense accounts belong on the income statement, while accounts showing the company's financial position belong on the balance sheet). After the group understands the basis for separating the accounts, discuss a proper format for preparing the income statement and the balance sheet. Ask as many questions as you can to push the participants into their own inferences and deductions.

4. ***Group inquiry.*** Provide examples of an income statement and a balance sheet for a company. Ask participants to study the examples in order to figure out how the two processes differ. Volunteer no further information, but encourage participants to ask you as many questions as they like. Using their own powers of inquiry and discovery, participants should be able to understand the concept being taught.

5. ***Information search.*** Create quiz questions on the difference between a balance sheet and an income statement. Give out a short reading assignment that effectively describes and illustrates the two processes and have the participants, individually or in small teams, search the material for answers to the questions in the quiz.

6. ***Study group.*** Give participants the reading assignment described in the previous suggestion; then form small groups so that they can clarify with each other the contents of the reading assignment. Reconvene the full group and answer any questions. Make *brief* lecture points where necessary.

7. ***Jigsaw learning.*** Pair up participants. Give one member of the pair information about a balance sheet and the other member information about an income statement. Ask them to teach each other what they have read and to figure out the difference between the two.

8. ***Learning tournament.*** Form teams and give them reading material about balance sheets and income statements. Stop their study session and quiz them on the difference between the two. Compare the scores of each team. Have the teams return to study the reading material; then quiz them again about the details of balance sheets and income statements.

Now consider a very different challenge. Imagine that you want participants to have a solid grasp of the twelve ways to improve meetings listed in Figure 5–8. What alternatives to lecturing would you select to teach this material? Compare your thoughts with the suggestions that follow.

1. ***Demonstration.*** Illustrate the twelve ways to improve your meetings by simulating a meeting with your participants. Use such topics as summer party planning or monthly budget evaluations. Give participants a checklist (such as a copy of the twelve suggestions) to guide their observations of your techniques.

2. ***Case study.*** Hand out a case description of two meetings held one week apart: an ineffective one and one that was productive from beginning to

---

FIGURE 5–8. TWELVE WAYS TO IMPROVE YOUR MEETINGS

1. Send out agendas in advance.
2. Be prepared with supporting facts and opinions.
3. Select problems that can be managed and solved.
4. Don't waste time. Stick to the issues at hand.
5. Agree on a definition of the problem before moving to solutions.
6. Allow adequate time for each problem-solving step.
7. Encourage positive confrontation.
8. Focus on the issues, not the people.
9. Take turns chairing long meetings.
10. Vary the pace of the meeting between reporting and discussion.
11. Rank alternative solutions before deciding on the best ones.
12. Determine a date on which to check on implementation of the decision.

end. Ask participants to figure out how the improvement might have been achieved.

3. ***Guided teaching.*** Put up on the wall two sheets of flip-chart paper that are blank except for the titles "Good Meetings" and "Bad Meetings." Ask participants to recall their own experiences in meetings, and volunteer suggestions as to what made the meetings positive or negative. List suggestions on the charts; then compare them to the lecture points you have in mind.

4. ***Group inquiry.*** Hand out a copy of the twelve ways to improve meetings. Divide the participants into small groups. Ask each group to come up with three questions that they would like you to answer concerning the information on the handout. Answer the questions in a large-group format.

5. ***Information search.*** Provide brief examples of the twelve ways to improve meetings without identifying which example illustrates which suggestion. Have pairs work together to match examples to the suggestions on the list.

6. ***Study group.*** Divide participants into small groups and ask each group to study the twelve ways to improve meetings, clarifying each point and discussing their opinions of its worth.

7. ***Jigsaw learning.*** Divide the twelve points into three sets of four each. Divide participants into trios and give one set to each member to read. Reconvene the trios and give each trio the task of using its members' respective information to improve the effectiveness of a meeting in which none of the twelve ways are present.

8. ***Learning tournament.*** Create teams of two and give members the list in Figure 5–8. Tell each pair that they have two minutes to memorize the list. Give teammates one minute to test each other. Then ask each team to write down the twelve ideas from memory. The team with the highest number recalled wins the tournament.

Now consider a topic from your own training situation. How could you avoid lecturing about it? As you think about this, remember that the methods can also be combined. For example, group inquiry can almost always follow one of the other alternatives. Used in this way, it serves as a way to debrief the training activity. Likewise, a study group can precede many of the other methods in order to provide a knowledge base for later application.

WORKSHEET

FINDING ALTERNATIVE METHODS TO LECTURING

Use the following worksheet to design an alternative to the lecture presentation you selected in Chapter 4.

Topic: (*check one*)

_____ Demonstration

_____ Case study

_____ Guided teaching

_____ Group inquiry

_____ Information search

_____ Study group

_____ Jigsaw learning

_____ Learning tournament

Design Outline:

_____

_____

_____

_____

_____

_____

_____

_____

_____

_____

_____

_____

_____

_____

_____

_____

◆　◆　◆

Chapter Six

Using Experiential Learning Approaches

*A*ctive training promotes learning by doing. As I have indicated, even a lecture has to be designed to involve the participation of the learner and, at times, it can be replaced by one of several methods that facilitate more direct acquisition of information. Still other methods place an even greater premium on active, participatory learning.

Experiential learning approaches are particularly suited for affective and behavioral training goals. They help participants to become aware of their feelings and reactions to certain issues and new ideas. In addition, they allow participants to practice and refine new skills and procedures. In this chapter, I will examine and illustrate six major experiential learning approaches:

1. **Role playing**
2. **Games and simulations**
3. **Observation**
4. **Mental imagery**
5. **Writing tasks**
6. **Action learning projects**

ROLE PLAYING

Role playing is a staple in any active trainer's repertoire. It is the best-known way to help participants both experience certain feelings and practice certain skills. Let's say, for example, that your training objective is to have participants get in touch with their feelings about confronting others (something many supervisors and, indeed, people in general avoid). You can set up a dramatic situation in which participants are required to confront someone else and then discuss the feelings generated by the role-playing experience. In addition, you can design a role-playing exercise to enable participants to practice constructive methods of confrontation.

Scripting

You have many choices when designing role-playing exercises. One set of choices has to do with the **scripting** of the drama. Scripting is concerned with the development of roles and the situation in which the drama is placed. Here are six options:

1. *Improvisation.* Participants can be given a general scenario and asked to fill in the details themselves. This approach promotes spontaneity and the opportunity to gear the scenario to one's own work experience. Because the situation is not clearly outlined, however, participants may have difficulty creating details on their own.

EXAMPLE: "Let's imagine that you are at a restaurant and your order is overcooked. Let's have Mary be that customer and request that the order be redone. What if Frank is the waiter and he gives the customer a hard time? Mary, you will try to persuade the waiter to redo the order. I'd like to see you both use all the skills we've been practicing so far."

2. *Prescribed roles.* Participants can be given a well-prepared set of instructions that state the facts about the roles they are portraying and how they are to behave. This approach gives you the most control over the script, so the dramatic tension you want to create is easily obtainable. However, participants may not identify with the roles and situation you have developed or they may get lost if the scenario is too complex.

EXAMPLE: "You are an accountant for an insurance company. You have been with the company since your graduation from college three years ago. You really like the company, feel you are doing well, and are looking forward to a promotion. You like your work except for writing letters, memos, and notes on your accounting reports. You've never admitted it to anyone, but you've always had difficulty in English. Your manager has just called you in. You're afraid it might be about your writing. You'll admit your deficiency only if your manager seems genuinely interested and concerned; otherwise, you will make up excuses."

3. *Semiprescribed roles.* Participants can be given information about the situation and the characters to be portrayed but not told how to handle the situation. By not prescribing how characters are to behave, this approach provides greater latitude for the participants. Some of them, however, may create a scenario different from what the trainer intended.

EXAMPLE: "You are a recently appointed supervisor of a support engineering group that has overall responsibility for maintaining and improving test equipment hardware and software at its repair centers. There are twenty engineers, differing widely in age and experience with the company. Each engineer is responsible for a specific list of test equipment. Up until now, staff members have not been called upon to work on test equipment that is not on their designated lists. This has meant that when one of them is sick or on vacation or has a priority assignment, it is difficult for anyone else to take up the slack.

"You have decided to assemble a small team within the group to develop Support Test Equipment Protocols (STEPs) that will provide the information necessary to support the various pieces of test equipment. With these STEPs, you will be able to establish a rotation system within the group. The people you have invited to be on the team include two senior project engineers and two hardware and software technicians.

"This is the first meeting of the group. Begin the meeting."

4. *Replay of life.* Participants can portray themselves in situations they have actually faced. This approach has the advantage of bringing the most realism to the drama. However, it can be difficult to re-create the actual situation and the role play may then flounder.

EXAMPLE: "I'd like each of you to think about the last time you gave a performance appraisal. Tell your role-playing partner what generally happened and reenact the situation, the first time keeping to the approach you took when you actually gave the appraisal and the second time altering your approach to include the suggestions I have demonstrated."

5. *Participant-prepared skits.* Participants can be asked to develop a role-playing vignette of their own. This approach provides them with time to create a role play and gives them a chance to rehearse before a final performance. Participants will respond especially well to this approach if they are invited to address their real-life problems and incorporate them into the skits. However, some of the spontaneity of the previous options is lost.

EXAMPLE: "I'd like you and your partner to take the three management styles we've just discussed and create a skit that shows a manager using each of the styles while giving project instructions to an employee. Base your skit on your own experiences. Take about ten minutes to prepare your skits. When you're ready, let me know and we will take a look at what you've come up with."

6. *Dramatic readings.* Participants can be given a previously prepared script to act out. This approach creates the least anxiety of any of the previous options and allows the least skill practice.

EXAMPLE: "Here is a script of an exit interview. It demonstrates very effectively some of the problems and some of the solutions we've been examining. In your pairs, one will be the interviewer and the other will be the employee who is leaving the company. Read your parts aloud to get a feel for the tension and relief experienced in the situation."

Of course, a trainer has the option of combining these scripted choices. For example, participants could be asked to read a script and then act out the same drama without the script in front of them. Or they could be allowed to prepare their own scenario, followed by a trainer-prepared scenario. Mixing scripting options in this manner helps to minimize the disadvantages of any single option.

Staging

Another set of choices has to do with *staging.* Staging is concerned with the format you use for the role play, regardless of the content. Here are six options.

1. *Informal role playing.* The role play can evolve informally from a group discussion. An informal format reduces the stage fright often experienced with role playing.

EXAMPLE: A participant says, "I can't get any cooperation from my boss." Wanting to understand the situation better, you spontaneously respond, "In order for me to have a clearer picture of what usually transpires between you and your boss, let me pretend to be your boss and you ask me for something you need from me. I'll respond the way I think your boss typically does, but if I'm off base, let me know. We don't have to set this up in any formal way. Stay seated where you are and just start off the conversation."

2. *Stage-front role playing.* One pair, trio, or the like can role-play in front of the group, which will observe and offer feedback. Staging a single-group role play focuses the class on a single drama for later discussion and feedback and allows for maximum coaching and feedback by the trainer. Often, stage-front role plays are the most anxiety-producing for the participants chosen. In addition, the rest of the participants are relegated to an observer role.

EXAMPLE: "I need three volunteers who will portray for the rest of us a family discussing the college choices of their child, who is a high school junior. Would someone agree to be the father, someone the mother, and someone the student?"

3. *Simultaneous role playing.* All participants can be formed into pairs for a two-person drama, trios for a three-person drama, and so on and simultaneously undertake their role plays. A multiple-group format reduces anxiety and allows everyone to participate. However, the trainer may have difficulty

monitoring the dramas that unfold and the level of performance demonstrated by participants.

EXAMPLE: "I'd like you to pair up with the person seated next to you and turn your chairs around to face each other. You should move away from the other pairs so that you have some privacy. One of you needs to volunteer first to be the client; the other will be the salesperson. Each of you will then get to practice how to close a sale."

4. *Rotational role playing.* Actors in front of the group can be rotated, usually by interrupting the role play in progress and replacing one or more of the actors. Although this option involves a single-group drama, several participants can still be included. This approach is less demanding than a nonrotating stage-front drama.

EXAMPLE: "I'd like to set up a scene in which an irate customer is calling to complain that her claim check has not yet arrived and the claims adjuster somehow needs to remain courteous under great pressure. This time we'll do something a little different. After every thirty seconds of the conversation, I'll tap out the role players, and their parts will be picked up by the next person in line."

5. *Use of different actors.* More than one actor can be recruited to role-play the same situation in its entirety. This allows the group to observe more than one style or approach. The trainer has to be careful, however, not to encourage comparisons between the actors that would lessen somebody's self-esteem. Also, obtaining volunteers to be the actors can be difficult.

EXAMPLE: "I need three brave souls who will agree to handle, one at a time, a disruptive junior high school class. These volunteers will be asked to leave the room and decide who will do the role play first, second, and third. While you're gone, the rest of us will set up the scene and then ask the first "teacher" to come in the room and manage the situation. The other two volunteers will stay outside until their turn arrives. This way, none of the "teachers" will have seen any of the others role-play the situation before his or her turn. I realize that volunteering means taking a big risk, but the rest of the group and I would really appreciate the chance to see three different people handling the same problem."

6. *Repeated role playing.* Regardless of the staging option chosen, the role play can be reenacted. This is always a good idea when you want participants to have a second chance after the initial feedback.

EXAMPLE: "Now that you've had a chance to try out this problem situation once, I'd like you to try it a second time. This time make any changes you'd like that will improve upon your performance. Think of it as a dress rehearsal before going out to the real world and actually doing it. Good luck!"

Once again, there are many ways to combine these staging options. For example, simultaneous role playing can be followed by a stage-front format. Or rotational role playing can precede the use of different actors. Also consider the numerous choices generated by combining different scripting and staging approaches. In fact, with six of each, you have thirty-six different options. To introduce role playing to a reluctant group, for example, you can divide participants into pairs (simultaneous staging) and give them a prepared script to read (dramatic readings). To refine skill development later on, you might try the use of different actors to stage a semiprescribed role play.

Processing

A final set of six choices has to do with *processing* the role play. Processing pertains to reflective discussion or debriefing of the role play or to giving performance feedback to the role players.

1. ***Designated observers.*** One or more observers can be added to each role-playing group and given specific instructions about what to observe and how to give feedback. (If you are using a single, stage-front role play, choose specific participants to be feedback observers.) Peer feedback is a two-edged sword. Participants are less threatened by it but, at the same time, they may not value it as much as the trainer's feedback.

EXAMPLE: "In your trio, each of you will take a turn observing the other two. When a role play is finished, share with the actors the nonverbal behaviors you saw that didn't seem to match what was being said."

2. ***Self-assessment.*** The role players themselves can discuss their reactions to the experience. Ask open-ended questions first so that the role players are free to make observations on their own. Ask more pointed questions later on, probing gently about feelings, intentions, and reactions.

EXAMPLE: "Take a few minutes as a group and share how you felt about the role play. When did you feel effective and when did you feel that others were effective? What felt uncomfortable? What would you like to do better the next time?"

3. ***Open audience discussion and feedback.*** Invite the group as a whole to give their reactions and feedback to a role play. You can avoid a free-for-all feedback session by providing guidelines such as asking the audience to give positive feedback first or focusing on specific events rather than global impressions. Try to obtain several points of view because different observers notice different things.

EXAMPLE: "Now that we've seen how Brad handled the customer's complaint, I'd like you first to comment on the good points and then to suggest how Brad could do things differently."

4. ***Subgroup discussion and feedback.*** Assign a small group from the audience to each one of the role players and ask the members to discuss what they saw happening. This technique is especially effective after the format of use of different actors. Ask the subgroup members to use the time not only to give feedback but also to obtain the actor's self-assessment.

EXAMPLE: "Since we had three characters in this role play, I will ask the audience to count off by threes. The 'ones' will go off with Joan and discuss her reactions to the role play and the reactions they had to her performance. The 'twos' will go off with Don and do the same. The 'threes' will go off with Lee."

5. ***Trainer observations.*** You can give your reactions to the role play for everyone to hear. Because your feedback is often held in high regard, be careful to preserve the self-esteem of the role players and "own" the feedback by saying such phrases as "It seemed to me . . ." or "I'm not sure how others saw this, but I . . "

EXAMPLE: "This was terrific. I'm really impressed by the number of techniques you wove into your performance. I especially liked the way you handled Pat's resistance. Your empathy really disarmed him. You might consider, for fine-tuning purposes, pausing a little more to emphasize what you're saying. Is this feedback helpful?"

6. ***Benchmark comparison.*** The role players and observers can compare the performance to an ideal script. Be sure, however, to give participants the opportunity to disagree with the "ideal."

EXAMPLE: "Let's take a look at a textbook example of this sales presentation. Look over this script and find things in it that you wish you had done. But also identify what you don't like. We'll get back together in fifteen minutes, after you've had a chance to read the script and discuss it with your seat partners."

Video Feedback

In addition to the processing options just mentioned, a trainer can arrange for ***video feedback.*** Here are some guidelines when facilitating video feedback.

Prior to the Taping

- Give trainees adequate time to prepare for taping so that they perform well enough to have a positive learning experience.

- Lighten the mood so that the performance is as natural and relaxed as possible.

- Consider leaving the room of the videotaping session initially to encourage trainees to experiment and tape each other briefly. Do this to help them become less camera-conscious.

During the Taping

- *Don't* make teaching points when participants are recording. Hold off until later.

- *Do* make notes of what the trainee is doing well and what needs to be improved. Start to think about what parts of the recording you may want to review carefully with the trainee. (You may want to keep a running time notation system so that you can easily locate critical parts later on.)

After the Taping

- Give trainees uninterrupted time to make their own judgments of their performance first.

- Consider creating peer support groups that watch each other's tapes and give feedback.

- Develop a written checklist of specific behaviors that trainees can look for in analyzing their tapes.

- Review parts of the tape you have selected with each trainee. Use effective feedback techniques, such as being descriptive, being specific, focusing on dos rather than don'ts, and obtaining trainees' reactions to your feedback. Invite trainees to problem-solve as much as possible instead of giving your own advice first.

Active Skill Development

One of the common uses for role playing is skill practice. After demonstrating the skill, the trainer asks participants to do it themselves. When you are demonstrating a skill, it is important ***not*** to explain too fully what you are doing. By demonstrating a skill without explanation, you encourage ***participants*** to be mentally alert to what you are doing. Instead of explaining what you are doing, have the participants observe, figure out what you are doing, and explain it back to you.

Ask participants to take the following four steps:

1. ***Observe.*** Ask the participants to watch you perform the skill. Just do it, with little or no explanation or commentary about what you are doing. Give them a visual glimpse of the "big picture." Do not expect retention. At this point, you are merely establishing readiness for learning and providing an overview.

2. ***Recall.*** Form pairs. Demonstrate the skill again slowly, again with little or no explanation or commentary. Ask pairs to discuss with each other what they observed you doing. (Telling them what you are doing will lessen the

mental alertness of the participants.) Obtain a volunteer to explain what you did. If the participants have difficulty, demonstrate again. Acknowledge correct observations. (If you are demonstrating a skill to only one person, follow the same procedure but ask that person to explain what you did directly back to you.)

3. ***Question.*** Ask for questions! Because participants have been actively involved in the process of observing the skill, they will have more questions (and better ones) than if you had taught the skill in a traditional manner.

4. ***Do.*** Have the pairs practice the skill with each other. Tell them that you want them "to test themselves." Encourage them to practice until they have proved to ***themselves*** that they have mastered the skill.

Even ***before*** taking these steps, consider the possibility of asking participants to attempt the skill before you demonstrate it. Encourage them to make an attempt on their own. By doing this, you will immediately get participants mentally involved. Then have them watch you, as an expert, demonstrate the skill.

If some participants master the skill sooner than others, recruit them to silently demonstrate the skill to others and help them to practice it.

GAMES AND SIMULATIONS

Some trainers are hesitant to use games and simulations in their programs, fearing that participants will find them too contrived or will dismiss them as mere entertainment. And, certainly, like any other training method, games and simulations are not without risk. Used in the wrong way at the wrong time, they may do little good. Used appropriately, however, they can be an enjoyable and effective way to advance training objectives.

One of the advantages of games and simulations is the extent to which they encourage participants to confront their own attitudes and values. An excellent example is the Prisoner's Dilemma Game. This well-known game is set up in such a way that participants make a choice, often without realizing it, to compete rather than to cooperate. The effects of the choice become evident as the game proceeds. It's a terrific way to help participants become aware of their competitiveness. Many other games perform similar self-revelatory functions.

Games and simulations can also help participants grasp the total course content. An advantage of using a game at the beginning section of a program is that it can give participants a chance to experience the whole before discussing the parts. For example, starting a cross-cultural training program with a simulation game such as Bafá Bafá is a great way to prepare people being transferred abroad for the frustrations, joys, and insights that come from contact with a foreign culture. In Bafá Bafá, participants are separated into two groups.

Each group becomes a culture and is instructed in the culture's values and traditions. The two groups then exchange "ambassadors," who observe the other group and return to report on what they have learned about its culture. After consultation time, a different set of ambassadors is exchanged with the charge of interacting with the culture being visited. The game provides an excellent chance to help participants focus on what they consider normal, how they act within their own inner circle, and how they interact with strangers. They usually spend an hour playing the game and then up to five hours discussing how stereotypes are formed and perpetuated.

Games and simulations can also help test the behavioral style and performance of participants. Playing a game at the beginning of a course allows the trainer to identify the styles and skills that already exist and those that need to be strengthened. Playing a game at the end of the course enables the trainer to assess the instructional experience. Take, for example, a simulation exercise called Desert Survival. Players are told that their plane has crashed in the desert, that their only priority is to survive, and that only certain items are available to them. In the first part of the game, players must decide how to survive individually. Then the game is replayed, with groups working toward team consensus. A trainer could include this simulation exercise at the beginning of a course on team building to assess how well teams work toward consensus. Near the end of the course, a similar exercise, such as Winter Survival, could be employed to measure progress in teamwork.

The CD-ROM is becoming a popular medium for this type of experiential learning. For example, using digitized video, a pharmaceutical company was able to re-create conversations between sales representatives and doctors about one of their products. Learners could observe and evaluate the reps' approach and competency at each stage of the sales call. The video clips featured experienced representatives from different sales territories, not actors. At the conclusion of each sales call, learners received a synopsis of the call from an expert sales coach (Advanced Consulting Inc., 1997).

When designing games and simulations, there are several things to keep in mind.

The game or simulation needs to be relevant to the participants.

EXAMPLE: A module on project-planning methods began with a game called Sixty-Four Squares. On a flip chart, the trainer drew a large square and divided it into sixty-four smaller squares (see Figure 6–1). The trainer then selected a square and wrote its letter and number on a piece of paper, without revealing its contents to the group. The participants were challenged to find the "secret square" by asking only six questions. The questions were to be answered by a yes or no. Calling out questions without a plan, it took the group twelve questions to find the secret square. The trainer then commented that the most efficient path to the answer involves a binary approach in which each question reduces the number of eligible squares by 50 percent. For example, if participants had asked whether the secret square was in rows 1 to 4, they could have ascertained which half of the matrix the square was in. The trainer pointed out that there is also a critical path to follow when it comes to managing a project; the challenge is to find it. All the participants were impressed by the experience, in large part because the game drove home a lesson that was highly relevant to their work situations.

FIGURE 6–1. SIXTY-FOUR SQUARES

	1	2	3	4	5	6	7	8
A								
B								
C								
D								
E								
F								
G								
H								

The easiest way to create games and simulations is to mimic the format and character of well-known ones.

EXAMPLE: Technical information is often dry stuff to learn. Television quiz games can be easily adapted for training groups. Probably the most widely copied ones are "Jeopardy," "Wheel of Fortune," and "Family Feud." Board games often work, too. Trivial Pursuit is perhaps the most popular choice, since merely playing the game and learning the correct answers is a satisfying way to pick up information. A clerical staff trainer went one step further. She divided participants into teams and gave them an opportunity to teach each other as much information as possible. Then team members were pitted against members of other teams in a head-to-head individual competition of Trivial Pursuit, using questions from the information the participants had just learned. Thus, both cooperative and competitive methods were used in a gaming approach to learning technical information.

Well-known games and simulations can be modified to suit your needs.

EXAMPLE: A story called "Alligator River" (Figure 6–2) is the basis for a well-known values clarification exercise. After reading the story, participants are asked to rank the four characters from most to least objectionable. Typically, groups are then formed to seek consensus. In the process of the discussion, participants are forced to clarify their values. A trainer in a course on listening skills decided to use this exercise for a different purpose. She dropped the consensus-seeking assignment and instead asked participants to do everything they could to force the group to accept their own opinions. When strong differences of opinion emerged, she instructed the participants to assume the point of view of another person in their group. Often, this became impossible because people had barely listened to their antagonists. The trainer used the experience to reinforce an important lesson—that listening is poorest when communication is competitive. In this instance, both the purpose of the game and the instructions were changed to suit the trainer's objective.

Funlike, contrived games can be followed by more serious, less contrived ones.

EXAMPLE: The trainer of a course on creative thinking designed for the marketing team of a large training vendor wanted participants to learn and value team brainstorming. He began with a zany exercise in which the team was asked to brainstorm as many uses for dirty undershirts as it could think of. Afterward, the team was asked to select their two most original ideas. The team had a ball, easily generating several ideas and quickly choosing their two best. Next, the team was given an exercise in which they were to generate new ways

---

FIGURE 6–2. ALLIGATOR RIVER

Once upon a time there was a woman named Abigail who was in love with a man named Gregory. Gregory lived on one shore of the river. Abigail lived on the opposite shore of the river. The river that separated the two lovers was teeming with alligators. Abigail wanted to cross the river to be with Gregory. Unfortunately, the bridge had been washed out. So she went to ask Sinbad, a riverboat captain, to take her across. He said he would be glad to if she would consent to go to bed with him before the voyage. She promptly refused and went to a friend named Ivan to explain her plight. Ivan did not want to be involved in the situation at all. Abigail felt that her only alternative was to accept Sinbad's terms. Sinbad fulfilled his promise to Abigail and delivered her into the arms of Gregory.

When Abigail told Gregory about her amorous escapade in order to cross the river, Gregory cast her aside with disdain.

Source: Simon, Howe, and Kirschenbaum, 1978, pp. 291–292. Used by permission.

---

to market their training services. As each idea surfaced, the only response allowed was to ask a question to clarify each contribution.

The trainer noted that it would be impossible in this brainstorming assignment to select the best ideas as quickly as in the previous one. Instead of a process in which individuals argued for the ideas they thought were best, the team was asked to first develop a set of criteria by which to judge the proposals and to then evaluate each one against the criteria the team had developed. The last step was either to choose the best marketing plans from the original list or somehow to combine the best ideas. Nonetheless, the first exercise had served the purpose of warming the team up and setting the stage for the second and more important exercise.

Instructions for games and simulations need to be carefully thought out.

EXAMPLE: A simulation called "Instant Aging" is designed to sensitize participants to sensory deprivation and the normal process of aging. Participants were given eyeglasses smeared with Vaseline, dried peas to put in their shoes, cotton for both ears, and latex gloves for their hands. They were then asked to take out a pencil and paper and write down their name, address, telephone number, any medication currently being taken, and any known allergies. Next, they were told to take a walk outside the training room, opening the door and finding their way around. The simulation involved a number of directions concerning the order of applying the props, the specific details of the tasks the participants were asked to perform, and the manner in which they were to take turns assisting each other. When all goes well, this experience has a tremendous impact on the participants.

Games and simulations almost always need to be discussed afterward for the experience to be an effective teacher.

EXAMPLE: Talking about what has just happened is important not only to bring the learning into focus but also to take advantage of peer pressure toward positive change. In the middle of a week-long course for new managers at a manufacturing company, the trainer placed a box of Tinkertoys in front of the participants, who were seated in pairs. One member of each pair was to assume the role of a supervisor while the other was to be his or her employee. The supervisor's job was to assign the employee the task of building a four-sided object with "something hanging in the middle," and to instruct the employee to accomplish the task in only a few minutes. After the allotted time, each supervisor was asked to seek feedback from the employee about the supervisor's assignment methods and general leadership style. This exchange set the stage for a discussion about appropriate supervisory behavior and direction giving. Many participants enjoyed the experience and felt that they would remember the point of it back on the job. A few participants complained, however, that the exercise was merely a game and that it indicated little about their real work situation. The trainer admitted that the exercise was contrived but then asked others how they found that it applied to their company. Many examples streamed forth from the group and a lively discussion ensued. The resisters, impressed by their peers' insights, were won over.

OBSERVATION

Watching others without directly participating can be an effective way to experience learning. Although it is worthwhile for participants actually to practice something, observation by itself can play an important part in a training design. The key is for the observation experience to be *active* rather than *passive.*

Designing

There are several ways to design observation activities so that participants are actively involved.

Provide aids to help participants attend to and retain pertinent aspects of a demonstration they are watching.

When modeling how to conduct an exit interview, for example, make sure the participants take notice of its critical features by giving an overview of the demonstration and providing a visual display of a few key terms to describe the specific behaviors to be modeled. It may even be helpful to point to these descriptions as they are being enacted. After the demonstration is over, you can help participants retain the observation points by asking them to recall them from memory. You may even want to challenge them to write out an imaginary exit interview that includes all the steps. A pocket-sized card summarizing the features of an exit interview can be also be given to the participants for future use as a job aid.

When participants are observing a role play or group exercise, provide easy-to-use observation forms containing suggestions, questions, and checklists.

Having concrete guidelines helps participants to get the most out of the observation experience. Give them a chance to study the form before the actual observation. You may even want to provide a brief practice exercise. In addition, you can assign specific participants to observe specific behaviors. For example, while some are observing the verbal techniques employed in a sales presentation, others can watch the body language of the presenter.

Provide key questions to help observers focus their attention.

When you find observation forms too specific for your purposes, a few questions can still help to guide observers. For example, observation of group process can be enriched by asking observers to consider (1) who they are most aware of, (2) what that person is doing, (3) what her or his impact is on the group, and (4) how others are reacting to the person.

Expect observers to give constructive feedback in order to challenge them to observe carefully and apply what they have previously learned.

In a longer training program, for instance, you can include several opportunities for observers to provide feedback to each other. At first, these exchanges should be kept short and focused on the positive behaviors displayed. As trust develops in the group, the feedback can be more extensive and more critical. Giving this responsibility to participants pushes them to review what they have been taught and to use it as the basis for their feedback.

Be aware that observers can have strong vicarious experiences if what they are observing has personal impact.

Watching role plays that hit home, for example, often produces a kind of Greek chorus effect. Observers are moved to comment when they can readily identify with the role players. You can facilitate matters by asking observers to disclose the feelings they experienced while watching the drama and to lend emotional support to the role players. Vicarious participation can also be catalyzed by interviews or experiential exercises.

Formatting

Three formats are commonly used in the design of observation activities.

1. ***The simplest format is to use observers as the audience watching a demonstration, video, role play, and the like "on stage.":***

   EXAMPLE: Participants in a course on employee discipline watched a video that showed how a supervisor of an accounts payable department confronted one of his bookkeepers. The bookkeeper had been thirty to forty-five minutes late for work at least seven times in the last three weeks, had come back late from lunch on five occasions, and had made personal calls several times. Prior to the video presentation, the participants were given the observation check-list reproduced in Figure 6–3 for their review. When the video had ended, the

---

FIGURE 6–3. OBSERVATION CHECKLIST

---

1. What did the manager do to let the employee know he was listening?

   Maintained good eye contact _____

   Nodded head _____

   Leaned forward _____

   Rephrased well _____

   Other (explain) _____

2. Jot down an example or examples of the manager rephrasing what the employee has told him (for example, "So, let me make sure I understand . . .").

3. Did you notice the manager using any specific rephrasing techniques?

   Verbatim repeating _____

   Paraphrasing _____

   Partial restating _____

4. In general, do you think the manager fully understood the employee's emotion?

   Addressed it directly _____

   Ignored it _____

   Danced around the edges _____

   Other (explain) _____

5. Overall, do you think the manager fully understood the employee's viewpoint before responding? What else might you have asked or clarified?

---

participants wrote their responses on the checklist and compared notes with their seat partner. They then reassembled to poll the results of their collective observations.

2. *Observers can also be assigned to small groups to provide feedback after the small group performs.*

   EXAMPLE: On the morning of a three-day course for novice trainers, fifteen participants were divided into three groups. Each participant then gave a ten-minute lecture he or she had prepared the night before; the other four members acted as a training audience. After the presentation, audience observers gave the lecturer feedback on (1) things that were done well, (2) skills and techniques used that were previously demonstrated in the course, and (3) suggestions for improvement. Later in the day, participants were asked to reconvene in the same groups. One participant at a time was asked to leave the group for a short time. These people were told, upon their return, to deliver the opening segment of the lecture they had given in the morning. The rest of the members of each group were instructed to select one member each who would act as a troublemaker when the person returned to give the lecture. Other members would then observe and give feedback on how the lecturer handled the troublemaker. Finally, observers were asked to identify with the feelings of the beleaguered lecturer.

3. *Finally, participants can be arranged in a fishbowl format, where observers form a circle around the individuals they are observing.*

   EXAMPLE: Employees of a major defense contractor were taking a course on work team effectiveness. Midway through the course, after learning several work team skills, participants were divided into two equal-sized groups. The members of group A sat around a long conference table, and a member of group B sat directly behind each one of them. Group A was asked to hold a meeting for the purpose of targeting "the most important changes your work teams should make in the way they operate." The group B members were to observe the task and maintenance behaviors of the person in group A seated directly in front of them. After ten minutes, the meeting was interrupted by the trainer, who asked the group B observers to meet with their group A observees and give them feedback. Then, group B was asked to sit at the conference table and conduct the same meeting with group A observing. Again, after ten minutes, a feedback round occurred. This back-and-forth process was repeated two more times, with the net effect that each group had thirty minutes to complete its task and to watch another group undertake the same task. In addition, each participant received feedback three times.

MENTAL IMAGERY

Mental imagery is the ability to visualize an object, person, place, or action that is not actually present. Trainers can design six kinds of imagery experiences:

1. ***Visual imagery***—for example, seeing various colored shapes like a golden triangle, a violet circle
2. ***Tactile imagery***—for example, shaking someone's hand, feeling its surface and temperature
3. ***Olfactory imagery***—for example, smelling the clean mountain air in a pine forest
4. ***Kinesthetic imagery***—for example, driving a car, sensing each turn of the wheel
5. ***Taste imagery***—for example, attending to the taste and texture of a favorite food
6. ***Auditory imagery***—for example, listening to the sound of a voice calling one's name

Being able to design activities that help participants visualize adds a powerful component to your experiential learning repertoire. Although it can be utilized to help participants retain cognitive information, imagery has special value as a way to help them mentally rehearse putting skills into action and to bring feelings and events into focus.

Mental imagery exercises can be used to replace role playing. Since they are internal, they cause less anxiety to participants who are shy about performing before other people. Skills such as speaking before a group or acting assertively, for example, can be practiced successfully through mental imagery, although a minimal amount of role-playing practice must be interspersed with it.

Mental imagery exercises also stimulate discussion. Often it is hard to get a discussion on a particular topic off the ground without a boost. When participants are guided to visualize a real or fantasized experience, thoughts and feelings relevant to a particular topic can be activated. For example, in a workshop on interfaith relations, participants were asked to imagine walking invisibly into the homes of people of different religious faiths and watching how they celebrate different holidays. A discussion followed on the norms of different groups. It was a lively and honest exploration of religious differences.

Guidelines

When conducting mental imagery exercises, certain guidelines are important.

1. ***Help participants to clear their minds by encouraging them to relax.*** Use background music, dimmed lights, and breathing exercises to achieve results.
2. ***Conduct warm-up exercises to open the mind's eye.*** Ask participants, with their eyes closed, to try to visualize sights and sounds such as a rosebud, their bedroom, a changing traffic light, or the patter of rain.

3. ***Assure participants that it's okay if they experience difficulty visualizing what you describe.*** Some participants initially block before they are relaxed enough to visualize. Tell them to be patient with themselves. All participants find that other thoughts drift into their mind at times. When this occurs, suggest that they simply bring themselves gently back to the subject being described.

4. ***Give imagery instructions slowly and with enough pauses to allow images to develop.*** If you use imagery scripts written by others, practice reading them in advance so that your delivery is smooth and well paced. Keep your voice soft enough to be soothing but loud enough to be clearly heard.

5. ***Invite participants to share their imagery.*** Sharing should always be voluntary. Keep the reports brief (lengthy disclosures can be boring to the other participants). Participants can also recount their imagery experiences in a journal.

Examples of Mental Imagery Exercises

The following script can be used as a warm-up exercise to promote relaxation breathing with imagery:

"With your eyes closed, draw and exhale several very deep breaths. Notice the rising and falling of your abdomen. Each time you breathe in, imagine that you are taking in energy from the universe. This is exactly what you are doing. As you exhale, notice that your body is becoming more and more relaxed, more and more peaceful.

"Now imagine that you are seated on a large rock, overlooking a quiet pool of water in some pleasant forest or wooded area. Imagine that nothing disturbs the tranquillity of this scene except the occasional jumping of a small fish to the side of the pond. Imagine that, in slow motion, you have picked up a small round stone near where you are sitting, and in very s-l-o-w motion, you are lobbing this stone into the air and watching it descend s-l-o-w-l-y into the very center of the glassy pond. Watch the stone as it travels up and then down through the air. Watch it slowly enter the water, and watch the ripples begin to form. Watch the ripples spread slowly outward toward the edges of the pond. Watch the surface of the water until it is completely still once again.

"Stay with this scene until you are aware of feeling very relaxed and refreshed. When you are ready, notice the sounds around you in the room, gently open your eyes, and go about your day's activities."

Source: Richard McKnight, Ph.D., *Staying Relaxed in a Tense World,* Learning Project Press, 157 E. Lancaster Avenue, Wynnewood, Pennsylvania 19098. Used with permission.

Here is a sample script used to help lead a group of employees through the process of preparing to receive a performance appraisal.

"I'd like you to close your eyes for a few moments as we explore how to prepare to receive your next performance appraisal. Close your eyes, slow your rate of breathing down, and listen as I walk you through the evaluation process. (*pause*) First, I would like you to imagine yourself working at your job. Consider aspects of your job that you truly enjoy. (*pause*) Think about the satisfaction that you receive as you complete that task. (*pause*) Now, imagine how you would describe the accomplishment of that task to your closest friend. Go ahead, brag about yourself. Explain just how well you like doing that task and why. Consider why you do that task better than anyone else.

"As you continue to keep your eyes closed, I would like you to turn your thoughts in another direction. This time, I would like you to consider an aspect of your current responsibilities that you really do not enjoy. Think carefully about a task related to a responsibility that you do not enjoy. (*pause*) What is it about this task that you do not like? (*pause*) Consider all of the different components of this task. Are there any that you believe that you could improve upon? Imagine yourself improving your performance of this task. Consider how you would feel if you handled this task to the best of your ability.

"Now you are ready to walk into your manager's office. Instead of being nervous, you feel confident in your abilities. Think back on the images you have just seen. Consider that in an appraisal both positive and negative evaluations of work performance will be discussed. Think back to how you evaluated your own performance as you discuss your appraisal with your manager."

Source: Carol Auerbach. Reprinted with permission.

The following exercise is called "Visions and Values." It is used for team building in a hospital setting.

"Spend a little time getting as comfortable as you can . . . find a comfortable spot . . . clear your mind . . . relax . . . take a deep breath . . . as you breathe out, silently say, 'relax and let go' . . . feel yourself relax even further . . . as you think about each part of your body, allow that part to relax, feel all the tension flowing away, feel calm, comfortable, peaceful . . . each time you breathe out you will become more relaxed and feel the relaxation spreading slowly through your body.

"I want you to imagine yourself on a typical day, on your way to work. Picture yourself en route, in your car, on the bus, train, or however you normally travel to the hospital. As you are traveling, you are thinking about work and who you are . . . what your job is . . . the way you do it . . . how you'd like to feel more successful . . . what you would do differently . . . what you would change.

"As you get to work you suddenly realize it's not the same place it was yesterday . . . something has changed . . . something is different . . . suddenly it's YOUR IDEAL PLACE TO WORK.

"You enter the hospital, the same entrance you usually use . . . what do you see, what do you hear? You walk through the halls into your department . . . who is there, who do you see . . . what are people doing . . . what are people saying . . . what are you saying . . . what is different? You sit at your desk thinking about the day ahead . . . you have a busy schedule . . . you will be traveling all around the hospital today.

"The first thing you have is a Department Head meeting . . . most of your colleagues are there . . . who do you see . . . what do you hear . . . what are people saying . . . what is different?

"After the meeting, you walk through the halls of the hospital back to your department . . . you see your employees . . . what are they doing . . . what do you say . . . what is the interaction like?

"You need to follow up on a problem with another department head . . . you go to that department . . . it's very busy . . . you and your colleague talk about the problem . . . what is that interaction like . . . how are you acting . . . what are you saying . . . how does it feel?

"At lunchtime, you are in the cafeteria . . . what's it like . . . what do you hear . . . what do you see . . . how is it different?

"You have a busy afternoon . . . you spend time at your desk doing paperwork . . . how do you feel . . . what's it like . . . what's different than before?

"It's time to wind up the day . . . you are getting ready to leave . . . you think back on the day . . . think about the people you saw and talked with . . . think about the sounds . . . think about the work you did . . . what's different . . . what's better about now?"

Have group members slowly bring themselves back mentally into the room.

Stand and form a circle. Instructions: "One person will start by answering a question. The person to the left will go next. The questions will keep going around the group till I stop the flow. You may pass. Do not try to be original. If someone else gives the answer you would have, please repeat it."

Personal

1. What is a word that describes yourself at work?
2. What is something you'd like to express more of at work?
3. How would you like to be at work?
4. What do you want others to think or say about you?
5. What is a hidden quality you have that others don't see?
6. You had an option for passing . . . I want you to think about how often you passed . . . how typical is this for you? Think but don't answer out loud.

Organizational

1. Who is (*name of hospital*)? (We are!)

2. What positive qualities would you like to see more fully expressed by the people at _____?

3. What is one word to describe your vision of the full potential of _____?

4. What value would you personally like to guide and direct at _____?

_____

Source: Albert Einstein Healthcare Foundation, Philadelphia, Pennsylvania 19141. ©1988. Reprinted with permission.

WRITING TASKS

Yet another experiential medium to consider is writing. Like mental imagery, writing is usually an individual activity. It allows each participant to reflect slowly on her or his own understanding of and response to training input.

Writing activities range from short responses to long essays. The most common short form is a worksheet, like the ones at the end of each chapter in this book. A **worksheet** provides rather specific instructions concerning what the participant is to write. It can be used at any time during a design. For example, a trainer in a course on customer relations might ask participants to fill out a worksheet that asks for brief descriptions of recent encounters with customers. A worksheet might also be assigned at the end of such a course, perhaps asking the participants to set goals for applying course techniques back on the job. **Longer writing** generally works best in the middle of a training design; assigned at the beginning or the end, it can make a program drag. One example of longer writing comes from a course on dealing with problem employees. Participants were asked to recall an especially disturbing incident that happened to them in the past. Then they were asked to write an action account of the incident in the present tense, as if it were happening in the "here and now." This writing assignment was used to help the participants distinguish behaviors from the feelings that accompanied them.

In addition to being used to describe events, writing tasks are useful when any written skill, such as business correspondence, is being taught. Furthermore, trainers can ask participants to record plans, develop verbal scripts, and review material in written form.

Guidelines

When you are about to introduce a writing task, keep these five tips in mind.

1. **Help participants to get in the mood to express themselves in writing.** Do something beforehand to inspire or challenge them. Make them feel that the writing has a good purpose and is not just busywork.

2. ***Make sure your instructions are crystal-clear.*** If appropriate, you may even want to provide a model for participants to emulate.

3. ***Arrange a good work environment for writing.*** Provide a clear, firm surface on which to write. Provide workbooks in which all pages lay flat or ask participants to remove worksheets from loose-leaf binders. Establish privacy and quiet.

4. ***Allow enough time for writing.*** Participants should not feel rushed. They may need time to get started. On the other hand, don't be overly long. Involvement will slacken.

5. ***Allow enough time for feedback.*** When participants have finished, they often want to share what they have written. One alternative is to invite a limited number of volunteers to read their finished work. A second alternative is to have seat partners share their writing with each other.

Examples of Writing Tasks

EXAMPLE: In a training program on interviewing skills, participants were taught five steps to planning an interview: (1) study the job description, (2) gather information on the organization and career advancement, (3) study the résumé of the candidate, (4) list the skills to evaluate in the interview, and (5) write a list of open-ended questions to ask in the interview. At this point, participants were asked to outline questions for use in an interview they might actually conduct. Figure 6–4 reproduces the written instructions.

FIGURE 6–4. INTERVIEWING SKILLS: PLANNING THE INTERVIEW

INSTRUCTIONS:

Outline questions for the job description you developed earlier in class. Please list at least two technical questions and six categories of performance questions. Remember that you will be asking follow-up questions to discover situation, action, and result. Here is an example of a preplanned question outline.

You are interviewing a candidate for the position of fitness trainer for our class using the job description already prepared for you. The list of preplanned questions includes the following:

TECHNICAL

1. Are you certified to teach aerobics?

2. Do you have knowledge of first aid?

FIGURE 6–4. continued

PERFORMANCE

1. In the past, when you sensed that a previous class was losing interest in maintaining their workout schedule, what did you do? (team building)

2. When conflicts arose among class members concerning _____, what did you do? (problem solving)

3. Describe a typical class. (planning)

4. Suppose that several class members had back problems. What would you do to accommodate them? (adaptability)

5. Tell me about the largest group you've had and describe how you maintained control over the group. (controlling)

6. How would you design or market a new aerobics class for a fitness center? (organizing)

YOUR PREPLANNED QUESTIONS

TECHNICAL

1.

2.

PERFORMANCE

1.

2.

3.

4.

5.

6.

EXAMPLE: The writing task in Figure 6–5 was given as part of a workshop entitled "Helping Women Pursue Their Dreams."

FIGURE 6–5. YOUR IDEAL DAY

Below, write a description of your ideal day exactly as you would like it. Tell about this fantasy day in the present tense and in detail, describing each thing you would like to do, with whom (or alone), where, and when.

_____

_____

_____

_____

_____

_____

_____

_____

_____

_____

Now divide the events in your ideal day into the three categories below.

Essential   *Optional*   *Frills*

_____

_____

_____

_____

_____

Pair up with someone else, share your lists, and discuss these questions:

1. What elements, if any, of your ideal day do you already have?

2. Which elements are conspicuously absent from your present life?

3. What obstacles stand in the way of your having your "essential" ideal day tomorrow?

EXAMPLE: A vision is an inspiring picture of a desired future state. Figure 6–6 presents a writing task that was used for enabling managers to learn what a vision is and how to create one.

FIGURE 6–6. CREATING A VISION STATEMENT

1. Have participants make two columns on a piece of paper. Have them entitle the first column *"What Doesn't Work."* They are to write here any major or minor glitches in the department that impede its effectiveness. Give them plenty of time to write this list. Encourage them to state these problems negatively. Give them lots of possibilities, for example, "Our people are burning out from all the work."

2. The second column should be entitled, *"Instead, I Choose . . ."* In this column, they should transform the negative statements in the first column into very positive, desirable statements. For example, if the first column included "We have way too much turnover," the corresponding entry in the second column would read, "Our staff turnover is only 5 percent per year."

3. Now participants should be instructed to write a detailed description of how their unit would be functioning eighteen months from now *if anything were possible.* This description should address all of the following:

   • The unique contribution the unit is making to the company

   • How the unit is perceived by other units in the company

   • The effective ways people in the unit are relating to one another

   • How much fun people are having because they are a part of the unit

   Participants should now be encouraged to write this *as if it were true now.* This will include phrases such as "We are creating new approaches to customer service all the time." This should be so simple and clear that an eighth grader would be able to understand it.

4. Next, have participants write five to eight declarative statements about *what people in the department will be doing* to fulfill this vision. Examples are, "Everyone in the department takes personal responsibility for quality" and "We hold to the commitments we make." These may well come right out of what was written in step 3. They should be the most important ingredients of the scenario described in step 3.

5. The participants should be instructed to regard what was written in step 4 as a list of "means," not the "end." Now, it's time to write a brief sentence or two describing the end state. This is what most people think of as the vision statement.

FIGURE 6–6. continued

Some sample vision statements are

- (for a customer service unit) "We make customers glad they bought our product."
- (for a hospital dialysis unit) "Because of us, patients feel more dignity and hope."
- (for a manufacturing plant) "Our customers know when they operate one of our units they are operating the finest equipment money can buy."

Source: Richard McKnight and Associates, *Training for Leadership* (1988), Learning Project Press, 157 E. Lancaster Avenue, Wynnewood, Pennsylvania 19098. Used with permission.

ACTION LEARNING PROJECTS

Action learning involves assigning lengthy tasks to participants. These tasks should challenge them to obtain additional information not given by the trainer or to apply what they have learned back on the job. If you design action learning projects that participants find meaningful, you will find that this method has significant learning value. Naturally, time is the biggest constraint on including action learning in a training program.

We will describe and illustrate five kinds of action learning projects commonly used in training programs.

In-Basket Assignments

In-basket assignments are a form of the project method in which letters, memos, phone messages, and so forth are given to the participant playing an assigned role. The participant is then given time to write actual responses to the items in her or his in-basket. Figure 6–7 provides instructions for such an assignment. This assignment could be used in its present form as part of a time management program for managers.

FIGURE 6–7. IN-BASKET

For the purpose of this exercise, you are to assume the role of Pat Ladder, manager of the operations department in the J. R. Jones Company. As manager of the operations department, you report to the division head, Kelly MacDonald. The following people report to you:

- Jamie White, secretary
- Mike Crossman, facilities maintenance supervisor

FIGURE 6–7. continued

- Linda Stevens, property and supplies supervisor
- Stan Powell, security supervisor
- Jay Snyder, transportation supervisor

All of them are capable people and have been in their respective jobs one year or more. The situation this exercise deals with is as follows.

Today is Monday, December 14. You have been away for several days, so you have come into your office at 8:00 A.M. (early) to catch up and get ready for the day. The normal working day begins at 8:30 A.M. Promptly at 8:30 A.M., you must leave to attend a training meeting. Therefore, you only have about thirty minutes to organize your work, and you want to get as much done as possible. You do not expect to return to your office from the meeting until 10:00 A.M. As you reach your desk at 8:00 A.M., you find items in your in-basket.

As you go through the material, take whatever action is needed, assuming that you are Pat Ladder. Use your own experience as a basis for your decisions.

Make notes to yourself or to others by writing directly on the message, letter, or memo or by attaching notes (use notepaper provided by the facilitator). Draft or write letters and memos where appropriate. Note any phone calls you plan to make, including information about when you plan to make the call and whom you plan to call. Note follow-up dates when further action is necessary. Write on the items themselves where you want them sent, such as "Follow up 12/15" or "File."

After the exercise, you will have an opportunity to compare your actions with others in the group. Remember:

- Put yourself in the position of Pat Ladder.
- Today is December 14.
- You have come in before regular working hours. There is no one else available to help or call.
- You want to get as much out of the way as possible in the thirty minutes you have to spend organizing.
- Record (make mention of) every action you make or intend to make.
- Be prepared to discuss how you handled the exercise with the group.

Research Projects

If preparation time and the necessary data are available, asking participants to conduct some research and present their findings is a valuable form of learning. This research can be done in small teams or individually. Teams or individuals can have the same or different assignments. Data can be obtained either from people or from written materials.

EXAMPLE: An interesting example of a research project comes from a course for insurance claims adjusters. The trainer in the course wanted to avoid long periods of dry lectures intended to give participants a crash course in tort law and medical terminology, two things adjusters dealing with accident claims need to know. Instead, she divided participants into small research study groups. Every evening during this week-long course, participants were given assignments (and reference material) that they did individually. For one hour each afternoon, the groups met to study the information they obtained and to draw up test questions for the other study groups. Twice during the week, test questions were swapped among the groups and the answers discussed. In post-tests, knowledge of tort law and medical terminology was shown to have increased 60 percent over that gained in previous courses.

Field Observation

An excellent way to do action learning is to set up a "field trip" to a real-life setting relevant to the training topic. You might begin by dividing the participants into subgroups of four or five and ask them to develop a list of questions and/or specific things they should look for during their field trip. After the subgroups put their questions or checklist items on flip-chart paper, post them, and share them with the rest of the class, the total group can discuss the items and develop a common list for every person to use. You can then give them a deadline (for example, one week) and direct them to visit a site or sites, using their list of questions or checklist items to interview or observe. Allow participants to choose their own sites, or you may want to make specific assignments to avoid duplication or to get good distribution. For example, with customer service, participants could identify different types of organizations or businesses such as retail, fast-food, restaurant, health care, hotel, or car repair. They would then visit these businesses as customers and, using their checklist, record their experiences.

Be sure the questions are specific and lend themselves to comparison with each other's findings. For example, with customer service, the following observation items would be appropriate:

- How long did the employee take before acknowledging the customer?
- Did the employee smile?
- Was the employee courteous and polite?
- Did the employee ask open-ended questions to identify the problem?
- Did the employee use active listening techniques? Give examples.
- Did the employee resolve the problem?
- Were you as the customer pleased with the experience? Why or why not?

You might ask the participants to share their findings with the rest of the class through some clever or creative method, such as a skit, mock interview, panel discussion, or game.

Here is an example of action learning using field observation.

EXAMPLE: In a training session entitled "Implementing the Americans with Disabilities Act," participants were given handouts and other information identifying architectural barriers and what business owners are required to do in order to make their buildings accessible. The participants were divided into five groups, with each group assigned a particular "barrier" such as (1) entrances; (2) parking facilities; (3) workspaces, lounges, and lunchroom; (4) bathroom facilities; and (5) hallways. Each group developed its own checklist for the barrier assigned and identified businesses to visit in order to determine how well the business or organization was meeting the Act's guidelines. They sought answers to the following questions:

Entrances

1. Is there a ramp to the entrance?

2. Are the doorknobs three feet from the ground?

3. Is the door light enough to be opened by someone in a wheelchair?

Parking Facilities

1. Are parking spaces reserved for people with disabilities?

2. Are the parking spaces near the entrance to the building and twelve feet wide?

3. Are there curb cuts so that people in wheelchairs can pass easily?

Workspaces, Lounges, and Lunchroom

1. Are the aisles in these rooms at least thirty-two inches wide?

2. Are there work stations, desks, tables, and so on that are high enough so that a person in a wheelchair can roll up closely enough to sit comfortably?

3. Are the lunchroom and lounges accessible?

Bathroom Facilities

1. Are the doorways to the bathrooms at least thirty-three inches wide?

2. Are the sinks low enough to be used by someone in a wheelchair?

3. Are there grab bars in the bathroom stalls?

Hallways

1. Are there flashing lights for fire alarms so that people with hearing impairments will know there is a fire?

2. Are there picture signs to show the purpose of each room so that people who cannot read will know where to go?

3. Are there Braille markers on the door and in the elevators?

Teaching Projects

It is said that someone really has learned something if she or he can teach it. Another project assignment is to ask participants to teach new information or skills to each other. The teaching can be performed by either individuals or teams in front of the full group or in small groups.

EXAMPLE: In a four-week course on family therapy, participants were formed into teaching teams. Each team was assigned one model of family therapy. In the last week of the course, the team was expected to teach others about the assumptions, key concepts, and intervention methods of its assigned model. Teams were urged to use active training methods. A natural competitiveness usually developed among the teams, which had the effect of producing teaching designs that were creative and of high quality.

EXAMPLE: A team-building trainer assigned teams to demonstrate one of the following attributes: flexibility, interdependence, trust, and openness. Some groups composed skills, some conducted meetings, and some used visual aids such as flip charts or banners in their teaching exercises. Once the demonstration was complete, the rest of the participants critiqued it, highlighting the positive aspects.

Task-Force Projects

The purpose of these kinds of projects is to give participants confidence in their ability to do the same task back on the job. Typically, groups are asked to generate a plan or other specific outcome that can be used by other participants in the actual work situation.

EXAMPLE: In a course on planning and organizing skills, participants were given a planning task based on a real case situation in their company. Task-force groups were formed, relevant materials were given out, and each group was asked to complete its work on a specific form, which was then duplicated and shared among the groups. A debriefing of the work of the task forces followed. The case study (minus the exhibits) and the planning chart that was to be completed are presented in Figure 6–8.

FIGURE 6–8. TASK-FORCE ASSIGNMENT

You are the director of distribution services and planning and you have been given approval by the president of XYZ Company to pilot a new teleselling program (or telemarketing as it is more commonly called). You have been waiting some time for this moment and the decision represents a victory for your department. Now the hard work of planning and organizing the project must begin.

BACKGROUND

The teleselling approach is a new one for XYZ. In teleselling a small, highly trained team uses advanced telephone technology to sell to a broad group of customers. To be successful, the teleselling team needs strong training in product knowledge as well as in telephone selling and communications techniques.

Typically, the XYZ sales force has operated on a face-to-face basis. The teleselling team would not supplant the regular sales force. Instead they would be an adjunct to the sales force and would help it reach smaller accounts more efficiently.

Upper management feels that teleselling would be especially useful in reaching accounts between $500 and $2,500 with a special emphasis on products other than hypertensives. In 1985 the company had fifteen thousand Class 19 accounts with total sales of just over $6 million for the year. Teleselling is viewed as a way to boost these sales.

Most of these accounts are too small for regular visits and detailing by the sales force. On the other hand, they would represent an excellent source of business if there were a way of reaching them efficiently. That is why upper management at XYZ finds teleselling so attractive.

But there are problems, too. For one thing, the wholesalers would feel that XYZ was impinging on their turf. The wholesalers are a key link between XYZ and its customers, both large and small, and relationships with the wholesalers would have to be handled carefully.

There are also turf issues within XYZ. The sales force feels that teleselling should be under its control. On the other hand, regional sales offices are located at most of the distribution centers that also handle inventory and transportation control. Ultimately, upper management decides to put the administration of the teleselling program in the hands of distribution, but the sales force will set the criteria for whom to call and what to sell and will provide the training. Thus, to be successful, the program will require excellent relations between sales and distribution personnel.

CURRENT STATUS

It is now August 1 and the president has passed on to you final approval to pilot the teleselling program in the Chicago region. Ultimately, he would like to see four teleselling locations set up, including the pilot. He wants the pilot up and running by the beginning of November. The company has set the following objective for the program:

FIGURE 6–8. continued

- Provide consistent coverage of mid- to low-volume Class 19s and allow more detailing time to field sales
- Increase market penetration
- Increase coverage of ethical and consumer products
- Improve XYZ's image with customers
- Increase sales at less contact cost

The president has given you a list of target products and has suggested that you work closely with the sales and marketing groups on strategies for promoting these products through special offers and other approaches. You have on your desk the draft of an introductory letter to be sent to accounts in the Chicago region by the branch operations manager.

You have also been working up proposed staffing and budgets for the program. Current plans call for two part-time telesell workers at the Chicago pilot site who will each work four hours per day. Each worker should be able to make thirty calls a day. You know that a key issue will be training and continued motivation for those involved in the program. From what you have been reading about telemarketing, burnout among workers in such a program can be very high. The total budget for the Chicago pilot program will be $152,000.

Under current plans, distribution will handle the operations of the teleselling program but will work closely with sales representatives. The division manager will send a list of all accounts below $2,500 to the sales representative. The sales rep will in turn determine which of these accounts should be called under the teleselling program and this information will be given to the branch operation manager.

You have very little time to put the program together and you are now mulling over how to plan and organize the work for the pilot. You are reviewing a memo prepared by a member of your staff on some of the key issues that will arise in the program. You know that the first and perhaps the most important step is to organize the work well and to plan for any contingencies that might arise.

PLANNING CHART
Prioritized Action Steps   Time Reference

_____   _____

_____   _____

_____   _____

_____   _____

_____   _____

_____   _____

_____

Source: Training Management Corporation, 600 Alexander Road, Princeton, New Jersey 08540. Reprinted with permission.

WORKSHEET

USING EXPERIENTIAL LEARNING APPROACHES

Now that you have been introduced to these experiential learning approaches, consider which ones you would want to utilize to achieve the objectives in your next training program.

_____ Role playing

_____ Games and simulations

_____ Observation

_____ Mental imagery

_____ Writing tasks

_____ Action learning projects

Strategy Outline:

_____

_____

_____

_____

_____

_____

_____

_____

_____

_____

_____

_____

_____

_____

_____

_____

_____

_____

_____

◆　◆　◆

Chapter Seven

Designing Active Training Activities

With objectives set and a variety of training methods at your disposal, you are in a position to develop all of the specific training activities you will need in an active training program.

THE THREE MAJOR INGREDIENTS OF ANY DESIGN

Earlier, we compared opening exercises to appetizers at the beginning of a full meal. Continuing with this delectable analogy, let's consider all the separate activities in an active training program as items on a menu or, if you prefer, dishes in a meal. Each item or dish has certain ingredients. Individual training activities have three: an **objective,** a **method,** and a **format.** How the objective, method, and format combine together is the basic recipe for the design. Your decisions about what is to be accomplished (objective), how it is to be accomplished (method), and in what setting it is to be accomplished (format) will determine the design you wish to create. Let's examine two activities to illustrate these points.

The first example is an activity called "The New Contract." In this activity, the following major decisions have been made:

1. The **objective** is to compare the "old contract" that described the historical employee-organization relationship to the "new contract."

2. The **method** employed is jigsaw learning, described in Chapter Five.

3. The **format** is pairs.

Figure 7–1 presents the details of this design.

FIGURE 7–1. THE NEW CONTRACT

---

1. Make the following points:
   - Change in the workplace is happening at an unprecedented rate.
   - Change is fueled by globalization and technology.
   - Change is likely to be ongoing, and things will not return to their original state.
   - Understanding change and developing strategies to thrive in it have been shown to be very helpful.
2. Ask the participants to form pairs.
3. State that many people today believe that a shift is taking place in the workplace. We are moving from the old implied social contract, which promised lifelong employment in exchange for hard work and loyalty, to a new contract where work is based on situational need and productivity rather than longevity.
4. Ask each pair to assign the number 1 or 2 to each of its members. Hand out the form below and ask the 1s to read about the "old contract" and the 2s to read about the "new contract."

Old Contract

Organizations value longevity and reward it through benefits programs.

Organizations expect you to work hard and be loyal.

Organizations are hierarchical in their reporting structure.

Organizations are paternalistic and take care of their employees.

Employees' career paths are directed and decided by managers.

Employees are expected to do work assigned to them by their managers.

Employees have job security for life if they work hard and are loyal.

Putting time in and doing the job is highly valued.

Employees expect regular promotions and pay raises if they do the job well.

New Contract

Organizations value productivity.

Organizations expect you to work effectively, producing results.

Organizations value employees who keep their skills and knowledge up to date.

Organizations are made up of clusters of teams that direct their own work.

Organizations empower employees by giving them decision-making authority.

Organizations provide learning opportunities for their employees but do not force employees to participate.

Employees manage their own careers.

Employees remain employed as long as they can make a contribution and their skills and knowledge are needed by the organization.

Organizations are flat and employees may have several lateral moves during a career.

Organizations value employees who are multiskilled.

Employees get pay raises and promotions when they do work that merits them.

Employees are loyal to their professions and engage in lifelong learning.

FIGURE 7–1. continued

---

5. Ask pair members to explain to each other in their own words what they read.

6. Encourage pair members to discuss these different contracts with each other.

7. Reconvene the entire group and facilitate an open discussion on the new contract.

Source: Mundhenk, 1997, p. 33. Used with permission.

The second example is a follow-up activity to "The New Contract" called "Point-Counterpoint." In this activity, the following major decisions have been made:

1. The *objective* is to clarify the virtues and liabilities of each contract.

2. The *method* employed is a debate.

3. The *format* is a fishbowl (group-on-group), followed by a meeting of the full group.

Figure 7–2 presents the details of this design.

FIGURE 7–2. POINT-COUNTERPOINT

---

1. Divide the participants into two teams and assign a contract to each team, with one team getting the "old contract" and the other getting the "new contract."

2. Explain that the teams are going to debate the virtues and liabilities of each contract.

3. Describe the debate as follows:
   - The old contract team sits on chairs in the middle of a circle formed by the new contract team.
   - One old contract team member starts by reading the statements from the form describing the old contract.
   - All participants in the inner circle engage in a discussion defending the old contract, using their experience and imagination.
   - The teams then change places and repeat the process with the new contract team defending the new contract.

4. Reconvene the entire group and ask participants to add additional insights.

5. State that the new contract isn't necessarily better, that there are benefits to both contracts, but that most supporters see it as liberating and, since it is here to stay, it's important to understand how it is changing our work lives.

Source: Mundhenk, 1997, p. 34. Used with permission.

For many topics, it is possible to make a variety of choices concerning the objective, method, and format of the designs intended to cover them. Let's take, for example, the topic of leadership behavior and, in particular, the concepts of authoritarian, democratic, and laissez-faire leadership styles. Your objectives as a trainer may range from deepening participants' understanding of the consequences of each style (cognitive learning) to allowing participants to experience their differing levels of comfort with each style (affective learning) to providing them with practice in utilizing each style in appropriate situations (behavioral learning). Just as the same menu item can be prepared with different recipes, so, too, can each of these objectives be achieved by a variety of methods and group settings. For example, participants could experience their comfort levels with each style through role playing, mental imagery, or a writing task. Any of the basic formats (full-group, individual, pairs, small-group, or intergroup) could serve as well. In training, as in cooking, art, or music, a desired end can be accomplished by varied means.

BASIC QUESTIONS ABOUT ANY DESIGN

When shaping a design, there are several considerations to take into account.

1. *Does the design achieve the activity's objective?* This is the most important consideration. To take an obvious example, a demonstration may show participants a skill or procedure in action without giving them actual practice. Even when the choice of method is appropriate, a particular design may not achieve its purpose. For example, a role play, if poorly designed, may provide little skill practice for participants.

2. *What knowledge or skill level does the design require of participants?* Your assessment of participants is often critical in creating a specific design. For example, a complicated task-force exercise on project planning might be premature for novice project managers. Or another design might not be sufficiently challenging for a particular situation.

3. *How much time will it take?* At any particular point in a program, you may feel that time is limited or, conversely, that a longer design is perfect for the occasion. In general, it is a good rule to keep afternoon activities shorter than morning ones. Further, it rarely pays to skimp on time when you are seeking to accomplish an especially important objective. You would not want, for instance, to give only ten minutes to a discussion of a company's controversial system for disciplining employees.

4. *Is the design slow-paced or fast-spaced?* Regardless of the overall time needed for a design, some activities are slow-moving and others have a quicker pace. Fast-paced activities work best to get the total group involved. Leisurely activities are more appropriate in a small-group format.

5. ***Is it suited to the size of the group?*** Some designs simply don't work well with large groups. For instance, dyadic role-playing practice is very hard to monitor when the training group consists of more than thirty people. On the other hand, some designs require a critical mass. For example, it can be uncomfortable to participate in a mental imagery exercise in a very small group (fewer than seven people); the anonymity of a somewhat larger group helps participants to relax.

6. ***What skills are required to conduct the design?*** It's important to assess how much expertise or facilitation skill a design demands. For example, a study group approach to cognitive material requires less in the way of Socratic skills than does a guided teaching mode.

It is not always possible to answer these questions in advance. Experience is the best teacher when it comes to designing; often the most you hope for is to anticipate what might occur if a particular design is used. Taking small risks is absolutely essential to your development as a trainer: the only way to find out if a design will work for you is to give it a try. A good approach is to change the design of *one* part of your module or course every time you teach, in order to expand your repertoire.

THE REMAINING DETAILS

When the objective, method, and format for a single design have been chosen, several details remain:

1. ***Time allocation.*** How many minutes will the design take?

2. ***Buy-in.*** What will you say or do to get participants involved?

3. ***Key points and/or instructions.*** What are the major ideas in the presentation, and what exactly do you want participants to do?

4. ***Materials.*** What do you or the participants need in the way of materials to implement the design?

5. ***Setting.*** How should you set up the physical environment for the design to succeed?

6. ***Ending.*** What remarks do you want to make and/or what discussion do you want the participants to have before proceeding to the next activity?

Once these decisions have been made, a design is complete. Let us illustrate this process.

EXAMPLE: Assume that you are conducting a course on assertive behavior for a group of sixteen managers. You are using a large training room with four windows. Participants are seated around U-shaped tables, which occupy only half the room. It's right after lunch. During the morning, you discussed and demonstrated the differences between nonassertive, aggressive, and assertive styles of coping with conflict. Your goal for the early afternoon is to teach how body language is a large part of style. *You decide that the purpose of your first design is to introduce the topic of body language in a dramatic way and to help participants become aware how they now use body language during a power struggle.*

The next decisions concern method and format. Looking over several possibilities, *you decide to use a game that involves every participant.* This decision allows for a fast-paced, active activity, which is desirable after lunch. With sixteen people to accommodate and with the need for practice time later in the afternoon in mind, *you decide to use pairs as the most efficient format for the game.*

With these tentative decisions in mind, you now need to find a game or, if necessary, invent a game that will achieve your purposes. Luckily, a colleague has told you about a nonverbal "persuasion" game that might suit your purposes. The only problem is that this game usually takes forty-five minutes and appears to you to be too threatening for your clientele. You decide to redesign the game, paying attention to such details as time allotment, buy-in, activity instructions, materials, physical setting, and ending. Your final design might resemble the one in Figure 7–3.

FIGURE 7–3. NONVERBAL PERSUASION

After greeting the participants who have just returned from lunch, say the following:

"I thought it would be a good idea to wake us up after lunch with a lively activity. It will help us to introduce the topic of body language and its effect on our style."

No materials are needed for the activity, but the instructions are very important and the physical setting plays a role. With those factors in mind, do the following:

1. Ask participants to pair off with a seat partner and to establish whose birthday falls earlier in the calendar year.

2. Give the person with the earlier birthday in each pair an index card with the following instructions: "Leave your seat and go somewhere else in the room (for example, look out a window, stand in the corner of the room, play with some object). Soon, your partner will come to fetch you and will want to bring you back to your seat. Resist him or her, saying or doing whatever you like. Don't go back to your seat until you feel persuaded to do so."

3. After these participants leave their seats, ask their partner to go and fetch them. Explain to them that they can approach the task in any way they like except for one condition: *they may not talk (or write) during the entire time they are trying to get their partner back to his or her seat.* (Allow the "resisters" to overhear your instructions to the "persuaders.")

FIGURE 7–3. continued

---

4. When all participants have eventually returned to their seats, ask the resisters to privately give feedback to their persuader. Urge them to identify which kinds of nonverbal communication were effective and which were ineffective. (Effective nonverbal communication tends to include some of the following: good eye contact, decisiveness, firm but gentle physical movements, persistence, and calmness.)

5. Ask the resisters to brag about their partner's effective nonverbal behaviors to the rest of the group.

6. Invite the partners to reverse roles and redo the exercise.

7. End the activity by stating that research indicates that the nonverbal aspects of communication (vocal, facial, and postural) influence the impact of our messages more (some even say 93 percent more) than does the verbal content. Write on a flip chart: "It's not what you say but how you say it." Invite participants to react to the statement.

THREE TIPS FOR CREATIVE DESIGNS

Many trainers wish they were more creative. However, creative designers are not a special breed; they *work* at being creative and use several tricks to help them do their best. Here are some of their tips.

One Design Can Accomplish Two Things at Once

Economy is the trademark of a good design, and with a little care, most designs can serve double duty. For example, you could brief participant observers about nonverbal aspects of communication to watch for while their peers are giving sales presentations. By watching how you change your own facial, vocal, and postural communication during the briefing, the observers could gain observation practice before trying it out for real. Or suppose that you wanted to help a participant through a role play requiring the participant to coach a confused employee. As you did this, you could provide a demonstration of effective coaching behavior.

The Same Design Can Often Be Used for Different Purposes

Many creative trainers have a few exercises in their repertoires that they use over and over again with different topics because the exercises are easily adaptable. Here is an example.

EXAMPLE: For an energizer late in the afternoon, a trainer of a team-building course had participants make paper airplanes and attempt to hit a target. Noticing that some participants helped each other out with their airplane designs while others did not, he initiated a dramatic discussion about teamwork.

At a problem-solving course, he used the same exercise to point out that many people changed their designs when their first attempts didn't work while others repeated the same essential solution (design) with each attempt.

Published Designs Can Often Be Modified to Suit Your Own Needs

Whenever you examine a published design, think how you might change its purpose, its direction, its length, and so on to achieve the design you are seeking. Here is an example.

EXAMPLE: A well-known activity based on a drawing that is either a young girl or an old woman, originally published in *Puck* in 1915, uses the ambiguous picture to examine stereotyping and group pressure on perception. Typically, participants are asked to relate their feelings and opinions about the woman they see in the drawing, not realizing that it can be viewed in two different ways. Instead of using this drawing for its traditional purpose, a trainer used it as the basis for an interesting coaching or teaching exercise, employing the following instructions:

1. Obtain two volunteers. One is to serve as a teacher. She should be a person who has previously seen the drawing. (You will always have some participants who have seen it.) The other volunteer is to portray a student who needs assistance in seeing both women.

2. The teacher should try to show the student how to see both women. (If the student is successful in a matter of seconds, replace him with someone else.)

3. After the student has seen both women, observers should tell the teacher in terms as descriptive as possible what she did to cope with the student.

4. Then discuss what behaviors were helpful or harmful in loosening up the student's perceptions of the drawing. Compare these behaviors to common teaching or coaching situations.

EXAMPLE: In a popular exercise, teams compete to build the best construction-paper tower. The towers are judged by height, aesthetic appeal, and sturdiness. A trainer was looking for a team-building activity to help in the development of new teams that would eventually work cooperatively with each other. He decided to change "towers" to "houses" and asked each team to construct a model of the dream house in which all members would like to live. Instead of using construction paper, teams were given index cards. With these noncompetitive instructions, three completely different and highly creative designs emerged and each team was able to proudly display a model of its dream home. Through a simple change in design, the activity had gone from a competitive to a noncompetitive experience.

WORKSHEET

DESIGNING A TRAINING ACTIVITY

Try your hand at designing a training activity. Choose an objective of your own and develop a creative design with the suggestions you have been given.

Objective:

Method:

Format:
____ Individual
____ Pairs
____ Small-group
____ Full-group
____ Intergroup

Outline:
(include time allotted, buy-in, key points and instructions, materials, physical setting, and ending)

_____
_____
_____
_____
_____
_____
_____
_____
_____
_____
_____
_____
_____
_____
_____
_____

♦   ♦   ♦

Chapter Eight

Sequencing Active Training Activities

What you do as a trainer is not all that counts. Equally important is *when* you do it.

No matter how well you design a particular activity or presentation, its impact and value for the participants may diminish greatly if it is misplaced in the overall sequence of events. For example, participants may be tired just when you need them to be alert. Or the group may not be able to grasp abstract ideas before experiencing concrete examples.

Further, an active training module is not a string of exercises. Nothing could be a greater waste than having participants go through one activity after another without a thoughtful plan. How well you weave activities together is of paramount importance to your overall effectiveness.

Sequencing is partly an art; some trainers just know where to place different pieces in their overall design and how to obtain a good mix and flow. Most trainers, however, learn to master sequencing through experience and trial and error. Nonetheless, some basic guidelines remove the mystery from effective sequencing.

BASIC SEQUENCING GUIDELINES

The following guidelines apply to most sequencing of training activities and should be considered fundamental to effective designing.

1. *Build interest and introduce new content before you delve more deeply.* Set the stage for learning by using an activity that hooks participants' interest or gives the big picture.

2. *Place easy activities before demanding activities.* Get participants settled in and warmed up before you put them through hard work.

3. ***Maintain a good mix of activities.*** Vary training methods, the length of activities, the intensity of activities, the physical setting, and the format. Variety is the spice of good training.

4. ***Group together concepts and skills that build on each other.*** Generally, we learn more easily when one idea is an outgrowth of another.

5. ***Provide subskills before practicing complex skills.*** It's better to learn the parts before the whole.

6. ***Close training sequences with discussion of "so what" and "now what."*** Have the participants consider the implications of the course content for themselves and plan their next steps back on the job.

How would you apply these guidelines to specific situations? Figure 8–1 presents an opportunity for you to try your hand at sequencing. There are no correct answers. Use your own judgment.

FIGURE 8–1. SEQUENCING ACTIVITY

You have been asked to design a training module for supervisors on giving feedback to their employees. The design is to be based on the handout containing the following text.

WHAT MAKES FEEDBACK USEFUL?

Constructive feedback is a way of helping other people to look at their own behavior without putting them on the defensive. It is communication to a person (or group) that gives that person information about how she or he affects others. If we wish to avoid creating defensiveness with our feedback, we must not appear to be attacking the person but rather commenting on the behavior.

Here are some criteria for useful feedback:

1. ***It is descriptive rather than evaluative.*** Describing one's own reactions leaves the individual free to use or not use the feedback or to use it as he sees fit. Avoiding evaluative language reduces the need for the individual to react defensively.

2. ***It is specific rather than general.*** Telling someone that she is "dominating," for example, would probably not be as useful as saying, "Just now when we were deciding the issue, you did not listen to what others said. I felt forced to accept your arguments or face attack from you."

3. ***It takes into account the needs of both the receiver and giver of feedback.*** Feedback can be destructive when it serves only our own needs and fails to consider the needs of the person on the receiving end.

4. ***It is directed toward behavior that the receiver can do something about.*** Reminding a person of some shortcoming over which he has no control only causes frustration.

FIGURE 8–1. continued

---

5. *It is solicited, rather than imposed.* Feedback is most useful when the receiver herself has formulated the questions that those observing her answer.

6. *It is well timed.* In general, feedback is best offered as soon as possible after the given behavior (depending, of course, on the person's readiness to hear it, the support available from others, and so on).

7. *It is clear.* Feedback is worthless if the receiver misinterprets it. One way of checking is to have the receiver try to rephrase what he has heard to see if it corresponds to what the sender had in mind.

The training activities you have chosen to support the handout include

A. Asking participants to assess themselves as *givers* of feedback

B. Setting up role plays so that each participant can practice giving feedback to a difficult employee

C. Dividing participants into small groups and asking them to discuss and clarify the handout

D. Setting up skill-building exercises to practice each skill suggested by the handout

E. Asking participants to discuss what they value when *receiving* feedback

F. Having participants identify employees to whom they would be willing to give feedback according to the guidelines in the handout

In what order would you sequence these activities? Why?

1. _____

2. _____

3. _____

4. _____

5. _____

6. _____

Bear in mind that there are many viable sequences. Here is one way to sequence the module in Figure 8–1:

1. E. Ask participants to discuss what they value when *receiving* feedback. (A good lead-in to the handout)

2. C. Divide participants into small groups and ask them to discuss and clarify the handout. (A study group method for teaching about feedback)

3. A. Ask participants to assess themselves as *givers* of feedback. (A useful way of reviewing the handout and motivating participants to improve their skills)

4. D. Set up skill-building exercises to practice each skill suggested by the handout. (An activity that allows the group to learn the subskills of giving feedback)

5. B. Set up role plays so that each participant practices giving feedback to a difficult employee. (An opportunity for participants to pull together the skills learned in the previous step)

6. F. Have participants identify employees to whom they would be willing to give feedback according to the guidelines in the handout. (A consideration of on-the-job application of the skills taught in the module)

APPLYING SEQUENCING GUIDELINES

Active training programs contain sequences of activities or modules that adhere to the six guidelines presented at the beginning of this chapter. Figure 8–2 presents an example of a two-hour training sequence for teaching ***force field analysis,*** a well-known problem-solving tool based upon the concepts of Kurt Lewin. As you read the design, note (1) the use of several methods described in previous chapters (partners, initial case problem, headlines, demonstration, and so on) and (2) the way in which sequencing guidelines are respected (interest building, easy activities first, a good mix, and so on).

FIGURE 8–2. TEACHING FORCE FIELD ANALYSIS

I. Introduction

Participants are invited to write down a personal and/or work-related problem they are currently experiencing. They are told that a suitable problem is one in which they have been pursuing or thinking about pursuing a goal (for example, stopping smoking or obtaining more business) but have thus far not succeeded.

Next, they are introduced to the term *force field analysis* and told that it is a tool for obtaining *unattained* goals such as those they have just listed. By contrast, it is *not* a tool for making decisions (for example, should I quit my job?).

FIGURE 8–2. continued

A request is then made for a few participants to share with the group one of the problems they have selected. The trainer either verifies that the problem chosen will "work well" with force field analysis or helps to modify the problem statement so that it does.

II. Lecturette

The trainer discusses with the groups some common patterns people use when they have trouble obtaining desired goals. One way to describe these patterns is to utilize the following list:

Procrastination—not dealing with the problem and perhaps even denying it

Fretting—continually stewing about the problem but taking no clear directions with it

Scheming—generating many solutions to the problem but not committing oneself to implementing any of them

Repeating—utilizing basically the same solution over and over again even though it fails to produce change

III. Partner Discussion

Participants are invited to pair off and share with each other the patterns that they use most frequently. It is suggested that the participants especially consider the patterns used with the problems each has identified in section I.

IV. Lecturette

The trainer emphasizes that force field analysis is an effective way to counteract procrastination, fretting, scheming, or repeating. It is a useful tool because it provides a focused framework for solving problems and builds in social support for implementation.

The trainer proceeds to identify four principles in force field analysis: (1) getting clear about what is happening right now with the problem, (2) defining more precisely the goal one is seeking, (3) identifying some of the obstacles that prevent goal attainment, and (4) selecting a concrete place to begin solving the problem.

V. Demonstration

Participants are given form A below. This form streamlines the process of force field analysis by eliminating the identification of helping forces (that is, factors that promote change). It also uses simple language.

FIGURE 8–2. continued

FORM A

  I. The situation as it is now:

  II. The situation as I want it to be:

  III. What will keep the situation from changing?

  IV. My top-priority obstacle:

  V. Possible action steps: Resources needed:

Next, the participants watch a prerecorded case demonstration in which an interviewer asks probing questions to help a "client" identify responses to each of the five steps on the form. Form B shows the results of an interview with a client who distributes watches.

FORM B

  I. The situation as it is now: *Over 25 percent of our accounts complained that they did not receive their Christmas order in sufficient time.*

  II. The situation as I want it to be: *In the future, our accounts should receive their Christmas order by November 10.*

  III. What will keep the situation from changing?
    Delivery delays
    My own disorganization
    Our drivers don't want to work overtime
    Orders from our accounts are late

  IV. My top-priority obstacle: *Orders from accounts are late.*

  V. Possible action steps: Resources needed:
    Survey accounts re: their obstacles   *Ask ass't. to develop survey*
    Establish discount for early orders   *Get fiscal projections*
    Establish deadline for order date   *Meet with shipping*

FIGURE 8–2. continued

VI. Skill Practice

Participants are asked to pair off with their partner from section III. Each is instructed to interview the other as per the case demonstration. The problem selected for each interview is one previously identified by the participant.

VII. Ending

Participants are invited to share their reactions to and questions about the skill practice activity. The trainer may discover that some participants were plagued by a problem which was not sufficiently concrete. Some resistance to the limits placed by the process (for example, selecting only *one* obstacle) may be anticipated and deflected with assurances that problem resolution begins with specific first steps that are actually implemented. The trainer should also encourage participants to announce publicly those action steps they intend to undertake and suggest that one's partner be used as support during the process.

Source: Silberman, 1986. Reprinted with permission.

Another sample sequence is given in Figure 8–3. Taken from a parenting course, the topic is that of obtaining support from other adults. Again, take notice of the techniques and guidelines as they are employed. Notice, in particular, how each part of the design flows into the next part.

FIGURE 8–3. OBTAINING SUPPORT FROM OTHER ADULTS

This session is devoted to how a parent obtains support from (and gives support to) other adults who care for their child, such as spouse, relative, teacher, and child caregiver. The key assumption is that parenting does not occur in a vacuum. There are always other significant adults who can support or undermine an individual parent's efforts.

    I. *The Lone Ranger* (Game)
       A. Ask participants to stand up and form a line. If they see themselves as a person who usually faces personal problems alone, they should go to the head of the line. By contrast, if they typically seek the help of others in solving their personal problems, they should find a place to the rear of the line. Participants who do not identify with either choice should find a place somewhere in the middle. Don't allow participants to "bunch up" in the middle. Urge them to create a "single-file" line. Use humor to help participants feel relaxed during the activity.

FIGURE 8–3. continued

B. When the lineup is completed, ask participants to form a semicircle so that they can see each other while keeping their place.

C. Interview the two participants at each end of the semicircle as to the factors influencing their self-placement. Ask them if they feel good about their position in the line.

D. Indicate that a parent needs to combine both ends of the spectrum: he must stand on his own two feet and also be willing to involve others in the problems posed by his children. Compare this notion to the Lone Ranger, a rugged individual crime fighter who nonetheless had someone to depend upon: Tonto.

II. *The Need for Support, Feedback, and Planning* (Lecturette)

A. Ask the group to sit down.

B. Write *support, feedback,* and *planning* on a chalkboard or newsprint.

C. Point out that adults in charge of the same children need to give and receive these three things in order to maximize their effectiveness as a team. *Support* is available if you can count on someone else to help out, listen to your frustrations, and appreciate your efforts. *Feedback* is a constructive evaluation of your strengths and weaknesses as a parent. *Planning* is a joint commitment to discuss rules, expectations, and discipline strategies for specific problem behavior.

III. *Your Own Resistance to Team Collaboration* (Discussion)

A. Indicate that every parent has some resistance to including others in the parenting of his or her children. Share your own resistance in order to give participants an example of what you mean. Perhaps you consider yourself more interested, better informed, and more capable of helping children than someone else. This attitude, although understandable and maybe even true, nonetheless blocks a team approach to parenting.

B. Request participants to form pairs and share with each other some of their resistance to including others in the parenting of their children.

IV. *How Adults Disqualify Themselves* (Guided Teaching)

A. Illustrate the five major ways adults "disqualify" each other:

• Allowing others to parent their children

• Keeping a rigid role division

• Acting impulsively

• Not standing on their own two feet

• Directly interfering with the other adult

B. Ask participants to provide examples from their own lives.

FIGURE 8–3. continued

V. *Guidelines for Team Parenting* (Study Group)

   A. Divide participants into small groups and ask them to read and discuss a handout—"Guidelines for Team Parenting." Be sure to indicate that these are general guidelines, not hard-and-fast rules.

   B. Ask participants to share their questions and comments about the five guidelines. Remind participants that the major activities done in this course are useful to do with their partners.

VI. *Making Requests* (Mental Imagery and Role Playing)

   A. Share with participants that they are more likely to practice team parenting if they feel comfortable and skillful making specific requests of other adults.

   B. Ask participants to select someone (spouse, relative, teacher, child caretaker, and so on) to whom they wish to make a request. The request should be something they want from that person that will improve their relationship with that person or the person's relationship with his or her child. Invite the participants to relax (perhaps closing their eyes) and then ask them to imagine making the request of the person they selected. Ask further, "When would you do it?" (wait fifteen seconds), "Where would you be?" . . . "What exactly would you say?" . . . "How do you think the person you selected would respond?" . . . " How would you respond back?" . . . "Can you make your request more specific?"

   C. Ask a volunteer to describe the dialogue he or she just imagined. Role-play the scene with you as the other person. If the person experiences difficulty, provide coaching.

   D. Ask participants to pair off and role-play making their request to their partner.

VII. *Quaker Meeting* (Ending Activity)

   A. As a closing event, ask participants to share their completions to any of the following sentence stems:

      1. Something I'm going to do as a result of tonight's session is

      _____.

      2. I'm still not sure that _____.

      3. Tonight, I learned _____.

   B. Explain that participants can share any of these thoughts as the spirit moves them (as in a Quaker meeting). There is no need to raise hands or agree or disagree with what others have said.

Source: The Confident Parenting Program, 26 Linden Lane, Princeton, New Jersey 08540.

Figure 8–4 contains one more example of a training sequence. It is a module from a day-long training program on conflict management. Its purpose is to help participants assess "what they bring to conflict situations." Note the variety of training activities.

FIGURE 8–4. WHAT YOU BRING TO CONFLICT SITUATIONS

Over their lifetime, most people have developed an approach they take in conflict situations. Although a person's *conflict style* often influences how she or he will behave in a given situation, many people are unaware of their own style. This module helps participants to reflect on their own *conflict style*.

I. *Feelings About Conflict* (Physical Continuum)

A. Ask participants to stand up and form a line. If they see themselves as people who usually "hate" being in conflict situations, they should go to the head of the line. By contrast, if they typically "relish" conflict situations, they should find a place to the rear of the line. Participants who do not identify with either choice should find a place somewhere in the middle. Don't allow participants to bunch up in the middle. Urge them to create a single-file line. Use humor to help participants feel relaxed during the activity.

B. When the lineup is complete, ask participants to form a semicircle so that they can see each other while keeping their place.

C. Interview the two participants at each end of the semicircle as to the feelings influencing their self-placement. Ask other participants to share their feelings about conflict. Note that discomfort with conflict is rather normal.

II. *Looking at Your Conflict Style* (Game)

A. Use one or more game-like exercises that place participants in a conflict situation.

B. Examples are

- Thumb wrestling.

- Debating someone. Find an issue that two partners truly disagree about such as abortion, capital punishment, or American foreign policy.

- Breaking balloons. Have each participant blow up a balloon and tie it to his or her ankle with a string. Then give a signal to begin a game in which participants try to break one another's balloons by stepping on them. The last person to have an unbroken balloon is the winner.

C. Process participants' feelings of aggression, defensiveness, defeat, and victory. Note strategies or styles for coping with conflict.

FIGURE 8–4. continued

III. *Assessing Your Conflict Style* (Questionnaire)

   A. Distribute the Conflict Management Style Survey and ask participants to complete and then score their survey.

   B. Allow participants time to share their results with people seated near them. Obtain reactions and questions.

IV. *Experiencing Different Conflict Styles* (Role Play)

   A. Divide participants into groups of four (if possible). Explain that each group will be asked to pretend that they are a group whose job is to distribute $10,000 to one cause.

   B. Before starting their meeting, give participants a copy of the attached form.

   Discussion Styles

	Person 1	Person 2	Person 3	Person 4
Round 1	C	P	I	R
Round 2	P	I	R	C
Round 3	I	R	C	P
Round 4	R	C	P	I

   Key: C = Confrontative (aggressive, judgmental)
   　　　　P = Persuasive (assertive, standing up for oneself)
   　　　　I = Introspective (analytical, somewhat conciliatory)
   　　　　R = Reactive (withdrawn, accepting)

   C. Ask each group to designate who will be person 1, 2, 3, and 4. Explain that the meeting will be interrupted every five minutes, thereby creating four "rounds." During each round, each participant will behave with the style she or he is assigned on the chart. Thus, over the twenty-minute discussion, each member will adopt each one of the four styles (though in a different order).

   D. Suggest that participants act out their style in subtle ways. It is generally not helpful to exaggerate any style.

   E. When the four rounds are completed, invite each group to process the experience. You might use these questions:
   • Which style or styles were easy or hard for you to perform?
   • What feelings did you have from this experience about each style?

V. *Your Conflict Style Is Situational* (Checklist)

   A. Explain that we tend to vary our style depending on the situation and, in particular, the relationship in question. Some people are confrontational with one person and reactive with another.

FIGURE 8–4. continued

B. Ask participants to assess this matter for themselves by completing the following checklist. (After writing the names of three significant others, ask them to check how they see their predominant style when interacting with each person.)

Name	Confrontative	Persuasive	Introspective	Reactive
1.				
2.				
3.				

C. Have participants show this checklist to a partner and discuss it with each other.

Source: Adapted from Silberman, 1992b, pp. 42–44

THE FINER SIDE OF SEQUENCING

Now that we have looked at some basic rules of thumb about sequencing, we can explore more subtle sequencing issues. Trainers have a number of sequencing choices at their disposal. In this respect, they can be compared to musical composers. Although composers follow certain "rules" in writing music, they still have a seemingly endless variety of directions to take. Sometimes, like Beethoven, they may even pull off breaking the basic rules and obtain a stunning result. Likewise, the content you are teaching may seem to dictate a certain logical sequence, but content is not the only determining factor.

Imagine, for example, that you were teaching somebody how to use a manually operated thirty-five-millimeter camera. If the student knows little about such a camera, what would you do first? We've posed this question to several groups of trainers, and the most common response we get is to "start from the beginning"—show how to load film into the camera and then explain the camera's parts (shutter, lens, and so on) and their function. It seems logical, doesn't it? Yet starting at the end could be just as effective. You could show a series of photographs, some unfocused, some too light, some too dark, and so on, then invite your student to speculate about why these results occurred and lead the student, in a Socratic fashion, to the unfortunate actions taken by the photographer. Along the way, you could explain the parts of the camera and how they interact to get different results.

In this example, the learner, rather than the content, influences the sequence. By beginning with the end result, you immediately involve the student, stirring up curiosity and grabbing his or her attention from the start. Nor is this method the only alternative to the more traditional approach. There are many other possibilities. The critical thing to avoid is to continually use the same sequence. *The hallmark of active training programs is the variety of sequences employed to keep participants not only awake but also learning.*

Let's consider four ways to alter a training sequence:

1. ***Your design can go from the general to the specific or from the specific to the general.*** You are teaching participants how to establish customer credit. You could define what makes a good payment record and then give a case example illustrating the positive payment history of one customer. Or you could reverse the sequence by providing the case example followed by the definition.

2. ***When teaching a procedure, you could start with the first step or the last step of the procedure.*** You are teaching participants how to compile a profit-and-loss statement. You could start by explaining the basic elements and proceed with a step-by-step demonstration of compiling the statement. Or you could present a completed financial statement and work backward, showing how the bottom line represents a profit or loss.

3. ***You could place an experiential activity before a content presentation or follow a content presentation with an experiential exercise.*** You have decided to discuss four manipulative communication roles people play (blaming, distracting, placating, and intellectualizing). To reinforce the presentation, you have designed a role play in which the different members of groups of four each exhibit one of these roles. Placing the role play before the presentation would allow you to hook immediate participant interest and provide examples to refer to in the presentation. However, placing the role play after the presentation would also work well, helping to clarify (experientially) what has already been presented (didactically).

4. ***You could teach from theory to practice or from practice to theory.*** You begin a counseling module by explaining how direct confrontation increases resistance in defensive employees. You follow your theoretical input with a chance to practice indirect ways to correct performance and lower resistance. Alternatively, you might begin by practicing indirect approaches and then discussing why employee resistance is lower when this strategy is used.

In addition to reversing sequences, you can also place design components in a variety of *positions*. Take, for example, practicing a complex skill. The practice session usually is placed **at the end** of a long sequence of explanation and demonstration. It often makes sense, however, to have participants practice a skill **at the beginning** without benefit of prior instruction just to see how well they do. You can then go back and examine the skill, piece by piece. Frequent practice sessions can also occur **during** the explanation and demonstration phase.

The trainer can show the skill as a whole, and the participants practice it; the trainer then focuses on a specific aspect of the skill, and the participants practice the entire skill again. Each time, the skill is broken down further and further by the trainer, but the participants always attempt to practice it as a whole.

The success of an effective training sequence often lies in the *flow* from one piece of the design to the other. The worst kind of training sequence is a steady progression of topics with little regard for building participant interest, highlighting the links between pieces, recycling earlier material, or concluding satisfactorily. Here are some tips to improve the flow of a design:

1. Use what Ruth Clark (1989) calls the "Zoom Principle." When introducing participants to new information, give them a broad picture before going into the details. The learner needs what Clark calls an "advanced organizer" before being able to sort new information out. After presenting the big picture, the trainer "zooms in" on some detail, returning to it periodically to show the participant how each detail relates to the whole. Clark provides the following example.

   When teaching the customer service representative job to new hires, you could describe the process flow of work among functional units in the customer service department. Then you might proceed with an explanation of the representative job, returning at critical moments to the flowchart to show the interfaces between the job and other departmental functions. The new customer service representative could also be presented with an overview of the major types of customer calls he will be taking and how they relate to each other. Then, as detailed information is given about each call type, the big picture can be presented again, giving more detailed information on how the call types relate to each other.

2. A training sequence should look like a spiral rather than a straight line. Reintroduce later on skills and ideas taught earlier in a sequence. If the skill or idea in question is complex, introduce it first on a simple level and then teach it at greater levels of complexity as the course unfolds. Training in conflict management provides a good example.

   A core skill in conflict management is the ability to listen attentively to one's opponent. Typically, active listening skills are stressed early in the program. As she introduces mediation and negotiation techniques, the trainer can easily point out how active listening is the basis of these more sophisticated tools. Moreover, being in the difficult spot of mediating or negotiating these intense conflicts of interest dramatically tests the ability to listen attentively.

3. Avoid the urge to plunge right into an important part of your design. Add a brief activity or short presentation to set up the main event and build motivation. Before an important task, warm up a group with a lighter exercise similar to but not as serious as the one to follow. Sometimes, a shift in the

design that widens or redirects the focus is necessary for the next experience to be more effective.

In team-building or leadership development programs, a crucial moment occurs when each participant is about to receive serious peer feedback about her or his behavior in the program thus far. The anxiety level of the group rises precipitously. Before giving the final instructions, a trainer can use the following analogy: "Feedback is like a gift. Take it as such. Like any gift, you may not like it. But, if it's from a reputable source, you can always return it 'to the store' without the giver knowing." Inserting this piece in the design helped to reduce the tension, and participants were more receptive to their first experience receiving peer feedback.

4. From time to time, build a training sequence around a critical incident, a problem to be solved, or a task to be accomplished rather than a set of concepts or skills to be learned. Often, trainers employ didactic teaching methods when the participants can learn instead from their own inquiry. Inquiry modes of learning are always more active than trainer-dependent ones.

Novice bank tellers are required to learn how to identify counterfeit bills. The usual training sequence is an orderly presentation, with handouts, of the flaws to watch for, such as the whiteness of the portrait, broken sawtooth points around the rim of the seal, uneven spacing of the serial numbers, and blurry lines in the scrollwork surrounding the numerals. A more active approach would be to ask the trainees to attempt to distinguish between counterfeit and noncounterfeit bills without benefit of prior instruction, sharing their evidence as they do so. The trainer could then point out other telltale signs of forgery. Yet another approach would be to ask the trainees to examine some genuine bills and develop hypotheses about how they are printed to discourage counterfeiting.

5. Closing a training sequence can be climactic or reflective. Sometimes a sequence should end with a bang to emphasize the accomplishment. For example, a dramatic finish could consist of a scintillating final lecture, an intergroup competition, a role play that serves as a dress rehearsal for later application, or a challenging case study. At other times, however, it may be more appropriate to wind down by processing reactions to the material, making connections to skills previously learned, or generating final questions about topics that are still unclear.

In designing the closing of a training module on how to assess the roles played by members of an alcoholic family, the trainer might use two approaches. One is to end with a live interview of a family in treatment so that, watching and listening, participants could test in their minds how they would assess the family roles in an actual situation. The trainer would easily be able to arrange such an experience, and it certainly would be memorable. The other approach is to end with a panel discussion in which participants would take turns answering questions posed by the moderator (that is, the trainer).

EXPERIENTIAL LEARNING SEQUENCES

The sequencing of strongly experiential training requires special consideration. In such training, learning flows not from didactic presentations but from what participants discover for themselves as a result of powerful experiences the trainer has designed for them.

The value of any experiential learning activity is enhanced by asking participants to reflect on the experience they just had and explore its implications. This reflection period is often referred to a *processing* or *debriefing* period. Some experiential trainers now use the term *harvesting*. Figure 8–5 describes a three-stage sequence for harvesting a rich learning experience, called "What? So what? Now what?"

FIGURE 8–5. WHAT? SO WHAT? NOW WHAT?

What?

Take participants through an experience that is appropriate to your topic. These experiences might include any of the following:

- A game or simulation exercise
- A field trip
- A video
- A debate
- A role play
- A mental imagery exercise

Ask participants to share **what** happened to them during the experience:

- What did they do?
- What did they observe? Think about?
- What feelings did they have during the experience?

So What?

Next ask participants to ask themselves **so what?**

- What benefits did they get from the experience?
- What did they learn? Relearn?
- What are the implications of the activity?
- How does the experience (if it is a simulation or role play) relate to the real world?

Now What?

Finally, ask participants to consider **now what?**

- How do you want to do things differently in the future?
- How can you extend the learning you had?
- What steps can you take to apply what you learned?

The best way to explain each step is to do so with an example. As mentioned in Chapter Six, many games resemble the classic competition-cooperation exercise, the Prisoner's Dilemma Game. One example is a game appropriately called The Game of Life. Figure 8–6 presents the instructions.

FIGURE 8–6. THE GAME OF LIFE

This is a game to be played by six groups of any size, although adjustments can be made to accommodate fewer groups. Each group should have approximately the same number of players. The objective is for each group "to win as much as you can."

Procedure

There are six rounds to the game. For each round, each group chooses either Y or X (without knowing what the other groups have chosen) and writes its choice on a slip of paper. All slips are handed to the trainer, who tallies them and announces the results. Each group's payoff depends on the combination of choices made by the groups. For six groups, there are seven possible combinations:

Combinations	*Payoffs*
All choose X	All lose $2
Five choose X; one chooses Y	Xs win $2; Y loses $10
Four choose X; two choose Y	Xs win $4; Ys lose $8
Three choose X; three choose Y	Xs win $6; Ys lose $6
Two choose X; four choose Y	Xs win $8; Ys lose $4
One chooses X; five choose Y	X wins $10; Ys lose $2
All choose Y	All win $2

Other payoff schedules can easily be generated for fewer than six groups.

After the third and fifth rounds, allowance is made for a ten-minute negotiation session between single representatives from any group that wishes to participate. The negotiations, if held, are to be loud enough for everyone in the room to hear. Before these opportunities for negotiation, the trainer announces that the payoff (wins and losses) will be tripled for the fourth round and multiplied tenfold for the sixth (last) round.

After experiencing The Game of Life, participants will have many reactions, especially anger at teams that did not cooperate (the six groups rarely choose to cooperate by all choosing Y) and disdain for any groups that used deceit. Some participants will protest, "It's only a game," while others will take it very seriously. In the ***what?*** portion of the process, it is crucial to obtain these reactions and observations in order to realize the potential of this experiential activity. The biggest mistake is to analyze the game too quickly before allowing feelings to be expressed.

After noting what happened during the game and what participants were feeling, the skilled facilitator guides the group into the ***so what?*** stage. Here, participants begin to develop many insights. They note that the world is not simply divided into good guys and bad guys. They understand that behaviors could have occurred during the negotiations that would have inspired trust and cooperation. They also observe how groups that were losing heavily often behaved like victims and failed to see that they had the power to turn their fortune around.

After achieving these insights, participants can now be helped to do some generalizing. Among the principles and learnings that might emerge are these:

- All parties in an organization are responsible for creating its ultimate climate.

- The actions of one unit invariably affect the actions of the others.

- Groups with power are reluctant to negotiate.

- Negotiation is most effective when each side acknowledges its needs in a straightforward fashion and acknowledges its differences with others in a nonblaming manner.

At this point, participants are usually motivated to start applying the experience to their own organization in the final, ***now what?*** step. When all participants belong to the same organization, discussion can address the intergroup competition within their own ranks and ways to alleviate it. When participants come from different organizations, individual participants can share case situations for the advice and counsel of peers.

As you can see, following this cycle allows you to base an entire training sequence on one experience. Two ingredients are key to an effective experiential training sequence: a structured ***experience*** that is rich in potential and a set of ***questions*** to follow it up, including these:

1. What happened?

2. How did you feel about it?

3. What did you observe about your behavior and the behavior of others during this experience?

4. What can we learn from this experience?

5. How can you apply these learnings to your life or work?

WORKSHEET

SEQUENCING ACTIVE TRAINING ACTIVITIES

Consider all the sequencing ideas in this chapter and select one or more to use in designing or redesigning your own training module. Outline your thoughts below.

Objectives:

Areas for change:

___ Obtaining a different mix of activities

___ Improving the flow

___ Reversing commonly used sequences

___ Altering placement of activities

___ Improving beginnings and endings

___ Providing experiential learning cycles

Outline:

_____

_____

_____

_____

_____

_____

_____

_____

_____

_____

_____

_____

_____

_____

_____

_____

_____

_____

_____

♦   ♦   ♦

Chapter Nine

Providing for Back-on-the-Job Application

..........................*M*any training efforts never get off the ground because they are not integrated into the workplace. What truly separates effective from ineffective training is the explicit attention given to back-on-the-job application. Without it, the benefits of even the best training are not realized.

The application phase is often the most neglected part of a training design. It is also the most difficult part of training, in both design and implementation. Happily, there are many ways to design your program so that the training sticks and back-on-the-job application occurs. My suggestions will cover three time periods: *before the training event begins, while it is in progress,* and *as it concludes.*

PRIOR TO THE TRAINING PROGRAM

Perhaps the single best insurance policy you might obtain to ensure that participants will transfer what they have learned from classroom to job is to pretrain their supervisors. When they receive such training, supervisors are able to serve not merely as managers but also as mentors, coaches, role models, and encouragers. When training sessions are followed up with on-the-job support, up to a 300 percent return is realized on every dollar invested. Conversely, little retention of skills occurs after training if management fails to reinforce it.

Of course, such an insurance policy is initially expensive, time-consuming, and hard to come by. (Here is an instance where computer-based or distance training programs can be a godsend!) If you cannot pretrain supervisors, you will frequently have the chance to brief them about the training their employees are receiving. In such briefings, it is important for you to discuss the following:

- The objectives of the training program
- The course outline
- The kinds of training activities utilized in the program
- Course materials
- Suggestions for facilitating further practice and application of skills

This approach will work well if you have built your training program with organizational objectives in mind. That way, management will trust that trainees will find a connection between their new skills and the organization's goals and priorities.

Another way to make supervisors your allies is to enlist their cooperation with regard to any precourse preparation you may ask of their employees. Giving the participants time off from their regular responsibilities to read advance materials or complete precourse assignments is a real contribution. It is even better when supervisors sit down with their employees and help them define a personal case problem or two to bring to the training program. This problem then becomes the basis for real-life problem solving in your instruction. Here is such a case.

EXAMPLE: For a course on managing difficult employee behavior, the trainer requested participants to write up brief descriptions of two incidents in which subordinates acted irresponsibly. These incidents were to be discussed in small groups during the program and were also to serve as a basis for role-playing exercises. The trainer asked participants to select incidents in consultation with their own supervisors. After the training program, they would be able to share with their bosses what they had learned.

Prior to the training program, it is also possible to ask participants and their supervisors to select a project to undertake as a result of what the participants learn. When participants come to the training program with a project in mind that has already been discussed with upper management, back-on-the-job application is built into the program design.

Of course, the best way to obtain management support is to invite supervisors to conduct training programs for their own team. Once a rarity, this possibility is becoming more frequent. In large part, this is due to the availability of low-cost, high-quality off-the-shelf training materials. For example, workshops from my own series, *20 Active Training Programs* (Volumes I, II, and III) have been utilized by many managers who are seeking easy-to-use training designs. Participants often report that manager-led training is successful as long as managers are well prepared to conduct training on their own.

**DURING
THE TRAINING
PROGRAM**

As you teach new skills, you can do certain things to promote retention and on-the-job application. A first tip is to *allow enough practice time for skill mastery.* Some trainers have a tendency to move quickly from skill to skill without enough rehearsal. For example, they may give participants the opportunity to role-play conducting a hiring interview and provide (or have peers provide) feedback on their performance but neglect to provide a chance for participants to redo the role play based on the feedback received. Some degree of over-learning is required in order for participants to feel confident about exercising a new skill. Skill mastery is like the process of breaking in new shoes. At first, it feels unnatural but, with enough wear, the shoes begin to feel comfortable. Confidence grows even more when participants master exercises of increasing levels of difficulty. Eventually, they feel that they truly own the skill. Here is a case in point.

EXAMPLE: In a training program on conflict mediation, participants practice mediation skills in a variety of situations. Experience has shown that when role-playing practice is limited to certain types of clients, trainees often have difficulty applying the skills in real life, where clients vary considerably. Because of this, a conflict mediation trainer designed a series of role plays that included a broad range of clients. Participants underwent two days of video-taped practice before seeing real clients under supervision. Frequently, role plays were redone after video feedback. Participants were pleased by the ample opportunity to practice and felt confident that they were ready for the real thing.

Participants are more apt to use skills back on the job if they have been able to practice them realistically. The more similar the training situation is to the back-on-the-job situation, the more likely it is to last. Even re-creating the physical environment of the job can be helpful. For example, bank teller training is greatly enhanced if the classroom is fitted with realistic teller stations.

As participants learn new skills, they should be encouraged to express their attitudes about the skills being taught and their feelings about their performance. Paradoxically, participants are less likely to resist changes if they have the chance to express their reservations and trepidations about them. Some trainers hard-sell the value of the skills, ideas, and procedures they are advocating. It is far better to encourage participants to draw their own conclusions. Ultimately, they are the ones who will decide whether to use what you have taught them. Here is a case example in which this process was encouraged.

EXAMPLE: Using a fishbowl design, a trainer invited participants to examine their feelings about his company's performance appraisal system. One-third of the group was asked to participate in the first fishbowl discussion. The trainer suggested that they begin by describing their positive and negative re-actions to the system. After ten minutes, a second third was brought into the fishbowl to react to the discussion of the first group. Then the final third re-placed their predecessors and wrapped up the discussion. By providing ample time to air viewpoints, the trainer gave a clear message about his respect for the participants' views.

A final tip can be implemented if you are able to arrange for time back on the job in between training sessions. *Give assignments to be completed in the participants' own work settings.* When you resume the training, you can ask the participants to share how well the real-life practice went and to pose any questions they may still have about the skills they have been learning.

EXAMPLE: In a course on overcoming shyness, the trainer requested that participants complete a between-sessions practice sheet. The sheet required the participants to identify one situation that occurred between sessions in which they attempted to be less shy than usual. Also required was information about who else was present, what the participants said and/or did, what (if any-thing) they wished they had done instead, how they felt during the situation, and how they felt after the situation.

AT THE END OF THE TRAINING PROGRAM

Before ending the training program, you can employ several strategies to en-courage application back on the job.

Self-Assessment

Ask participants to evaluate what they have learned about themselves, includ-ing their knowledge, behavior, and attitudes. Taking stock of oneself is a great motivator of change. A wide variety of techniques can help participants with their self-assessment. Make use of questionnaires, post-tests, and final role-play-ing performances. Activities such as the following ones can be appropriate.

EXAMPLE: At the end of a one-week management development program, participants evaluated the extent to which they saw themselves along three style spectrums: (1) *directive* versus *delegating,* (2) *well planned* versus *spon-taneous,* and (3) *challenging* versus *nonthreatening.* For each spectrum, they were asked to stand up and place themselves in a line according to how they viewed themselves. For example, if they saw themselves as more directive than other participants, they went to the head of the line. By contrast, if they saw themselves as more delegating than others, they went to the rear of the line. Participants who did not identify clearly with either choice were to place them-selves somewhere in the middle. Each physical continuum was discussed, with participants disclosing their reasons for placing themselves where they did and commenting on the self-placement by their peers. Finally, they were asked if they wanted to change their "place in line" and to indicate what they would need to do back on the job to achieve this.

EXAMPLE: At the beginning of a customer service training program, the trainer asked the participants to form subgroups and charged them with developing a list of guidelines for new customer service representatives. The participants' initial list included the following:

- Get people in and out quickly.
- Don't eat in front of customers or chew gum.
- Don't talk on the telephone.
- Smile.
- Refer an irate customer to the manager.
- Adhere to company policy.

At the end of the training session, the trainer displayed the initial list and asked the participants to produce a new, improved list. This is the list they produced:

- Tell people what you can do, not what you can't.
- Whenever possible, give people choices.
- Put yourself in the customer's shoes.
- Go the extra mile.
- Use the customer's name.
- Try to solve the problem yourself.
- Acknowledge the customer immediately.

Job Aids

Job aids include checklists, worksheets, and a variety of other forms that are used as course materials. These aids provide a structure that helps participants to remember and apply what they have learned in the course. Job aids are most effective when they are explained and tried out first in the course itself.

EXAMPLE: Participants in a management training program were given the checklist in Figure 9–1 to use in preparing their upcoming interviews with problem employees.

FIGURE 9–1. CORRECTIVE INTERVIEWS CHECKLIST

1. Begin on a positive note.
2. State your purpose.
3. Identify the changes desired.
4. Obtain and listen to the employee's point of view.
5. Get agreement.
6. Involve the employee in generating solutions.
7. Have the employee summarize corrective actions.
8. Express support and encouragement.

EXAMPLE: Participants in a course on project management were urged to remember Murphy's Law when they were back on the job: "If something can go wrong, it will." For this reason, participants were given the Project-Protection Chart (see Figure 9–2) to use as a job aid in predicting and responding to what might go wrong. It asks the project planner to do the following:

1. Identify what is likely to go wrong with elements of the project.
2. Identify how and when the project planner will be informed that something is wrong.
3. Identify what, when, and how something will be done if something goes wrong.

Reentry Advice

Any training program might end with a closing session on reentry advice. Such a session should present some realistic first steps for applying the training on the job. First steps might include setting up a meeting with one's supervisor to discuss the training program and how to use it, consciously identifying tasks that would use skills learned in the program, or networking with others who have taken the course or similar courses to compare experiences and applications.

EXAMPLE: As a program on improving technical training skills was ending, the training consultant advised the employees of a large retail organization to begin observing each other's work. She urged the group to adopt this practice as the best way to build support and continued reinforcement of what they had learned in the training program.

EXAMPLE: Participants in a training program on business writing skills were urged to request writing assignments from their supervisors that would enable the participants to practice the skills learned in the training program.

FIGURE 9–2. THE PROJECT-PROTECTION CHART

Project: _____

_____

Project Element	What Is Likely To Go Wrong?	How and When Will I Know?	What Will I Do About It?	When Will I Do It?	How Will I Do It?
Quality					
Cost					
Timeliness					
Other					

Source: Stieber, 1992, p. 251. InterPro Development, Inc., Newtown, PA 19040.

Obstacle Assessment

Future planning must include a realistic assessment of the obstacles to applying training. Just as any dieter will have a hard time resisting a midnight snack, so a participant subjected to the pressures of his or her job may slip back into old ways of doing things. The most common obstacle is a lack of support from peers, supervisors, or others on the job. Another common obstacle is the lack of time to apply new skills consciously, assess how they've been used, and get feedback from others. In addition to offering reentry advice, a training program should build in time for participants to discuss some of the obstacles they expect to meet and ways to overcome them.

EXAMPLE: A stress management trainer was so concerned about the obstacles to carrying out the techniques he had taught participants that he decided on an unusual strategy. Instead of giving his usual pep talk at the end of his course, he asked participants to predict the circumstances of their first moment of faltering. Using a mental imagery approach, he encouraged participants to visualize the scene in great detail. He then asked them to develop positive images of coping with the situation that they would be able to keep in their mind's eye when the predicted negative scenario began to unfold in the actual work setting.

EXAMPLE: At the end of a team-building course, teams were asked to identify "threats" to their future effectiveness. Using a SWOT (strengths, weaknesses, opportunities, and threats) analysis, teams were challenged to convert these threats into "opportunities" for future development.

Peer Consultation

One of the best designs I know to bring together the learnings from a training program and to encourage back-on-the-job application involves peer consultation. Participants are arranged in small groups for the purpose of discussing a specific back-home issue for each member. After each issue is clarified, the client (the participant with the issue) receives advice from the consultants (the other group members). This process gives participants the opportunity to summarize and apply the knowledge and skills they have gained and to try out their new expertise.

EXAMPLE: At the end of a workshop on managing cultural diversity, participants were formed into quartets. Each participant took turns being a client with a specific problem (based on her or his own work situation) concerning racism or sexism. The job of the other group members was to recall and select concepts and action ideas examined earlier in the workshop that might apply to the problem posed by the client. By taking part in this process of peer consultation, participants were able to prove their expertise to one another and to pull together the contents of the workshop.

EXAMPLE: At the end of a workshop on managing change, peer consultation was used in the following way. Each participant was asked to develop a plan to effectively handle a change in his or her work unit. Then participants were paired with someone from a different work unit who served as a "peer consultant." After the workshop was over, partners consulted with each other on the progress of their respective change management plans.

Peer Teaching

An excellent way to master new ideas and skills is to try to teach them to someone else. Teaching others is also bound to increase one's own commitment to actually using what is being taught. Consequently, there is considerable benefit in encouraging participants to present to others what you have taught them. This can be done within the program by assigning participants to different projects and having them present their findings to others in the training group. Participants may also be able to present the material to peers back on the job who have not yet received the training.

EXAMPLE: Half the members of a sales staff were given training in how to build rapport with different types of clients. Each participant was then paired up with a salesperson who had not received the training. Pairs were expected to meet with each other three times to share the ideas and skills gained from the training. The trained salespeople did such a good job that it was unnecessary to conduct a program for the other half of the staff.

EXAMPLE: A similar approach was used in a computer training class. Participants were invited to teach the database management techniques they learned in the class to colleagues who had not yet taken the class.

Self-Monitoring

A well-known technique in behavior modification is to ask clients to monitor their own behaviors. For example, in a weight loss program, clients might be asked to note everything they eat on the assumption that increased awareness will bring about greater self-control. Likewise, you could suggest to participants that they closely monitor their own behavior back on the job as a way to make training benefits last. Keeping a personal diary is one way to perform self-monitoring. The use of ready-made checklists is another approach. Whatever tools are chosen, they ideally should be tried out before the training program ends so that participants can gain comfort with the procedure and understanding of it.

EXAMPLE: At the end of a business-writing seminar, the trainer asked participants to design their own checklist for monitoring their future business memos. The training group received guidelines on checklist construction and a sample checklist as a working model. The trainer then divided the group into teams, each of which developed a series of checklist questions covering such areas as organization ("Have I used subheadings?"), conciseness ("Do I make my point in the fewest words possible?"), sentence and paragraph length ("Do I use too many choppy sentences?" or "Are my paragraphs short?"), redundancy ("Do I repeat ideas instead of elaborating on them?"), phrasing ("Have I used antiquated phrases like 'pursuant to your request'?"), passive language ("How tentative is my language?"), tone ("Is my style conversational or stuffy?"), spelling ("Is the memo free of spelling errors?"), and grammar ("Do my subjects and predicates agree?"). Each participant then devised a checklist suited to her or his needs based on the input of the group.

EXAMPLE: In a session on time management, the trainer asked the participants to brainstorm reminders to help them manage their time more effectively back on the job. Using the sentence stem "Remember to . . .," the participants came up with the following reminders:

Remember to . . .

- Make a "to-do" list every day
- Make an appointment with myself
- Jot down notes and ideas on index cards
- Set priorities based on importance, not urgency
- Create a "to-read" file and carry it with me when I travel
- Skim books and articles quickly, looking for ideas
- Answer most letters and memos right on the item itself
- Delegate everything I possibly can to others
- Consult my list of lifetime goals once a month and review them if necessary
- Save up trivial matters for a three-hour session once a month

Participants were then asked to select the three reminders that they felt had the most relevance to them and to place them on a card to be posted in their work space.

Contracting

A popular device for promoting the application of training is a simple written expression of the intent to change one's behavior in some respect or to undertake a particular action appropriate to the goals of the training program. The contract can be made with oneself or with others (a coparticipant, the trainer, one's boss, or a colleague). The format of the contract can be formal ("The undersigned hereby commits himself to . . .") or informal (a letter to oneself). Often, trainers will offer to collect the contracts and mail them back, by regular or electronic mail, to participants for review in one month. Pairing participants who commit themselves to exchanging contracts and supporting each other is an excellent way to conduct this process. Following up with e-mail, a phone call, or a get-together helps to cement the contract.

EXAMPLE: The peer contract shown in Figure 9–3 was used in a career exploration seminar.

FIGURE 9–3. PEER CONTRACT

As a result of our training on career exploration, I want to incorporate the following ideas:

1.

2.

3.

4.

Signed _____

I will follow-up with the above person in one month.

Signed _____

Date _____

EXAMPLE: At the end of a facilitation skills workshop, the trainer asked participants to write a letter to themselves indicating what they had learned about facilitating team meetings and how they were going to apply it. Here is one participant's letter:

"I hereby resolve to be less directive in conducting team meetings. I will ask open-ended questions and allow team members to give complete answers without interrupting them. If no one answers immediately, I will be patient and not jump in to fill the void created by silence. I will avoid giving my direct opinion immediately. When asked a direct question, I will direct it back to the team members to answer before I respond. I will make a real effort to facilitate group interaction instead of controlling the meeting."

Action Plans

A more detailed tool for future application is the action plan. In this approach, the participant defines appropriate outcomes and the steps to achieving them as a result of the training program. Obstacles are anticipated as well. In a work setting, an action plan is often utilized as a mechanism by which the participant and his or her supervisor agree on a project that has benefits for the organization. An action plan can also be viewed as a self-motivational tool for the employee without specific monitoring by the supervisor. Figure 9–4 shows a typical action plan used in many training programs.

FIGURE 9–4. DEVELOPING AN ACTION PLAN

1. List three actions you would like to undertake as a result of this program.
   a.

   b.

   c.

2. Choose the action that you would like to plan to do first and enter it below.

3. List the potential roadblocks to implementing this action:

4. Discuss with your seat partner how you might overcome these roadblocks.
5. Describe in detail the action you will undertake and the steps you will take to ensure that it will happen.

Action plans have the virtue of pushing writers to be clear about what they are going to do. In the form in Figure 9–5, the writer is asked to specify how and when he or she will be assertive in the near future.

FIGURE 9–5. AN ASSERTIVE ACTION PLAN

I want to be more assertive with (*person's name and title*) in this situation:

The skills I will use:

Roadblocks that could get in the way:

Sample script or conversation:

I will make my first attempt by (*date*)

Figure 9–6 reproduces an elaborate example of action planning used in a management development program. It involves a serious commitment on the part of the participant and others in the organization to apply what has been learned in the training program and simultaneously to benefit the organization.

FIGURE 9–6. ACTION PLAN DESIGN AND DEVELOPMENT GUIDELINES

Directions for Use

One of the greatest shortcomings of management development programs is the absence of any tools to measure their effectiveness. To be sure, the participants can complete an evaluation sheet that asks what they like most, least, and so on. However, such questions are not able to fully gauge the impact of training.

The only true measure of impact is the degree to which the participants return and use the skills learned in the program. In order for this to happen, two conditions must be met:

1. The participant must work on a plan of action that spells out the specific steps for implementing change.
2. This plan is shared with the mentor and manager and supported by them.

This ACTION PLAN is designed to assist participants in meeting these two conditions, thereby enabling both them and XYZ Company to realize a return on the investment made through participation in the program.

Subject

Many topics are covered in this module. Select a project (one of those covered or one of your own) that you plan to focus on. As you complete your ACTION PLAN, try to be as specific as possible in stating your subject. For example, if you were writing an ACTION PLAN for communication, "Written Communication" would be too broad. A more specific subject would be "Developing a Highlight Report Format for the Department."

Within the subject you have selected, state your purpose or reason for selecting it. This will be a brief description of your intent or goal. Using the example of "Developing a Highlight Report Format," the goal might look like this: "Highlight reports contain numerous details. They need to be organized so that the details appear in a logical sequence. After obtaining permission from my manager, I plan to format one of my manager's highlight reports using an eye-opener, transition one, supporting details, transition two, and action conclusion."

Goals are stated in broad terms; objectives are quite specific and should include measures by which your progress toward them can be determined. Objectives are the things you must achieve (deadlines, performance indexes, and so on) in order to meet your goal. Building on the same example, the objective might look like this: "To spend one day formatting a highlight report that can be used as a model for subsequent highlight reports."

To achieve your goal, you must schedule activities to move toward it. This section is your blueprint and timetable for reaching the goal. Following our example above, the activities list might look like this:

FIGURE 9–6. continued

Activities	*Time*
1. Meet with mentor to explain my ACTION PLAN	1. One morning next week, two hours
2. Meet with my manager to explain my ACTION PLAN and obtain three latest highlight reports written by manager	2. One morning next week, two hours (after meeting with mentor)
3. Read over my manager's highlight reports	3. Two hours following week
4. Develop a format for organizing a highlight report	4. Two hours same week as item 3
5. After obtaining necessary highlight facts, data, and so on, write an actual highlight report for my manager	5. Four hours before report is due

As you carry out your schedule of activities, problems or barriers inevitably occur. Sometimes these can be anticipated in advance. Other times they may not. This section of the plan asks you to list and number all problems, present and potential, that you foresee as barriers to completing your activities. Next, state how you plan to deal with each problem, numbering each solution to agree with the problem it addresses. Following the example, this section might look like this:

Problems	*Solutions*
1. Manager may not be able to get me all the facts and data needed to complete the actual highlight report	1. Work directly with manager in writing highlight report

Resources

Some ACTION PLANS are easy to carry out, requiring no resources other than your own time. Others may need help to be implemented (from your manager, other professionals, other managers, and so on). This section asks you to detail other sources you are depending on.

Costs and Benefits

Some activities you plan may involve a cost to the organization. If you don't know actual costs, estimate them. For example, the cost of completing our sample ACTION PLAN includes "Word Processing Services from Support Staff." Then list the payoffs you expect to realize from carrying out the ACTION PLAN. Some may be intangible (improved morale, a systematic approach, an increase in performance, better customer service, and so on). If possible, estimate the dollar

---

FIGURE 9–6. continued

---

value of your benefits, both tangible and intangible. For example, one benefit of the plan is "developing a format usable in writing highlight reports."

Commitment

Finally, the last section asks you, your mentor, and your manager to make a commitment to carry out the plan. As described in the directions, you will review the plan with your mentor and agree upon any changes. Then you will want to review the plan with your manager.

Then you, your mentor, and your manager should sign the plan confirming your intent to carry out the plan. You should set one or more dates for reviewing progress.

Source: Training Management Corporation, 600 Alexander Road, Building 2, Princeton, New Jersey 08540. Reprinted with permission.

Follow-Up Questionnaire

A clever strategy for raising participants' consciousness about the training program long after it is over is to use a follow-up questionnaire (Johnson and Carnes, 1988). It also serves as a way to stay in touch with participants.

Here are the steps to take to use this approach:

1. Explain to participants that you would like to send them a follow-up questionnaire one month from now. The questionnaire is intended (a) to help them assess what they have learned and how well they are doing in applying the training and (b) to give you feedback.

2. Urge them to fill out the questionnaire for their own benefit. Ask them to return the questionnaire if they so desire. (Using e-mail might make it easier for participants to reply.)

3. When you develop the questionnaire, consider the following suggestions:
   - Keep the tone informal and friendly.
   - Mix the questions so that those that are easiest to fill out come first. Use formats such as checklists, rating scales, incomplete sentences, and short essays.
   - Ask about what they remember the most, what skills they are currently using, and what success they have had.
   - Offer participants the opportunity to call you with questions and application problems.

Figure 9–7 contains an example of a follow-up questionnaire sent to participants after a training program on stress management.

FIGURE 9–7. FOLLOW-UP QUESTIONNAIRE

Hello! How are things going? I hope you have had the opportunity to work on your management of stress. As I promised, I'm sending you this questionnaire to help you review and assess your ability to obtain the goals you are seeking. By sending this questionnaire back to me, you will also help me to evaluate the impact of the training program. Thanks!

1. Please rank the situations below in order of difficulty to you. Use the following scale: (1) least difficult to (5) most difficult.

   ___ Managing time effectively

   ___ Keeping physically fit

   ___ Maintaining healthy nutritional habits

   ___ Staying relaxed

   ___ Being able to say "no"

2. Briefly describe a recent stressful situation in which you managed things effectively: _____

   _____

   _____

   _____

3. Describe a recent situation in which you did not manage stress effectively and regretted it: _____

   _____

   _____

   _____

4. Please circle the strategies below that you have found useful:

   a. Identifying negative self-thoughts and distortions

   b. Scheduling in fun, relaxation, and recreation

   c. Delegating responsibility to others

   d. Striving for realism, not perfectionism

5. Check one of these statements:

   ____ Please call me. I'm having difficulty with _____.

   ____ Everything's going well. There's no need to contact me.

WORKSHEET

PROVIDING FOR BACK-ON-THE-JOB APPLICATION

Now is your chance to think about strategies for back-on-the-job application of your training program. Use the worksheet to guide your planning.

Strategies Prior to the Program:

_____

_____

_____

_____

Strategies During the Program:

_____

_____

_____

_____

Strategies at the End of the Program:

___ Self-assessment

___ Job aids

___ Reentry advice

___ Obstacle assessment

___ Peer consultation

___ Peer teaching

___ Self-monitoring

___ Contracting

___ Action plans

___ Follow-up questionnaire

Notes:

_____

_____

_____

_____

◆　◆　◆

Chapter Ten

Planning Active Training Programs

At this point in the design of your active training program, you've established your objectives and sequenced activities to support them. You've also taken into consideration back-on-the-job application of the skills and information your program is intended to teach. You have now reached the point where you can organize all of your design ideas on a given topic into a complete program. This final step in designing involves the creation of the outer shell of the program, sometimes referred to as the *macrodesign*.

THE MACRODESIGN OF AN ACTIVE TRAINING PROGRAM

In the introduction to Part Two, I proposed that an active training program was characterized by

- A moderate level of content
- A balance between affective, behavioral, and cognitive learning
- A variety of learning approaches
- Opportunities for group participation
- Utilization of participants' expertise
- A recycling of earlier learned concepts and skills
- Real-life problem solving
- Allowance for future planning

With these characteristics in mind, I would like to present a macrodesign for a total program. If your time is limited, it may be difficult to employ all five aspects of this plan. In this case, you might eliminate the middle and advanced activities.

Opening Exercises

Design activities that build interest in the entire course and introduce some of the major ideas of the first part of the program. Also use this time for group building and learning about the participants. An initial case study that invites participants to start thinking about the subject matter may be a good starting point. This is also the time to solicit participants' initial questions about the topic being studied. If the course is skill-oriented, ask participants to try out the skills without the benefit of prior instruction just to see how well they do.

Building Blocks

Design activities that both teach the basic knowledge and/or skills and explore participants' attitudes and feelings about the topic. Actively involve the participants by interspersing lecture presentations with opportunities for group participation. Utilize alternative methods to lecturing and experiential learning approaches for variety.

Middle Activities

Design activities that help participants review the building blocks and introduce ideas to be covered at the next stage of the program. Role playing, simulation, and observation exercises; case studies; assigned projects; and other comparable methods can be featured.

Advanced Knowledge and Skills

Design activities that teach the course material at a more advanced level. Emphasize real-world problem solving. Be careful to recycle the information and skills presented earlier. Be especially mindful of utilizing the participants' expertise. Draw out their feelings about what they are learning.

Application Activities

Design activities that help participants test their knowledge and skill and encourage them to apply these activities to new problems and on-the-job (or back-home) situations. Allow time for goal setting, action planning, and consideration of on-the-job or back-home application issues.

A CASE EXAMPLE OF AN ACTIVE TRAINING PROGRAM

To illustrate this five-part macrodesign, I have chosen to present in Figure 10–1 a training program on coaching and counseling skills that I designed as part of an ongoing development program for a group of new managers in a large pharmaceutical company. The details of each activity have been eliminated so that you can easily follow the general outline of the macrodesign. As you read this outline, keep in mind that the program design was developed as an intensive two-day seminar. If the program had been longer in duration or allowed for time back on the job during it, the specific designs of each section could have been quite different. A program you are designing may differ because of the nature of your training topic, your assessment of the participants, and your overall training objectives. Still, you should find this macrodesign adaptable to your situation.

FIGURE 10–1. COACHING AND COUNSELING PROGRAM

This two-day program is designed to increase a manager's skills as a coach and as a counselor. As a coach, the manager identifies a need among employees for instruction and direction, usually related directly to their current work assignments—for example, an employee may be having difficulty learning a new computer system. In a coaching relationship, employees are open to advice and show little defensiveness. As a counselor, the manager identifies a problem that is interfering with employees' work performance—for example, an employee may be suffering from burnout and lack interest in the work. A manager needs to switch from a coaching to a counseling mode when employees are not as open to his or her input. In a counseling relationship, the manager builds trust by approaching the employee in an especially supportive, nonthreatening manner.

The program gives equal weight to affective, behavioral, and cognitive aspects of the topic. It builds on training that participants have already received about the Myers-Briggs Type Indicator (MBTI), a tool in which the effects of personality type on performance as a manager can be examined.

I. Opening Exercises

   A. *Introduction and Objectives*

      1. *Key terms*

         a. **Coaching**

         b. **Counseling**

      2. *Objectives*

         a. To value the role that coaching and counseling play in a manager's work

         b. To learn and practice coaching skills

         c. To learn and practice counseling skills

(*The trainer begins with remarks about the terms* coaching *and* counseling *and shares her or his objectives with the training group.*)

   B. *The Role of Coaching and Counseling*

      1. *Discussion:*   Ask, "What experiences have you had being coached and counseled by others?" "What coaching and counseling behaviors have been effective and ineffective?"

FIGURE 10–1. continued

---

   2. *Activity:*   Have participants identify specific examples in which coaching and counseling have taken place (or might take place) in your work as a manager.

   3. *Discussion:*   Ask, "What are the benefits of coaching and counseling effectively?"

   4. *Videotape:*   Watch "Coaching and Counseling" (an overview of the two skills).

(This section is a sequence of activities designed to achieve team building, on-the-spot assessment, and immediate learning involvement. Although participants already know each other, they become reacquainted by discussing their prior experiences and current views. At the same time, the trainer can assess participants' attitudes about the training topic. The video is used not only to clarify further the distinction between coaching and counseling but also to stimulate interest in further skill development.)

II. Building Blocks

   A. *Coaching Employees*

     1. *Activity:*   Do a paper-tearing exercise that proves that coaching is not merely telling someone what to do.

     2. *Activity:*   Have participants observe a role play in which someone is learning something new.

     3. *Activity:*   Have participants practice teaching a new skill or procedure to an employee.

     4. *Discussion:*   Ask, "How does your MBTI profile affect how you coach employees?"

(The first major training sequence begins with an exercise demonstrating common foibles in coaching another person. Participants are then asked to observe effective coaching procedures and apply what they have observed in their real-life work situation about teaching a skill or procedure to another participant. The sequence concludes with an interesting exchange between participants with contrasting MBTI profiles concerning the needs each has in a coaching situation.)

   B. *Counseling Employees*

     1. *Discussion:*   Ask, "How do you feel when you have to counsel a resistant employee?"

     2. *Lecturette:*   Provide guidelines for giving performance feedback.

     3. *Activity:*   Have participants practice feedback skills.

FIGURE 10–1. continued

---

4. *Activity:*	Have participants learn ways to actively listen, reflect back what people are saying, and ask probing questions.
5. *Demonstration:*	Have participants participate in a counseling interview.
6. *Activity:*	Have participants practice counseling interviews.
7. *Discussion:*	Ask, "How does your MBTI profile affect how you counsel employees?"

(The second training sequence begins with an affective consideration of the problems inherent in counseling employees. It then presents basic counseling skills [feedback, listening, questioning, and reflecting] and provides opportunities for practice. At the end of the sequence is a second discussion of the MBTI, this time examining how contrasting styles affect the success of the counseling experience.)

III. Middle Activities

A. *Case Review Problem*

1. *Activity:*	Have participants determine whether a case situation requires coaching or counseling and outline the actions needed.
2. *Discussion:*	Ask, "What questions remain for you concerning when and how coaching and counseling skills are applied?"

(Before launching into advanced topics, the trainer asks participants to reflect on what they have learned by clarifying their understanding of the respective roles of coaching and counseling.)

IV. Advanced Skills

A. *More Issues in Coaching and Counseling*

1. *Demonstration:*	Demonstrate dealing with anger and resistance.
2. *Activity:*	Have participants practice dealing with anger and resistance.
3. *Demonstration:*	Demonstrate motivating higher performance.
4. *Activity:*	Have participants practice motivating higher performance.
5. *Discussion:*	Ask, "How confident do you feel about handling your role as a coach and a counselor?
6. *Activity:*	Have participants perform, critique, and redo role plays of a variety of coaching and counseling situations.

FIGURE 10–1. continued

(The purpose of this section of the program is not only to consider new issues [anger or resistance and motivating higher performance] but also to process emerging feelings and polish difficult skills. The last two activities recognize that coaching and counseling are a confluent mixture of affective and behavioral elements. Participants are asked to rehearse their newfound skills in a variety of situations to maximize the transfer of training back on the job.)

V. Ending Activities

    A. *Peer Consultation*

        1. *Activity:*   Have participants use fellow participants as consultants on back-on-the-job problems with difficult employees.

    B. *Action Planning*

        1. *Discussion:*   Discuss the steps needed to ensure retention of skills.

        2. *Activity:*   Have participants develop a self-contract for improving their coaching and counseling skills.

(When the trainer asks participants to act as consultants for each other, the peer consultation activity becomes a review of the knowledge participants have gained. Action planning is incorporated into the design to motivate back-on-the-job application.)

WORKSHEET

PLANNING AN ACTIVE TRAINING PROGRAM

Use the space provided in this worksheet to outline a total active training program of your own. Check the results against the characteristics of an active training program.

Opening Exercises

_____

_____

_____

_____

_____

_____

_____

_____

_____

_____

Building Blocks

_____

_____

_____

_____

_____

_____

_____

_____

_____

_____

Middle Activities

_____

_____

_____

_____

_____

_____

_____

_____

_____

WORSHEET continued

Advanced Skills

_____
_____
_____
_____
_____
_____
_____
_____
_____
_____

Ending Activities

_____
_____
_____
_____
_____
_____
_____
_____
_____
_____

Qualities of my program:
_____ Moderate level of content
_____ Balance between affective, behavioral, and cognitive learning
_____ Variety of learning approaches
_____ Opportunities for group participation
_____ Utilization of participants' expertise
_____ Recycling of earlier learned concepts and skills
_____ Real-life problem solving
_____ Allowance for future planning

◆　◆　◆

Part III

Conducting an Active Training Program

A question was posted on the Training and Development listserv on the Internet (trdev-l @ psuvm.psu.edu): "What do top-notch trainers do?" A myriad of responses followed, including the following:

- Involve participants in an activity in the first five minutes.
- Frequently check for understanding.
- Modify plans based on participant feedback.
- Use self-disclosure and humor to develop an open climate.
- Listen carefully and match what's happening to the needs of the participants.
- Use a wide variety of learning methods.
- Give participants the "what-why-how" for every training activity.
- Review where the group has been, give an overview of where it's going, and summarize periodically along the way.

Yes, you can build active learning into the design of your program, but it is in the delivery of that program that your efforts are truly tested. As I have already stressed, designing is not complete at the time of delivery. Instead, the delivery phase of a training program is a period of continually adjusting, refining, and redesigning.

Ensuring the successful delivery of a training program is a process that actually begins before the participants arrive. Preparation is one of the most important ingredients for success. Since much will happen during the actual program, you need to make sure that materials and equipment are ready and that the physical layout of the training room is suitable. As the trainer of this event, you need to be mentally prepared as well. Greeting participants, establishing early rapport, presenting your training agenda, and inviting feedback are also important beginning steps.

Once you have *connected* with your participants, you have the opportunity to *lead* them through the program. Your credibility as a leader depends on your ability to set group norms, eliminate training time wasters, get the group's attention, win over wary participants, and manage difficult behaviors. This can be a daunting task for many trainers. Fortunately, there are many techniques to help you gain control and establish yourself as an effective leader of the training group.

The challenge of delivering an active training program is most apparent during the middle section of the program, where the majority of your content is covered. Here, you have two different roles as a trainer: as a *stimulator* when you give presentations and lead discussions and as a *facilitator* as you guide participants through structured (and often team-based) activities. At this point, your success will depend upon how well you present information, lead discussions, direct participants through exercises, and make effective transitions from one event in the program to another.

Concluding a training program can be as difficult as beginning one. Among the key skills are how you review the program, handle remaining questions, guide back-on-the-job application, and evaluate training results.

The five chapters that constitute Part Three focus directly on your actions in the training room as you conduct active training programs. (In some instances, they also apply to training delivered out of the classroom.) Chapter Eleven tells you how to prepare yourself mentally and arrange the physical layout of the training room and illustrates four ways to establish immediate rapport with participants and introduce the training program. Chapter Twelve suggests ways to foster constructive group norms, control timing, assert positive authority, and use humor to handle difficult situations that occur in training programs. Chapter Thirteen describes ways to overcome anxiety, make eye contact, maintain a natural and positive body language and voice quality, handle props, and make smooth transitions. It also outlines a ten-point menu of training behaviors that facilitate discussion. Chapter Fourteen explains how to motivate participants to buy into a training activity, give clear instructions, manage group behavior, and assist participants in processing what they have learned and examining its implications. Special suggestions are made for fostering collaboration in long-term learning teams. Finally, Chapter Fifteen identifies techniques for reviewing program content, eliciting final questions and concerns, promoting self-assessment, focusing on back-on-the-job application, and expressing final sentiments. Specifically, it describes how to obtain ongoing feedback and determine the focus, tools, and timing of evaluation.

Each of the chapters in Part Three is filled with examples of how the ideas it contains have been translated into many different types of training programs covering a wide variety of content areas. Every chapter also ends with a worksheet where you can practice applying the suggestions to your training situation.

At times, it will be helpful to refer back to the design ideas in Part Two as you apply the suggestions for conducting active training. Be alert to instances where material from Part Two should be considered side by side with material from Part Three.

◆   ◆   ◆

Chapter Eleven

Beginning an Active Training Program

You have assessed your group participants in advance, have designed course objectives and activities, and are now ready to conduct your active training program. If you have designed some effective opening exercises, you're likely to have a strong beginning. For added insurance, however, it is wise to think about these questions: How are you going to arrange the physical setup of your facility? How are you going to establish rapport with participants as they walk in the door? What are you going to say to introduce your program once it starts?

No training program can be totally successful based upon the written design alone. Programs that look gorgeous on paper can lose their effectiveness quickly if the trainer does not have the delivery skills to carry out the design requirements. In this chapter, we will give you tips for conducting the beginning portion of a previously designed training program.

PREPARING YOURSELF MENTALLY

All trainers are a little nervous when starting a program. However, it is usually the anticipation rather then the training itself that is the worst part. If you have planned your activities and are well organized, there is a good chance that the butterflies will pass. If, on the other hand, you forget to take care of preparation details until the last minute and do not carefully think out your design, you will have a far greater chance of losing the confidence necessary to help sell the group on your ideas.

The preparation of materials and activities for a training program may begin weeks or days before the participants walk into the classroom. Typical preparations include determining the date and time for the course, reproducing manuals and course materials, arranging for room space and audiovisual equipment, and confirming course attendance. People who are not directly involved with training themselves usually don't consider all of the little things that go into making a program successful—that is, until something "inconsequential," like a miscommunicated date and time or a training room without enough chairs, interferes with the overall conduct of the session. Attention to all of the details required to put together a successful active training program sets an atmosphere of order, organization, and professionalism.

In addition to preparation, you will find that making the effort to connect with participants before you begin will reduce your tension and build your confidence. This way you avoid the self-absorption that breeds anxiety. Remember that it is the participants who are responsible for producing skills or information as a result of the training experience. The purpose of their coming to training is not so that they can be impressed by you; it is so they may take something back with them when they leave the training session. Here is a case of someone who needed this advice.

EXAMPLE: One trainer in a large service organization was famous for theatrics during his normal one-day training programs. Employees were always anxious to sign up for his classes because they were known to be fun. The trainer's style seemed to be fine until he was asked to deliver a five-day program for midlevel managers. After three days, the theatrics had worn thin and attendance began to drop. By the fifth day, the trainer had lost half of his group and the participants who remained weren't able to demonstrate anything except that they had been entertained by the experience.

Another consideration is your own comfort level with the course content. Creating a training program from scratch and delivering it for the first time can be tremendously exciting as you participate in the learning process step by step with the participants. The drawback to presenting new material is the hesitancy and uncertainty with which you may deliver the course content.

If you are not well versed in the subject matter, you might be especially concerned about questions from the participants. Remind yourself that one way to handle questions when you don't know the complete answer is to draw upon group expertise: throw the question out to the group as a whole to determine if collectively they can discover the answer. Another possibility is to write down any questions that you are unsure of and promise to find out the answer as soon as possible. Make sure to get back to the participants once you have the correct answer to their questions. Here is an example of how one trainer fielded a participant's question.

Participant: How will our documents be archived once the new system is in place?

Trainer: I'm not sure that I can answer that question right now. I'll have to check with our systems administrator to find out how archiving will be handled in the future. If I don't have the information by the end of today's class, I'll make sure to send the archiving procedures to you by the end of the week.

A different kind of mental preparation is needed if the course content is something that's second nature to you. Boredom with subject matter is a problem faced by anyone who teaches a subject repeatedly. If you are in the position of teaching course material that you could recite in your sleep, try to remember that although the information is not new to you, it is new for your group members.

EXAMPLE: A sales trainer was asked how she could possibly look forward to conducting a session on customer relations the next day in light of the fact that she had conducted the same session every other day in the past three weeks. Her answer was simple: "I just tell myself to focus on the participants and not myself. I find it interesting to watch the way that they respond to what I'm saying and try to find as many opportunities as possible for them to contribute to the discussion. In that way I can learn from their experiences and add their contributions to the subject matter the next time I teach the course."

Other ways to prevent trainer burnout are as follows:

1. *Be flexible with your lesson plans and designs.* Use repeat sessions of the same program to try out new ways to deliver the same material or to try out new activities.

2. *Vary the location and the environment.* If you always teach in the same room, see if a different one is available instead. If conditions permit, try bringing your program to the participants' work area rather than having them come to your training facility.

3. *Watch others train the same program.* If an outside vendor offers a similar program elsewhere, attend the class to get new ideas on how to handle the same subject matter. If you can observe other trainers within your organization, take the time to do so to pick up new delivery techniques and styles.

As a professional trainer, you may be asked to conduct a program many times more than you would prefer. However, the preceding tips may help you to extend your endurance and postpone burnout a bit longer than you would ordinarily expect.

One final recommendation as you mentally prepare for your training program ahead: remember that what works well for one audience may not work at all with another group of people. The course content may not vary from one session to the next, but the mix of people most likely will. Success in an active training program will depend upon your ability to modify the content and design of a course according to the overall goals of that particular group of participants. All course time should be centered around the particular knowledge, skills, or attitudes that are supposed to be learned. Walk through your program with the participants you are currently training in mind. Try to be as flexible as possible as you think through your program, always considering a backup exercise if a planned activity does not fit the characteristics of your current training group.

If you could design a training room from scratch with an unlimited budget, what would be at the top of your list of preferences? Most trainers, I would guess, would include some of the following:

- A fully controllable lighting and sound system
- Infinitely flexible furniture
- Magnetized walls
- PC hookups to a network
- Wiring or cabling to accommodate videoconferencing
- Carpeting and plush swivel chairs
- Liquid crystal display panels and computer projection
- Reliable temperature controls

The physical setup of a training facility is the first impression that participants will have as they begin their session. Large corporate training centers are available with hotel-type accommodations and extensive recreation areas, but your program may very well be scheduled for an unused classroom in a church basement or elementary school. Regardless of the level of luxury in your surroundings, take into consideration the number of ways that you can directly affect the physical layout of the training classroom.

By considering the physical arrangement of a room to be a continually flexible backdrop to your active training program, you enable your training room to provide continued action and support for your activities. Don't be afraid to move the furniture within your classroom, even with the participants' help. By asking the participants to work with you to rearrange the room differently than it was originally set up, you offer them the chance to change things around, make use of the existing surroundings, and in a very subtle way make it their own. Training that is conducted in a less-than-optimal environment is sometimes more successful than training undertaken within the best possible facilities, because everybody has to pitch in to make things work. Here is a case in point.

EXAMPLE: A trainer walked into a classroom with twelve rectangular tables arranged in three rows (see Figure 11–1). Since there was little time to rearrange the tables, he decided to leave things as they were for his opening remarks. When he needed participants to be seated as subgroups, he asked them to help him do some interior decorating, rearranging the tables as in Figure 11–2.

FIGURE 11–1. TABLE ARRANGEMENT 1

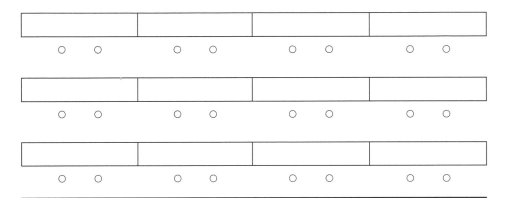

FIGURE 11–2. TABLE ARRANGEMENT 2

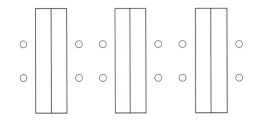

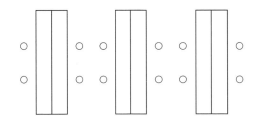

Later on, when he wanted a fishbowl design (one group surrounding another group), he used the arrangement shown in Figure 11–3.

FIGURE 11–3. TABLE ARRANGEMENT 3

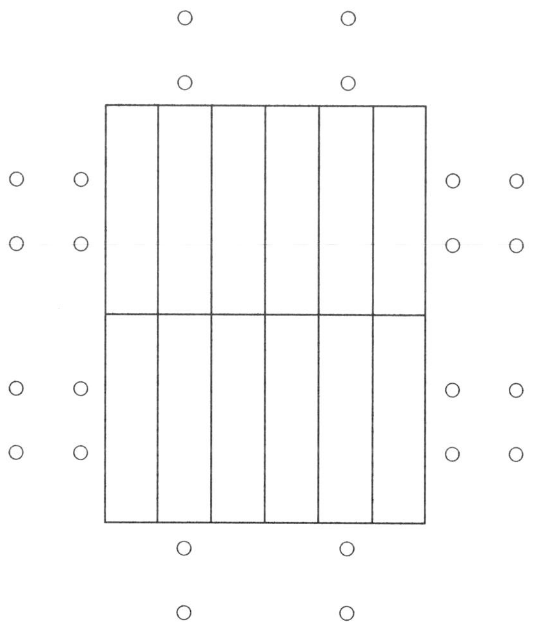

There are times, of course, when nothing can be physically changed to create new arrangements. Even then, however, all is not lost, as evidenced by this case example.

EXAMPLE: A trainer had designed a fishbowl activity as part of a course on conflict management. She walked into a small room furnished with one large rectangular conference table and space enough only for chairs around it. Her solution was to treat each side of the table as a potential fishbowl group. Participants along one side of the table at a time became the center of the discussion, with all those seated elsewhere acting as observers (see Figure 11–4).

Even fixed seating in an auditorium does not have to inhibit interaction. Participants can still have dyadic conversations with seat partners and can also be divided into groups of four, with two of the participants sitting directly in front of or behind the other two.

FIGURE 11–4. MUSICAL FISHBOWLS

First fishbowl group

Fourth fishbowl group   Third fishbowl group

Second fishbowl group

Probably the most common seating arrangement in the training world is a horseshoe (see Figure 11–5).

The virtue of a U-shaped layout is that participants can see each other while a traditional teacher-in-the-front presentation is going on. Whenever the trainer wants to break into full group discussion, participants can interact face to face without having to move. The arrangement is also convenient for handing out materials as the need arises: the trainer simply moves into the U and

---

FIGURE 11–5. SEATING ARRANGEMENT 1

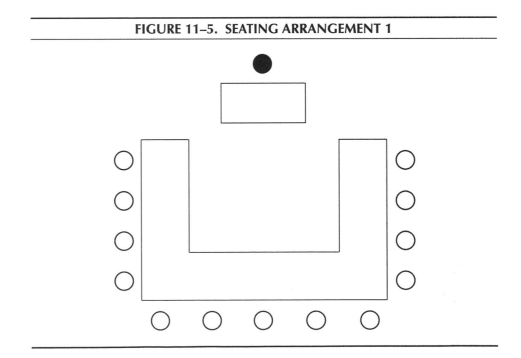

gives a stack of handouts to participants at each side of the horseshoe. If the room is large enough, participants can pull away from the tables and form small groups. For a more intimate full-group discussion, some participants can move their chairs into the mouth of the U to create a circle.

When your design calls for mostly full-group discussion with few trainer-led presentations or subgroup activities, furniture can be arranged in a circle or square (see Figure 11–6). Circles and squares afford the best view for each participant, although sometimes the room dimensions dictate an oval or rectangular arrangement.

FIGURE 11–6. SEATING ARRANGEMENT 2

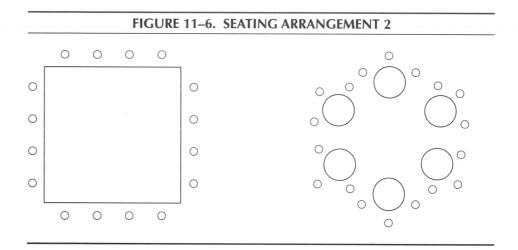

If you plan to have the participants work in subgroups, try to locate groups as far from each other as possible so that they do not disturb one another. In these circumstances, if you must address the full group at any time, keep your remarks brief because you will be too far away to connect with your entire audience for a long period of time. Use breakout spaces, if available, for maximum privacy for the subgroups, but do so only when the task is sufficiently lengthy to warrant physical isolation between groups. For short tasks, sending groups to breakout areas may be too time-consuming.

In the event that your design involves little need to write, take notes, or read from training manuals, you can do away with tables entirely. With only chairs to maneuver, any layout can be set up easily and quickly. Circles for small or large groups are easiest to achieve without any tables as obstacles.

GREETING PARTICIPANTS AND ESTABLISHING RAPPORT

The first moments of getting acquainted with group members can be an awkward time for both the trainer and the participants. Consider the following example.

EXAMPLE: Michael Taylor was responsible for putting together a one-day program on team building for two small manufacturing companies that had recently merged. The program was scheduled to run from 9:00 A.M. to 4:00 P.M. at the in-house training facility of one of the two companies. Participants had been informed by a preclass confirmation memo that coffee and donuts would be available at 8:30 A.M.

By 8:35, the first few participants had walked into the training room and had begun helping themselves to the refreshments. This was the first opportunity for employees from the two companies to meet each other, and, even within the same company, some of the faces were unknown to fellow workers. As more people entered the training room, small groups of participants began to form, with little interaction between groups. A few participants made no effort to socialize; after getting coffee, they began to read newspapers at their seat. Several other participants wandered around the room, looking unsure of where to put themselves.

The trainer, Michael Taylor, did not help himself to coffee and donuts. He was in his office around the corner from the training room doing some last-minute preparations for the day's class. When he looked at his watch and discovered that it was 8:50, he realized that he still had a chance to make a couple of quick phone calls before the official class start time. When he did enter the classroom at 9:00, he greeted the participants with a brief hello and launched into the program.

By 9:45, Michael experienced the first feelings that perhaps all was not going as well as he had hoped. Although he could not identify exactly what was wrong, he noticed that very few participants responded when he asked general questions. He had seen several people yawn openly as he talked, and many participants appeared to be restless. Two participants near the back of the room had begun a private conversation, and it looked as though others were more interested in this conversation than in the information that Michael was delivering.

Michael decided to give the class a morning break a little earlier than he had planned to give himself a chance to figure out why the group wasn't relating to his material. He kept asking himself, "What went wrong?"

Consider Michael's experience to be a warning of what can happen if you do not take the time to greet participants one by one and connect with your group as a whole. A simple way to ease those tense moments is to make sure that you are available and ready to greet participants at least fifteen minutes prior to the start of the program. Walk around the room casually as people enter, make eye contact, and try to shake hands with the participants as they make themselves comfortable with the training environment. *Learn as many names as you can. Introduce participants who don't know each other.* This getting-to-know-you process may relax your nerves as well, for you will begin to see the group members as individuals with whom you can share your interests. If you have not had a chance to do a thorough assessment of your group previous to the class, informal conversations with the participants can help you to gain valuable information before you begin the program.

Informal conversations are also valuable for establishing rapport with your participants. This can be very difficult with a new group, yet it is essential if you are to gain your participants' acceptance and respect. Consider the following approaches as you attempt to connect with your audience, whether in informal conversations or in the first moments of your training program. Not all may work for you, but utilizing even one of these approaches will create a bond between you and the participants.

1. *"I've got something for you."* Let participants know about your expertise and your ability to transmit it to them. Don't be boastful but do let them know that you are confident about your knowledge and skills.

   EXAMPLE: Management training is a difficult subject to deliver unless you can convince participants of your expertise and experience. In a management training class designed for newly promoted supervisors, one trainer began the session, "I'm pleased to be your trainer for this class. Luckily, I have both the management and the training experience to help you. For those of you who aren't familiar with my background already, I'd like you to know that I've worked at the bank for the last twelve years, eight of which were spent working at all levels in the branch system. In addition, I've worked in training for four years, three of which were prior to my most recent experience as a branch manager. I hope my experiences at the bank will enable me to relate to your questions."

2. *"I've been through this, too."* If you have been through the same training and work assignments as the participants, let them know that you can identify with them.

   EXAMPLE: A trainer used this approach to connect with her group when she was asked to deliver a training program for clerical employees in a production environment. The employees were responsible for processing high volumes of mail and were employed only at peak times of the year. Before beginning the training session on quality awareness, the trainer let the participants know that she had also worked an off-shift at one time in her career. She began the session by encouraging participants to compare stories about the difficulties of coping with an irregular work schedule. The group was pleased to discover that the trainer understood some of the pressures of their work. Without this mutual exchange of stories, it is doubtful that the employees would have paid as much attention to the new information presented in the training program.

3. ***"I admire you."*** Express your admiration for qualities that you respect in your participants. Praising their efforts, their intelligence, and their goodwill can help you to build a positive rapport.

   EXAMPLE: A trainer asked customer service representatives in a program on telephone skills to describe what it was like to be on the firing line with angry customers. The initial response was hesitant. Once the first story had been told, however, more and more participants joined what quickly became a very animated discussion. The trainer wrapped up the conversation by saying, "It's very interesting for me to hear about some of the frustrations you face on the job. I really respect you for having the patience and control to be able to deal with so many customers every day. I'm not sure I could do as well."

4. ***"You interest me."*** Get to know the participants and express interest in their backgrounds, life experiences, and concerns. The more you let participants know that you care about who they are, the more they will care about what you have to offer to them.

   EXAMPLE: A group of Indonesian managers came to the United States for a two-month training program. One of the trainers in the program began the first day of his section of the program by asking the participants if they already missed home. Most nodded affirmatively. A participant added that that day was a special national holiday back home. The trainer asked the group if they would sing their national anthem for him to hear. Immediately, all twenty-eight participants rose and sang in unison. The trainer tried to learn the melody by humming along. To the delight of the participants, he successfully got through the opening notes. A tradition was then started, and, during breaks in the program, the participants taught the trainer several Indonesian songs. Showing this degree of interest in the participants' native music enabled the trainer to form a strong bond with the group.

GETTING THE BEST FROM THE FIRST THIRTY MINUTES OF TRAINING

Any progress that you might have made toward establishing rapport with your group can go to waste immediately if you are not careful during the most important time period of your training program: the first thirty minutes. The first half-hour is a kind of "grace period" during which any overt hostility or antagonism will be submerged under a veneer of politeness, watchfulness, and reserve. It is during this initial segment of time, however, that participants decide how they perceive you, what role they expect to play during the training program, and what they intend to accomplish during the course. As a trainer, it is your responsibility to make sure that each of these concerns is resolved positively during the first thirty minutes of your program. Be aware that participants may be asking themselves any of the following questions about their involvement with you and the training:

1. When are we actually going to start learning? How long will this thing last? (impatience)

2. What am I doing here? I already know this stuff. Does the trainer really know what she's doing? (competence)

3. I don't think that I'm going to like this trainer. I wonder what the trainer thinks of me? (compatibility)

4. Is he really interested in solving *my* problems? I wonder if what I say in class will get back to my manager? (trust)

5. Who will handle my regular work while I'm here? Is somebody going to be able to get in touch with me if there's a problem at home? (out-of-class concerns)

Knowing that the first thirty minutes of your training set the tone for the entire program, try following these tips for making a positive first impression on your group:

1. **Impatience:** Begin the class promptly at the time previously announced for the start of the course. Work to focus the group on the course objectives, trying to hook the participants' interest onto the course content as opposed to what time they will be released for breaks and lunch.

2. **Competence:** Don't assume that everyone in a course needs exactly the same content delivered to the same degree. Assess the range of participants' knowledge, skills, and attitudes, either as part of a formal needs assessment or during informal conversations before the class. Opening exercises also can be used to explore participants' skills more fully. Let the participants know that you are confident in your abilities without pretending that you have all the answers or the final word, and never pretend that you know more than you really do.

3. **Compatibility:** Neutralize the traditional teacher-pupil relationship as quickly as possible during the opening moments of a training program. Let participants know that your purpose is not to preach *at* them, but instead to interact *with* them. Establish a community-like atmosphere in which contributions from the group are welcomed and supported by you and by the other members of the class.

4. ***Trust:*** Emphasize that you respect class confidentiality. Show the participants that you want to hear what they have to say and that you will be responsive to their needs.

5. ***Out-of-class concerns:*** Allow the participants the opportunity to speculate about how the training program will affect their work. Begin to establish the transition from the classroom back into the real world during the first, not the last, hour of the program. And, of course, inform participants of the schedule so that they can arrange communication with the outside world if necessary.

**REVIEWING
THE AGENDA**

No discussion of the beginning moments of a training program would be complete without a reference to reviewing the agenda or program objectives. After your introductory remarks, clue the audience into what they can expect out of the training program and what detail is expected of them. There are several ways to do this:

1. Include your training objectives in the participants' manuals. Briefly clarify what you mean by each objective. Giving participants a copy of the objectives up front allows them to be clear about what learning is expected of them. Figure 11–7 presents an example.

FIGURE 11–7. OBJECTIVES

After completing this time management course, you will be able to

- Complete a time-study analysis
- Specify time savers and time wasters that have an impact on your personal productivity
- Establish priorities to maximize your work in the future
- Develop a time plan to use both at work and at home

---

2. List what you hope to accomplish on a flip chart. You can make the flip chart ahead of time or can fill it in as you make your remarks. One way to do this is to list the issues to be covered in the program. Figure 11–8 reproduces an example from a training program on selling skills.

3. Orally describe the overall program objective to your group. This approach is suitable if you have a very short or informal program that you would like to keep casual in tone.

FIGURE 11–8. AGENDA
• How to feel more comfortable asking for business • How to improve group selling skills • How to draw out and understand client needs better • How not to subvert the salesperson if you are the manager

EXAMPLE: A trainer began a management training program for new supervisors by saying, "The transition from coworker to supervisor can be difficult. Many first-time supervisors ask questions such as these:

- How do I manage relationships with former coworkers?
- Do I need to keep my distance?
- How do I define my role as supervisor to them?

"Today's workshop is designed to help you adjust to your new position."

In addition to informing participants about your goals, you should be sure to tell them how the program will be run and what you need from them in order for the program to be successful. Include the following information:

1. A content outline
2. A description of the kinds of training activities you have designed
3. The schedule
4. Requests you will make of participants during the program
5. Housekeeping information (eating arrangements, location of restrooms, coffee breaks, telephone messages)

INVITING FEEDBACK TO THE AGENDA

One of the basic decisions that you will face at this point is the degree to which you will solicit participants' feelings about the impending program. Some trainers are reluctant to risk the possibility of opening a Pandora's box. They enthusiastically present their agenda and then proceed directly with opening exercises, bypassing participant feedback. There is little problem with this if time is limited and you have every reason to believe that the program is eagerly desired as it has been advertised. In most instances, however, you have much to gain by inviting feedback. How else can you check whether your agenda fulfills the participants' expectations?

The simplest approach is to ask directly, "Does this match what you hope to gain from this program? Is there anything you would like to add to the agenda?" By asking these questions, you are not implying that the agenda is up for grabs. You are merely expressing your willingness to consider any wishes the participants may have. Most participants will understand when their wishes cannot be accommodated.

Another common approach is to ask participants, once they have learned about your plans, what hopes and concerns they might have. This formula allows them to express a wide variety of wishes, from wanting the program to have more real-life application to allowing for smoking breaks. Some trainers prefer to separate the discussion into two parts. First they elicit from the group *what* they want to learn. Then they encourage the participants to discuss *how* the program will proceed and *how* they will work together as a group.

If you have gathered assessment data about the participants prior to the program, it makes a great deal of sense to summarize that information at this point. Let them know that you have done your homework and are aware of their needs. This recognition is particularly important if you learn that the participants have some resistance to the program. Instead of ignoring their resistance, you are better off bringing it out into the open. Showing interest in their misgivings is a sign that you are supportive and not afraid to listen to negative comments. Even if you do not agree with the participants' views, you can still empathize with their feelings and acknowledge their valid points without compromising your own beliefs concerning the value of the program you have planned.

By the time you have completed your agenda review, your training program should be well under way. You can now continue with the opening exercises outlined in Chapter Three. Remember that a well-planned beginning can save you hours of later frustration and prepares the stage for the rest of your active training program.

WORKSHEET

BEGINNING AN ACTIVE TRAINING PROGRAM

Use this worksheet to think about the beginning of your next program.

Physical Layout

    Shape of tables:

    _____

    _____

    _____

    Arrangement:

    _____

    _____

    _____

Establishing Rapport

    "I've got something for you" (*describe*):

    _____

    _____

    _____

    "I've been through this, too" (*describe*):

    _____

    _____

    _____

    "I admire you" (*describe*):

    _____

    _____

    _____

    "You interest me" (*describe*):

    _____

    _____

    _____

WORKSHEET continued

Reviewing the Agenda

_____ Flip-chart presentation

_____ Informal remarks

_____ Inviting participant feedback

Notes:

_____

_____

_____

_____

_____

_____

◆   ◆   ◆

Chapter Twelve

Gaining Leadership of the Training Group

In the early stages of a training program, your leadership needs to be accepted by the group. Even though all learning does not depend upon you, the active training program you have designed requires your direction and guidance. Setting appropriate group norms, controlling the timing and the pacing of the program, getting the group's attention, winning receptiveness to your message, and dealing with problem participants are all aspects of gaining leadership within a training group.

SETTING GROUP NORMS

One of the first steps in gaining leadership of the group is to set appropriate group norms. Consider what behavior you want to foster within the training and then focus on guiding the group in this direction. Establishing firm ground rules lets everyone understand how the training program will operate and where it will go. These ground rules should not just be set and forgotten; you should model and reinforce them continuously throughout the session. Group norms that are firmly established from the outset of the training program help to guide the remainder of the course.

The following group norms have been found to be helpful within an active training environment:

1. *Encourage participants to express themselves honestly.* Let them know that the open expression of ideas, concerns, and attitudes is appreciated and will enhance the overall learning process.

231

Sample script: "Please feel free to add your own opinions to our discussions; your ideas and experiences will contribute greatly to the value of this class for all of us."

2. ***Ask that confidentiality be respected.*** Let participants know that you want what everyone says during a session to remain confidential. Conversations about people outside the training group should not be disclosed to others once the session is over.

Sample script: "I realize that many of you know the same people within your organization. Let's have a rule of trust between us that whatever we say and do as individuals during the training session will remain in this room."

3. ***Urge risk taking.*** A training session is a unique opportunity for participants to step away from their usual roles and responsibilities and consider information from another point of view. Encourage participants to use the training environment to their advantage by taking risks that they normally would not consider.

Sample script: "Sometimes people shy away from role plays because they feel uncomfortable acting in front of the group. It is my hope that you will find role plays to be quite useful for examining your own behavior in a variety of situations and that you will feel comfortable participating in the activities planned for today."

4. ***Expect participation from everyone.*** Remind participants that if they hold back initially from participating, it becomes increasingly more difficult to join in as time goes on. Tell them that you have planned opening exercises designed to encourage participation.

Sample script: "Do you remember when you were a student in high school or college how the same people talked up in class each time it met? I don't want that to happen here, so I have put together some introductory activities designed for all of you to participate in right from the beginning."

5. ***Promote the value of performance feedback.*** Let participants know that they are expected to give helpful feedback to each other and that all comments, both given and received, should be considered constructive criticism.

Sample script: "As part of this interviewing skills training course, I will ask each one of you to participate in an exercise that will be videotaped and then critiqued by the class. I hope that you will view this as an opportunity to sharpen and enhance your existing skills and not see it as a personal attack on your own interviewing style."

6. ***Require participants to sit in different spots.*** This way more people meet each other, the social climate of the group evens out, and cliques cannot form.

Sample script: "We will be together for three days. I'd like you to switch seats twice a day so that you will get a chance to work with everyone in the group."

7. ***Reassure participants that their questions are welcomed.*** Let them know that you expect them to ask questions whenever they are confused and to speak up when they don't understand.

Sample script: "The best questions are those that, at first, you might think are dumb. These questions truly seek an answer and are asked at a risk. These same questions might also be on the minds of many others."

8. ***Insist on punctuality.*** Let participants know that you will be able to start and end on time as long as they return promptly from breaks and lunch.

Sample script: "We have a jam-packed program, and I need your cooperation to make it run smoothly. One thing that will help me a lot is if you are punctual when it's time to resume after a break. Even one person missing can be a problem because often we will be involved in team activities and therefore can't start until all members are present."

As an alternative to stating norms yourself, you can invite group members to express their own norms. Break the group up into pairs and have participants identify behaviors they want and don't want to occur. When pairs report their lists, there will probably be considerable overlap. Wishes expressed by more than one pair can be listed on a flip chart (ask a participant to jot them down). Attaching the list to a wall will serve as a reminder to all throughout the program.

EXAMPLE: In a public workshop with a diverse group, some participants expressed their wish that people could get to know others who were different from them. This encouraged the participants to seek out during breaks, lunch, and evenings people with whom they might not have been comfortable initially. This level of social integration would probably not have occurred if the wish to have different kinds of people get to know each other had been expressed solely by the trainer.

Norm setting does not, of course, have to rely on direct verbal statements. The opening exercises you have designed can set in motion positive group behavior without any direct suggestions from you. Setting positive group norms through opening exercises can go a long way toward preventing negative situations from arising within your training program.

CONTROLLING TIMING AND PACING

One way to lose a grip on your leadership is to lose control of time. Few feelings are worse than the panic a trainer experiences on discovering that only one hour is left to cover half a day's worth of material. Running out of material also can be embarrassing and can give participants the feeling that they have been cheated out of time that they have already allocated and purchased. And, although you may decide during the design phase of development how you would like to pace your program, it is not until you actually begin delivering that program that you will be able to ascertain the appropriate timing and realize its benefits. Both the participants and you will feel a sense of completion and organization when a program remains on target and moves at a steady pace through the planned agenda. On the other hand, a program that moves too slowly or too rapidly will leave participants either bored or breathless.

A leisurely pace should be considered for small-group activities to allow sufficient time for each person to be heard and directly involved in the activity. A much faster pace is necessary to keep the attention of all of the participants when you are working with the group as a whole. Regardless of the format, stay alert to signs of restlessness and conclude any activity before the participants' interest is lost. Keeping things moving will help to give the entire program a sense of organization and accomplishment.

Also make sure that no time is wasted during your training programs. This may mean giving short breaks, letting participants know that work will begin as soon as the break is over, and taking care not to waste time when you move from one part of your program to the next. Potential training time wasters and their more efficient alternatives are shown in the following list:

Time Waster	*Alternative*
Starting late after breaks or lunch	Start exactly at the time that you indicated. If all of the participants are not yet in the room, begin the session with a discussion or filler activity for which complete attendance is not necessary.
Starting an activity when the participants are confused about what they are supposed to do	Give clear and precise instructions. If the directions are complicated, putting them in writing beforehand will avoid the need for lengthy oral instructions.
Writing lecture points on flip charts while participants watch; recording all output from subgroups	Prepare flip charts ahead of time or ask a participant to record information as you moderate a discussion of

	responses; use only key terms; decide if recording is really necessary.
Passing out participant materials individually	Prepare stapled packets of handouts ahead of time; distribute packets to strategic areas so that several people can assist with their distribution.
Demonstrating every part of a new skill	Show only the parts of a skill that are new to the participants or are key for their understanding of the whole skill.
Having every subgroup report back to the whole group one by one	Ask participants to write key findings on flip-chart paper and post lists on the walls of the training room so that each group's work can be viewed and discussed at the same time. Or, going from group to group, have each team report only one item at a time so that everyone can listen for possible duplication. The groups should not repeat what has already been said.
Letting discussions drag on and on	Express the need to move on but be sure to call on those who were cut off during a subsequent discussion. Or begin a discussion by stating your time limit and suggesting how many contributions time will permit.
Waiting for volunteers to emerge from the group	Recruit volunteers during breaks in the program; call on individual participants when there are no immediate volunteers.
Pulling ideas or questions from a tired or lethargic group	Provide a list of ideas or questions and ask participants to select those they agree with; often your list will trigger thoughts and queries from participants.

You can affirm the value of your training program by monitoring how you allocate time within the session. A program that provides both adequate time for participants to learn and a quick pace to ensure participant attention helps to establish your control. You then keep that control by eliminating busywork and time wasters.

GETTING THE GROUP'S ATTENTION

In a school setting, a teacher calls the class to order in ways that often won't do for a trainer who wants to emphasize an adult-to-adult relationship. There are several friendly, unobtrusive, ways to accomplish the same task. For example, as participants are chatting, you can simply speak slightly over their voices and say nonapologetically: "May I begin?" To vary your cues over a longer program, try any of these attention-getting devices:

1. Flick a light switch ever so slightly. This isn't offensive if it is done tastefully.

2. Make a dramatic announcement. Grab attention by saying something like "Testing, 1, 2, 3. Testing"; "Now hear this, now hear this"; or "Earth to group, earth to group." Use a megaphone or microphone for large classes.

3. Create a verbal "wave." Instruct the class to repeat after you whenever they hear you say, "Time's up." In no time flat, the entire class is assisting you in indicating that it's time to stop what they are doing.

4. Use clapping. Instruct the class to clap their hands once if they can hear you. Within a few seconds, the first participants to hear your instructions will clap and, by doing so, will get the rest of the class's attention.

5. Play prerecorded music. Select music that can quickly grab attention. Decide by your selection whether you want to quiet down participants gracefully (for example, with meditative music) or with a bang (for example, with the theme song from the movie *Rocky*). (Be sure to abide by copyright laws when using music in your training session.)

6. Use a silent signal. Tell the participants to quiet down whenever they see you using a particular signal (for example, holding up your index and middle fingers). Encourage them to do the signal as well.

7. Use a sound signal. Anything will do, including gavels, bells, whistles, or kazoos.

8. Tell a joke. Inform participants that you have a storehouse of jokes or riddles (such as "How many _____ does it take to screw in a light bulb?") that you will use to serve as a cue to quiet down.

9. "Can we talk?" Use Joan Rivers's famous line as a way to reconvene the entire class for discussion.

10. Announce "break time!" This will surely get everyone's attention.

INCREASING RECEPTIVITY TO YOUR LEADERSHIP

The way a trainer talks to adult participants makes a big difference in how receptive they will be to her or his leadership. As you converse with your group, particularly in the early stages of the program, try to use some of the following approaches to win participants over.

1. Make "liking" statements:

    "I'd like to get the chance to know all of you."

    "I hope that, through the comments I give you, you will feel as though you're getting some personal attention."

2. Convey respect and appreciation:

    "Don't worry about waiting for a break to get your coffee."

    "Thanks for having me here."

3. Share what you have in common with participants:

    "I guess we all wear a number of different hats."

    "A lot of us don't plan."

4. Phrase your advice and directives indirectly:

    "I guess I'd like to start by asking you . . ."

    "Let me tell you how I propose to do this."

5. State what's positive about participants' contrary viewpoints:

    "It's exciting to me to try out these ideas with you."

    "It's always more interesting to get different points of view."

6. Encourage disagreement:

    "Nothing is carved in stone; I just want you to know that."

    "This is the aspect that people are most resistant to."

7. Convey a desire for collaboration:

    "You're going to have a lot of input in this program."

    "I'd like to spend most of today finding out how you would handle these matters."

HANDLING PROBLEM SITUATIONS

Any experienced trainer can tell you anecdotes about difficult moments with entire training groups or with individual participants. The unfortunate truth is that a trainer is an easy target for hostile participants' frustrations. Even more difficult can be the uninterested participants who would much prefer to be at home or at work rather than in your training program. Dealing with those feelings of hostility and lack of interest can be the most difficult aspect of delivering a training program.

Why might an ***entire group*** become hostile toward you? Quite simply, because participants are likely to turn on you any dissatisfaction or frustration that they are feeling at the time of the program. The hostility may have nothing to do with you personally but instead may stem from irritation at having to attend your program or anxiety about learning new skills. Additionally, the participants may make an "us-versus-you" distinction in which they perceive you as the natural opposition.

As we mentioned in Chapter Eleven, acknowledging class resistance is the first step to overcoming it and breaking through the us-versus-you barriers. A well-known strategy is to acknowledge that often participants do not come to a training program as voluntary, eager *learners*. Instead, they may have been sent by their managers and feel like *prisoners*. Or they might have just wanted a break from the daily grind of their job and may be attending essentially as *vacationers*.

You may want to tell the prisoners with gentle humor, "I'll try to keep your sentence as short as possible." To the vacationers, you might say, "We'll be having some fun and will be taking frequent breaks." In a more serious tone, you might try asking participants to identify their role and place themselves in a group with fellow learners, prisoners, or vacationers. Ask them to discuss these questions:

1. Why are you in this group?

2. Why do you feel the way you do?

3. What can you get from others in the room?

4. What can you give?

The more you encourage group members to explain their position, the better chance you have of reducing their hostility. This may mean leaving the course content for a while, but more productive learning in the long run will make up for the time spent dealing with the situation. An efficient approach is to use the conflict as a learning tool by incorporating it into the discussions and exercises planned for the course.

If you sense resistance when introducing a new skill or some new information midway through a program, you should again take the time to focus on the resistance and identify it before the situation gets out of control. Don't be afraid to stop the program, ask what's happening, and propose a discussion of the problem.

Negative behaviors of ***specific individuals*** create another difficult situation. Fortunately, you can prevent a lot of negativity by using active training methods. Further, the frequent use of pairs and subgroups minimizes the damage that individuals can do to you and the rest of the group. However, all problem behavior will not disappear in an active training program. Following is a list of some common behaviors you might face within the training environment:

1. *Monopolizing:* taking up a great deal of time

2. *One-upping:* trying to appear more skilled and knowledgeable than the others in the group, including the trainer

3. *Complaining:* continually finding fault with the procedures of the trainer

4. *Intellectualizing:* excessively rationalizing and justifying one's ideas and beliefs

5. *Withdrawing:* not participating (and sometimes distracting the group by doing so)

6. *Arguing:* taking vocal exception to any comments with which one disagrees

7. *Questioning:* stopping the flow of presentations by frequently asking questions

8. *Clowning:* joking at inappropriate times

The key to handling such behaviors is to not take them personally. There are several reasons for problem behavior by a participant that have nothing to do with you:

- She may have been ordered to attend the training to shape up.

- He may be hiding fears about failing to do well in the program.

- She may be a long-time employee who doesn't believe anything will change.

- He may feel too old to deal with new approaches.

- After years of hostility toward her boss, she may be displacing her anger toward you.

- He may like the attention he attracts with his behavior.

Coping effectively with participants' problems is an extremely important training skill. When a participant exhibits problem behaviors, the whole group likely will become involved and therefore will be distracted from the actual training program. Negative behaviors also tend to rattle the trainer and distract from the delivery of the course content.

Your responsibility is to the entire class and not just to one participant. You should not allow the disrupter to monopolize your attention to the point where the program begins to suffer. If you do need to say something to a participant

Here are potential solutions to these situations:

1. *Monopolizing*

   • Use small groups or pairs.

   • Summarize the participant's viewpoint (active listening), then move on.

   • Ask others for their input.

   • Ask the participant to hold off until a break.

2. *Tangents*

   • Ask the participant to hold off till later in the seminar.

   • Summarize the participant's viewpoint and move on.

   • Address directly the fact that a tangent has been raised—"That seems to be a different issue"—and restate the purpose of the discussion, asking others for input.

3. *Private conversations*

   • Use nonverbal methods to regain the participant's attention (make eye contact, move closer).

   • Lower your voice or pause.

   • Ask one of the participants a question (making sure to say the participant's name *first*).

   • Ask the participants to refrain from talking (privately, if possible).

4. *Jokes*

   • Ignore the jokes and resume the session after the humorous interjections (be as serious as possible).

   • Reinforce the person by complimenting his or her sense of humor.

   • Privately ask the participant to minimize jokes.

5. *Disagreeing*

   • Present hard data in a respectful manner.

   • Summarize the participant's viewpoint; ask others for their opinions.

   • Agree to disagree.

   • Agree *in part*, then state how you differ and why.

6. *Distractions*

   • Use nonverbal signals, such as eye contact, to get the participant's attention.

   • Ignore the behavior if it is not distracting from the session.

- Privately ask the participant to stop.
- Request that beepers and phones be switched to the vibrating mode.

7. ***Doing one's own work***

- Switch into pairs.
- Use nonverbal methods to get the participant's attention.
- If a group activity is under way, ask all to participate.
- Ignore the behavior if it is not affecting others.
- Privately ask the person to participate actively in the program.

8. ***Time schedules***

- Minimize the distraction of the latecomer by ignoring the behavior.
- Adhere to time schedules; don't let everyone suffer for one person's lateness.
- Remind participants of time frames.
- Privately request promptness (as a courtesy to the rest of the group, not just to you).

9. ***Nonparticipation***

- Use response cards.
- Ask direct but nonthreatening questions.
- Connect with the participant during breaks.
- Ask the participant to be the leader in a small-group activity.
- Leave such participants alone (just because they're not participating doesn't mean they aren't learning).

10. ***Sleeping***

- Walk near the person without being obvious.
- Vary your voice.
- Shift into pairs or subgroup discussion.
- Create a physical activity.

One final thought as you consider handling problem situations: remember that it may not be necessary for you to intervene every time a participant exhibits a problem behavior during your training program. Very often, other participants will make it known that they find such behavior inappropriate and unnecessary. A good guideline is to intervene only if the problem behavior is repetitive or affects the entire training program. Also, realize that participants who have been difficult often want to find a way out themselves. Give them some space to discover a graceful, face-saving way to change their behavior.

To effectively gain leadership of your training group, it is important to keep in mind that prevention and intervention are the keys to establishing and maintaining control. Setting positive group norms and modeling those behaviors throughout the session help participants know what guidelines to follow. Controlling the timing and pacing of your program prevents boredom and keeps participants focused on the course content itself. The way that you handle problem situations will give further credibility to your leadership, allowing you to concentrate on giving presentations and leading discussions.

WORKSHEET

GAINING LEADERSHIP OF THE TRAINING GROUP

Use this worksheet to think through how you will establish your leadership in your next training program.

Group norms to be encouraged:

_____

_____

_____

_____

_____

Time wasters to be avoided:

_____

_____

_____

_____

_____

Comments to win participants over:

_____

_____

_____

_____

_____

Ideas for preventing problem behaviors:

_____

_____

_____

_____

_____

◆　◆　◆

Chapter Thirteen

Giving Presentations and Leading Discussions

In Chapter Four, I suggested several ways to design presentations to build interest, maximize understanding and retention, involve participants, and reinforce the content. The tips and illustrations of successful delivery techniques provided here are intended to complement those ideas. In addition, this chapter will cover ways to make smooth transitions between phases of your program and facilitate lively discussions.

KNOWING YOUR GROUP

To many people both in and out of the training profession, the ability to deliver an effective presentation is the mark of a good trainer. Sometimes, sessions that are called training programs are really just forums for presentations by speakers with expertise in a particular area. If a presentation is the only component of your session, don't expect much retention or application. If you are including brief presentations at intervals during an otherwise active training program, you can expect better results.

To be effective, first consider the nature of the participants. What are their concerns, their backgrounds, and their reasons for attending? Tailoring your remarks specifically to your audience is the first step toward a successful presentation. If you originally designed a lecturette on writing techniques for college undergraduates, for example, edit your examples to make sure that they are appropriate in an adult working environment before presenting the same information to a corporate audience. The more aware you are of the composition of your audience, the better your chances of suiting your remarks to its needs. Following these other tips also will help you to connect immediately with your presentation audience.

1. ***Aim your initial remarks at the immediate concerns of your listeners.*** Participants will be attentive if they think that you are going to address the questions that matter most to them. Until these questions are answered to the participants' satisfaction, they will have difficulty relating to the information that you are trying to get across. Here are some typical concerns:

- "Why are you telling me this?"
- "How does this affect me?"
- "Why should I be here instead of elsewhere?"

If you do not address these concerns at the outset, you risk losing your listeners before you even begin and having to spend the rest of the time fighting to regain their attention and interest.

2. ***Understand why you are communicating this information.*** Have you been invited to speak as an expert consultant, a helpful intermediary, or a decision maker who is telling the group what is about to happen? If you have been asked to present information about a new benefits program that will require employees to make major concessions, are you prepared to handle the hostility and angry responses that are likely to come from your audience? If you are lecturing as an expert consultant, do you have the credentials to back up your statements? Anticipate your group's perceptions of your role and plan your reactions accordingly.

3. ***Use language familiar to your listeners to establish bridges between your experiences and theirs.*** Avoid jargon or unfamiliar terms that might confuse people or prevent your overall message from getting through. Provide examples that relate to your audience.

Following is a transcript of the beginning of a class given by a corporate trainer responsible for teaching employees how to use a new word-processing system. Pay attention to how the trainer attempted to answer the listeners' concerns immediately, explained her role, and used language accessible to the participants.

"Welcome to word-processing transition training. Today's class is intended to help you, as experienced word processors, to make an easy transition between what you are using currently and the new version of word processing that our company will be using in the future.

"Although a full conversion between the two systems will not take place until all word processors in your area have been trained, you will find that as of tomorrow morning the new system will be available to you on your terminals at work. It is important that you try out the new software on your own as soon as possible so that you can gain the full advantage from your hours spent in training today. I have been tracking previous attendees very closely and have found that the people who are having the best results use the new system immediately. I'd like to give you a follow-up call approximately three days from now to find out if you have accessed the new system and if you have experienced any problems when using it. Before I go any further, are any questions already forming in your mind?"

"Will we still be able to access the old version of word processing?"

"Yes, for a limited time period you will have access to both the new and old software. I will be explaining more about conversion time frames at the end of our class today.

"Let's start by finding out why our company has decided to change to a new version of word processing. The vendor that developed our system received numerous requests from word-processing operators for enhancements that the old system simply didn't have. The programmers decided to put all of the enhancements together into one new word-processing package, which is what you are going to be trying out today. I think that after you practice on the new version, you'll agree that the enhancements are really terrific and make our word-processing system much easier to use."

"What if I decide that I don't like the new version?"

"The truth is that our company has definitely decided that everyone will be converted to the new system by mid-October. Any time you move away from something that you're comfortable with you are bound to feel a bit awkward at first. However, I think that once you experiment with the new version and then try to return to the old system, you will say to yourself: 'I can't believe that I lasted with the regular word-processing program for so long.'

"Instead of just talking about the system, let's go ahead and have you try out some of the new features for yourself. Please sign on by entering your user ID and password."

In this extract, the speaker addressed the participants' potential concerns by identifying the reason why she was giving the presentation as well as the short- and long-term impacts of the new system on the word-processing operators. A concern that the trainer had overlooked (giving up a familiar word-processing system) was brought up by a listener very early in the presentation. The purpose of the session was clearly identified (to help word processors learn how to use the new system) and the trainer used jargon that the audience would understand ("software," "enhancements"). The trainer knew her audience and presented the information in a way that they could understand.

Here is another excerpt, this time from a lecture presented as part of a program entitled "Strategic Selling Skills." The immediate topic is sales presentations. As with the previous example, notice how the trainer focuses his initial remarks on the concerns of his listeners, understands his role in communicating this information, and uses a common language to bridge his experiences with those of the participants.

"Right now we're going to be focusing on the sales presentation framework. Taking a look at our list of course objectives from yesterday, you'll remember that several people had mentioned improving their sales presentation delivery skills as one of their personal goals for our training program.

"I know from my previous experience that making a sales presentation can be a very nerve-racking experience, especially if making these types of presentations is new to you. However, I think you will find that you may already possess much of the knowledge that you should have in order to be successful when you give a sales presentation. What you will see by comparing the information covered yesterday to what will be covered today is that there are a lot of similarities between a sales call, a sales telephone call, and a sales presentation. Let's look at the framework of the sales call as a review right now. [The following list appeared on a flip chart labeled "Framework of a Sale."]

- Opening
- Client's Primary Needs
- Probing Questions
- Listening
- Positioning Product Knowledge
- Resolving Objections
- Close
- Action Step

"The framework for a sales presentation will follow the framework of a sales call very closely because all of the elements are very much the same. The skills that are required for handling a successful sales call will also be required for successfully handling a sales presentation, with some extra attention given to specialized delivery techniques such as voice inflection and positive body language. We will have a chance to practice these delivery techniques later in today's program.

"Let's begin, however, by discussing the opening or the introduction within the framework of a sales presentation. When you start giving your presentation to a group of individuals, and by this I mean within a sales situation, one of the most important things to do is to immediately thank everybody in the room for the opportunity to speak to them. You are taking their time away from their work, so you want to thank them for coming to your presentation and giving you the opportunity to present your organization and your company's solution to them.

"Another thing that you want to do up front is to clarify just how much time you have to speak. Many of us will prepare for an hour's presentation only to have someone come in and say, 'I'm sorry, I have to leave in forty-five minutes,' or somebody might come in and say, 'You're going to have to cut your presentation to twenty minutes because we have a big problem and we have to run out on you.' Some advice that I'm going to give you is to always have a short program and a long program, because you never know what the situation is going to call for. Above all, you want to make sure that you save enough time to get through your major points, close effectively, and allow time for questions and answers.

"So, initially, prepare yourself for your presentation by planning for both a long and a short program, and don't forget to thank your listeners up front for the opportunity to present to them."

ORGANIZING YOUR PRESENTATION

Although the actual design of your presentation may vary widely from one course to the next, several organizational principles apply to all presentations regardless of content or structure. Some ideas to keep in mind as you organize your presentation follow.

1. ***Make sure your opening is effective.*** A good opening will help the rest of your presentation to go much more smoothly. If you have a great opening story or joke that makes sense within the context of the rest of your presentation, use it. However, don't think that your opening has to be entirely your responsibility. Poll the group or ask the participants a few initial questions designed to elicit their opinions before you launch into your presentation. Asking the group to participate immediately will be as effective as the most humorous or captivating opening story.

2. ***Provide a preview of information prior to an explanation.*** An overview can familiarize participants with what is to be presented. It should be short and precise, providing a statement of the overall idea to be presented, the importance of the information, and a statement that outlines the structure of the content to be presented.

3. ***Cover a few points of information thoroughly rather than many points incompletely.*** Set limits on how much you plan to cover and stick to those limits during your presentation. All listeners have finite attention spans, no matter how interesting or scintillating the speaker is. Trying to cram in as much information as possible can overwhelm your key points as well as confuse the listener.

4. ***Organize this information within a step-by-step sequence.*** Participants tend to get lost in verbal mazes. Carefully structure the presentation,

arranging information logically and breaking down material into clear, coherent, and explicit steps.

5. *Avoid tangents and getting off track.* Prevent yourself from going off the deep end when delivering your presentations, especially in response to participant questions. Stay on target and in focus, and pace your presentations so as to keep everyone's interest in your subject matter alive.

6. *Signal transitions between information.* Use statements that move from the introduction to the body of the presentation, between major points and subpoints, and from the body to the conclusion. Make transitions explicit and then relate the previous information to the new information.

7. *Be as specific as possible in your lecture points.* The clearer your message, the greater the likelihood that your audience will understand what it is that you are trying to convey. Give examples or make analogies that truly illuminate your points. Select ones to which participants can relate and that are dramatic.

8. *Provide for brief pauses at appropriate times during the presentation.* Give participants adequate time to process the information and take good notes. (Most people are capable of taking notes at only twenty words per minute.) Also, consider using guided note taking (see "Guided Note Taking" in Chapter Four).

9. *Review or allow participants to recap information frequently.* This helps to "save" the information for later retrieval. Reviewing is especially important after a stretch of difficult material and at the end of the presentation.

10. *Estimate the time each part of your presentation will take.* By doing so, you can alter your remarks as needed. Sometimes you will need to shorten certain parts of a prepared presentation to fit into the time constraints of a particular training group. Before delivering the presentation, decide which segments can be shortened or lengthened if needed.

WATCHING YOUR BODY LANGUAGE

Underlying all presentations are your body language and the expressiveness of your voice. The maxim "It's not what you say but how you say it" holds true. In fact, research shows that *what* you say accounts for only 7 percent of the impact of your presentation. The other 93 percent of how people will respond to you stems from *how* you are communicating nonverbally. The keys to effective nonverbal behavior are how you present yourself *vocally, facially,* and *posturally.* Remember that the participants will primarily be focused on you as the presenter. The effective communication of your message can be sabotaged by delivery techniques that are annoying or irritating to your listeners. Following these suggestions will enhance your personal presentation skills:

1. ***Establish your comfort level with the group through natural, positive body language.*** Maintain good posture and a firm stance as you address the group. Avoid putting your hands near your mouth or your face, as those gestures signal insecurity. Watch out for such bad habits as fidgeting, playing with your hair, or tapping a pencil, as they distract the participants from your message.

2. ***Individualize your audience by making eye contact with the participants.*** Resist the temptation to stare at your notes or read from a written page. You are speaking to an audience, not a piece of paper. Pick out two or three friendly faces and look at them frequently for support. Alternate looking at those specific people with a general panning of the group, allowing your eyes to rove from one corner of the room to another. If you decide to use notes for a presentation, number the pages or note cards so that you don't get lost midway. Try to look at your notes rarely and don't give in to the temptation to read your written information verbatim.

3. ***Be aware of the pace and volume of your voice as you speak.*** Try to speak slightly more slowly than you would in normal conversation so that all participants can catch what you are saying. Speak at a volume that is loud enough for all to hear yet not so loud that you find yourself shouting. Varying both the rate and the tone of your voice can help to keep the audience's attention, much as a master storyteller modulates her or his voice to complement the plot and characters of the story.

4. ***Alter speech habits that are annoying to your listeners.*** Fillers like "ah," "um," and "er" are irritating when used repetitively by a speaker. Especially guard against the continued use of "you know," which is a popular conversational phrase but is out of place in a lecture or presentation. Excessive coughing or throat clearing takes a listener's attention away from the information being presented and focuses it instead on the presenter.

As you try to make any desired changes in your nonverbal behavior, be careful not to overdo it. Eye contact that becomes a stare, a forced smile, or an overly enthusiastic voice will diminish your credibility.

Listening to a tape recording of yourself giving a sample presentation may help you to pick up annoying speech mannerisms of which you may be unaware. Viewing a videotape (ask a friend or colleague to help) is even better, since you can both hear and see your delivery style.

Changing your presentation style may be difficult at first. Your habits have probably developed over a long period of time and may be hard to break.

However, constant awareness of your body language and voice patterns while you speak in front of a group will help to ensure that your message not only is delivered, but also is heard and understood by your participants. If you wish, utilize the feedback form reproduced in Figure 13–1 to assess how you are doing.

FIGURE 13–1. FEEDBACK ON NONVERBAL BEHAVIORS

VOICE

Volume	(loud)	5	4	3	2	1	(soft)
Tone	(animated)	5	4	3	2	1	(monotonous)
Fluency	(smooth)	5	4	3	2	1	(halting)
Speed	(fast)	5	4	3	2	1	(slow)

FACIAL EXPRESSIONS

Eyes	(engaged)	5	4	3	2	1	(removed)
Mouth	(friendly)	5	4	3	2	1	(stern)
Forehead	(relaxed)	5	4	3	2	1	(furrowed)

POSTURE

Posture	(erect)	5	4	3	2	1	(slouchy)
Movement	(controlled)	5	4	3	2	1	(fidgety)
Hand gestures	(natural)	5	4	3	2	1	(robotic)

ADDING VISUALS

Doug Malouf (1992, p. 84) gives several reasons for using visuals in your presentation:

1. Pictures are processed by the mind with very little effort.

2. Pictures act as keys to the memory.

3. Pictures can easily illustrate tasks that words are not suited to.

4. Vibrant visuals provide a common focus for the audience.

5. Visuals allow the presenter to direct the attention of the audience to his or her goals.

6. Visuals allow the audience to pause, scan the message, linger for a moment, and then absorb the message more thoroughly.

7. Research has shown that presenters using graphics are seen as better prepared, more professional, more persuasive, more credible, and more interesting.

A *flip chart* is the least expensive and perhaps most effective visual medium to use in presentations to groups of fewer than thirty participants because it does not require lighting to be dimmed. A flip chart is also versatile, correctable, and portable.

When writing on flip charts, be sure to print big and use few words. Use uppercase block letters, if possible. If you have good handwriting, keep it consistent in slant and style. Write in different, robust colors. The most visible are black, blue, and green. Two colors are usually more eye-catching than one. Use bullets, shapes, and pictures to add graphic appeal.

A number of other flip-chart hints may come in handy:

1. Leave a blank page in between each already prepared flip-chart sheet in case you want to write spontaneously during a presentation. Or use a second flip chart for this purpose.

2. Number, paper-clip, or otherwise flag important pages so that you can locate and flip to them quickly.

3. Hide lines on the flip chart if participants' reading ahead will lessen the impact of your presentation. You can accomplish this with strips of paper or by folding up lower portions of the sheet.

4. Build curiosity and provide an opening summary of your presentation by posting all the flip charts you plan to use along a wall or blackboard.

5. Tear off and post around the room sheets from the flip chart that you want the group to be able to refer to throughout the program. Have strips of tape ready so that you can paper the walls quickly.

Although they are not as personal a medium as flip charts, **overheads or slides** can add impact to your presentations to large audiences, especially when they are clear, concise, and easy to read. The advent of software such as PowerPoint makes it easier than ever to produce appealing transparencies or slides.

Here are a few important tips for using overheads or slides:

1. If you supplement your presentation with overheads or slides, be aware of the "6–6" rule: there should be no more than six lines on each transparency or slide, and each line should contain no more than six words per line.

2. Limit yourself to one idea per transparency or slide and use graphics whenever possible.

3. In order to stay connected with your audience, turn the lamp off whenever the overhead projector is not in use or advance to a blank screen if you are using slides.

4. Be sure not to stand in front of an overhead projector, and use a pointer (a pencil will do) rather than your finger.

5. Make sure the room has enough light so that people can see you and any printed materials in their hands.

With today's technology, presentation visuals can now be electronic. There are several advantages to ***electronic presentations.*** Because they offer access to more information, you can use more visuals and can change from one visual to the next more quickly than with conventional slides. Electronic presentations also offer the ability to present information in a nonlinear manner. Buttons can be created within a given visual to jump to another visual. They also can be used to launch completely different software applications or to play multimedia modes such as sound, animation, or full-motion video. Finally, a major advantage to electronic presentations is the seamless transition from one visual to the next (Mucciolo and Mucciolo, 1994).

A ***handout*** spares participants the burden of note taking and provides a helpful reminder of the points that you covered in your presentation. Make sure, however, that your handout is concise and designed for easy reading. And think carefully about when you should distribute your handouts. Many trainers do so before their presentations and then wonder why they have trouble getting the group's attention when they begin speaking. If you want the group's full attention, let them know that handouts covering the major points of your discussion will be available after you speak. They will then be free to concentrate fully on what you have to say rather than on what you have written on the handouts. If you feel that participants will follow your presentation more easily if they have a handout in front of them, be explicit about asking them for eye contact when you need it.

You can do many things to add active learning to your handouts. Dave Arch (1996) offers seventy-five different ideas, including

- Templates that can be copied onto the back of handouts to transform them into content-related paper sculptures, closing activities, and review tools

- Graphics (optical illusions, simple magic tricks, and puzzles) that can be used to increase retention and training transfer

- Interactive activities for use with any handout

Following the suggestions outlined in this section should assist you with any presentation that you are asked to make, regardless of the size of the group or the subject matter. Well-designed visual aids can help you to communicate your message quickly and effectively to the participants in your training program.

MAKING SMOOTH TRANSITIONS

Earlier in this chapter, a segment from a lecture on strategic selling skills was excerpted. In this section, which considers linkages and transitions, we will be taking a look at another passage from that same lecture. This time pay attention to how the trainer leads the group from one topic to the next.

> "I hope that you didn't forget the framework of a sales presentation over lunch because it's important that you keep that framework in the back of your mind as we move on to our next topic. By taking a look at our agenda, you'll notice that we're now going to be discussing differentiation. Mark, I believe that it was you who asked me this morning about how to differentiate proposals, wasn't it? Now is the time when I finally get to explore your question in detail.
>
> "As you'll see on this overhead, I have listed three specific ways to differentiate your proposal from the competition's. The first method listed, team strategy, focuses on introducing the team of individuals that is with you when you make your sales presentation and the expertise of those individuals. It is important that you make sure to introduce whoever is accompanying you from your company and give the group a brief idea as to how and when they are going to be contributing to your presentation that day."

Making smooth linkages and transitions between one topic and the next in your lecture or presentation involves briefly reminding the participants of what you have already covered, then indicating what is to follow. The best transitions appear to be seamless and flowing, easily connecting what you have already covered to what you will be discussing next. There are several techniques for either tying together sections of your presentation or linking together various parts of your training program. Following are descriptions of these techniques and examples of how they can be used:

1. *References to periods of time.* Mentioning specific periods of time—"yesterday," "this morning," "today," "this afternoon"—helps participants to organize the sections of your training program in their mind and gives them a clear indication of where you are headed.

> "This morning, we took a look at what not to do in an interview; this afternoon we will be focusing on what positive approaches you can take to make the most out of an interview."

2. *Minisubject review.* Taking a few moments to review what was previously covered allows participants the chance to reflect on what they've already learned and to prepare themselves for the next part of your presentation.

"Let's quickly review what we've covered so far before we move on to our next topic of discussion."

3. *Agenda check.* Hanging your planned agenda on the wall not only helps to keep the group on track but also serves as an easy reference when you are making subject matter transitions.

"Taking a look at our agenda for today, you'll see that we have already covered writing and speaking communication skills and are now ready to address the topic of listening."

4. *Change of visual aid.* Introducing a new visual aid or changing to a different type of presentation tool indicates a transition to a new lecture topic.

"Turning to our flip chart, you'll see that I have listed the five assertive communication techniques that we will be discussing today."

5. *Change of group format.* Reorganizing the group into a new configuration is probably the clearest way of marking a definite transition from one segment of your program to another.

"I think that it makes more sense for us to be together in one group for our next discussion topic. If you would just move your chairs from the small groups we were in for our last activity and form a large circle, we can begin."

Logical linkages between sections of your presentation ensure that both you and your group are ready to address a new topic. With just a bit of practice, elegant linkages will become a natural part of your delivery style.

FACILITATING A LIVELY DISCUSSION

For many presenters, encouraging a discussion after a lecture consists of introducing a question-and-answer period with the classic line, "Are there any questions?" All too often what follows is an uncomfortable silence as the participants wonder who will dare to speak up first. After a few awkward moments, the trainer sighs and says, "Well, if there are no questions, I thank all of you for listening."

How do you coax a lively discussion out of a group intimidated by the quiet aftermath of a presentation or lecture? Starting a discussion is no different from beginning a lecture. You first have to build interest. Note how the following opening remarks are designed to generate a discussion about the benefits and problems with work teams.

"Now that we have looked at the nature of work teams, I'd like to take the next ten minutes to get your thoughts about their advantages and disadvantages. Everyone these days is touting work teams as if they discovered the Holy Grail. But maybe there hasn't been a critical enough look at when it makes sense to do things in teams and when it's better to get work done on an individual basis. I also know people who feel that work teams place an unfair burden on the "responsible" people who have to take up the slack of the team members who don't pull their weight. It's as if there can be no individual accountability in work teams. You have a lot of experience working here at ABC Corporation. What do you think about the pros and cons of getting work done around here using teams?"

Start off the discussion with an open-ended question (for example: "How do you feel about . . . ?" "What do you know about . . . ?"). Most experts agree that open-ended questions trigger better discussions than closed questions. Closed questions should be avoided because they are too restrictive and don't require participants to think. They can also make your audience defensive and stifle participation. Therefore, avoid questions that can be answered simply yes or no, such as "Did you like this training video?" The question, "What are some things that you liked and didn't like about this video?" invites a longer response. In addition, avoid questions that can be answered with a fact, such as "When did that occur?" or "Which action would you take?"

Remember that once a discussion topic is introduced, you can use many interesting formats to obtain further participation. In Chapter Three, I discussed the following methods:

- Open discussion
- Response cards
- Polling
- Subgroup discussions
- Partners
- Go-arounds
- Games
- Calling on the next speaker
- Panels
- Fishbowls

Many of these options allow you to sit back and let the participants take charge. You might, for example, ask participants to form small groups to discuss the question, "What do you think about the pros and cons of getting work done around here using teams?" and then summarize their conclusions on newsprint. Other options require your leadership. In such cases, your role is to facilitate the flow of comments from participants. Although it is not necessary to make an interjection after each person speaks, periodically assisting participants with their contributions can be helpful. Here is a ten-point facilitation menu to select from as you lead group discussions:

1. ***Paraphrase*** what someone has said so that the participant knows that she or he has been understood and the other participants can hear a concise summary of what has just been said at greater length.

> "So what you're saying is that you have to be very careful during an interview about asking an applicant where he or she lives because it might suggest that you are looking for some type of racial or ethnic affiliation. You also told us that it's okay to ask for an interviewee's address on a company application form."

2. ***Check*** your understanding against the words of a participant or ask a participant to clarify what she or he is saying.

> "Are you saying that this plan is not realistic? I'm not sure that I understand exactly what you meant. Could you please run it by us again?"

3. ***Compliment*** an interesting or insightful comment.

> "That's a good point. I'm glad you brought it to our attention."

4. ***Elaborate*** on a participant's contribution to the discussion with examples or suggest a new way to view the problem.

> "Your comments provide an interesting point from the employee's perspective. We could also consider how a manager would view the same situation."

5. ***Energize*** a discussion by quickening the pace, using humor, or, if necessary, prodding the group for more contributions.

> "Oh my, we have lots of humble people in this group! Here's a challenge for you. For the next two minutes, let's see how many ways you can think of to increase cooperation within your department."

6. ***Disagree*** (gently) with a participant's comments to stimulate further discussion.

> "I can see where you're coming from, but I'm not sure that what you are describing is always the case. Has anyone else had an experience that's different from Jim's?"

7. ***Mediate*** differences of opinion between participants and relieve any tensions that may be brewing.

> "I think that Susan and Mary are not really disagreeing with each other but are just bringing out two different sides of this issue."

8. ***Pull*** together ideas, showing their relationship to each other.

"As you can see from Dan and Jean's comments, personal goal setting is very much a part of time management. You need to be able to establish goals for yourself on a daily basis in order to manage your time more effectively."

9. ***Change*** the group process by altering the method of participation or prompting the group to evaluate ideas that have been raised during the previous discussion.

"Let's break into smaller groups and see if you can come up with some typical customer objections to the products that were covered in the presentation this morning."

10. ***Summarize*** (and record, if desired) the major views of the group.

"I have noted four major reasons you have suggested that may account for managers' unwillingness to delegate work: (1) lack of confidence, (2) fear of failure, (3) comfort in doing the task themselves, and (4) fear of being replaced."

Any of these actions can be used alone or in conjunction with the others to help stimulate discussions within your training group. You may find that, as participants become more and more relaxed about contributing their ideas and opinions, you shift from being a leader to being an occasional facilitator and perhaps just another participant with an opinion. As your role in the conversation diminishes, the participants make the learning process their own.

Finally, there are many special formats for stimulating lively discussions. One excellent choice is to set up an "active debate" that involves every participant in the class, not just the debaters:

1. Develop a statement that takes a position with regard to a controversial issue relating to your subject matter (for example, "There is too much new drug development today").

2. Divide the class into two debating teams. Arbitrarily assign the "pro" position to one group and the "con" position to the other.

3. Next, create two to four subgroupings within each debating team. In a class of twenty-four participants, for example, you might create three "pro" subgroups and three "con" subgroups, each containing four members. Ask each subgroup to develop arguments for its assigned position. At the end of their discussion, have each subgroup select a spokesperson.

4. Set up two to four chairs (depending on the number of subgroups created for each side) for the spokespersons on the "pro" side and, facing them, the same number of chairs for the spokespersons on the "con" side. Place

the remaining participants behind their debate team. Begin the "debate" by having the spokespersons present their views. Refer to this process as "opening arguments."

5. After everyone has heard the opening arguments, stop the debate and reconvene the original subgroups. Ask the subgroups to strategize how to counter the opening arguments of the opposing side. Again, have each subgroup select a spokesperson, preferably a new person.

6. Resume the "debate." Have the spokespersons, seated across from each other, give "counterarguments." As the debate continues (be sure to alternate between both sides), encourage other participants to pass notes to their debaters with suggested arguments or rebuttals. Also urge them to cheer or applaud the arguments of their debate team representatives.

7. When you think it appropriate, end the debate. Instead of declaring a winner, reconvene the entire class in a single circle. Be sure to "integrate" the class by having participants sit next to people who were on opposite sides. Hold a classwide discussion on what the participants learned about the issue from the debate experience. Also, ask participants to identify what they thought were the best arguments raised on both sides.

You can also use a debate format that is less formal and moves more quickly:

1. Select an issue that has two or more sides.

2. Divide the group according to the number of positions you have stated and ask each group to come up with arguments to support their issue. Encourage them to work with seat partners or small cluster groups.

3. Seat groups opposite each other.

4. Explain that any participant can begin the debate. After that participant has had an opportunity to present one argument in favor of his or her assigned position, allow a different argument or counterargument from another group. Continue the discussion, moving quickly back and forth between the groups.

5. Conclude the activity by comparing the issues as you, the instructor, see them. Allow for follow-up reaction and discussion.

WORKSHEET

GIVING PRESENTATIONS AND LEADING DISCUSSIONS

Answer the following questions.

1. What do I know about my audience?

   _____

   _____

   _____

   _____

   _____

2. What is the core organization of my presentation?

   _____

   _____

   _____

   _____

   _____

3. What nonverbal behaviors do I want to increase? To avoid?

   _____

   _____

   _____

   _____

   _____

4. What visuals will I use?

   _____

   _____

   _____

   _____

   _____

5. How will I make transitions?

   _____

   _____

   _____

   _____

   _____

WORKSHEET continued

---

6. How will I introduce a discussion?

_____

_____

_____

_____

_____

7. What facilitation methods do I want to pursue?

_____

_____

_____

_____

_____

8. What special techniques can I use to stimulate discussion?

_____

_____

_____

_____

_____

◆   ◆   ◆

Chapter Fourteen

Facilitating Structured Activities and Promoting Team Learning

*T*his chapter has two goals. One is to offer advice on facilitating structured activities used throughout an active training program. These activities typically utilize small-group formats *for short periods of time.* The other is to offer advice on promoting team learning. This endeavor involves placing participants in small groups or teams *for an extended period of time.*

STRUCTURED ACTIVITIES

In Chapters Five and Six, we examined alternatives to lecturing as well as several experiential learning approaches. Because these kinds of structured activities play a central role in active training programs, you will need to develop an array of facilitation skills to make them effective learning experiences. Listening to a lecture, watching a demonstration, or even participating in a discussion demand less effort and risk than does taking part in a role play, an exercise, or a project. Consequently, one of your basic responsibilities as a facilitator of experiential learning is that of *motivating participation.* Since it is difficult to get participants to do exactly what you want them to do, especially if any of your activities are complicated, you also need to become an expert at *directing participants' activities.* As an activity unfolds, the dynamics of the training group can impede success, so you will need to be comfortable with *managing the group process.* In the middle of any activity, energy may begin to flag and your task becomes one of *keeping participants involved.* Finally, at the activity's end, its meaning may be unclear. You now need to involve the participants in *processing the activity.*

Without the necessary skills in each of these areas, these mistakes commonly occur:

1. *Motivation:* Participants aren't invited to buy into the activity or sold on the benefits of joining in. Participants don't know what to expect during the exercise.

2. *Direction:* Instructions are lengthy and unclear. Participants cannot visualize what the trainer expects from them.

3. *Group process:* Subgroups are not composed effectively. Group formats are not changed to fit the requirements of each activity. Subgroups are left idle.

4. *Energy:* Activities move too slowly. Participants are sedentary. Activities are long or demanding when they need to be short or relaxed. Participants do not find the activity challenging.

5. *Processing:* Participants are confused and/or overwhelmed by the questions put to them. The trainer's questions don't promote the goals of the activity. The trainer shares her or his opinions before hearing the participants' views.

How can you avoid these mistakes? Many of the skills you need can be explained best in the context of a case situation. Imagine the following.

EXAMPLE: You have been asked to create a two-day training program on interpersonal effectiveness. You have pulled together materials from other communication skills classes that you have taught previously and have redesigned some key pieces to fit the group you expect. Today is the first time you have tried out the newly designed program.

So far, the session is going very smoothly: there are no latecomers and the total group comprises eleven participants—a comfortable number. Introductions were straightforward and the first activity, a needs assessment survey, was completed individually. You followed up the survey with a brief lecture that tied in the needs assessment to the overall learning goals for the course. It's now 9:45 and time for you to facilitate the first structured activity, a small-group exercise called "Making Connections."

The exercise calls for the group to form trios and discuss questions that relate to interpersonal communication skills. After the first question, two of the three group members will rotate to join new groups and discuss another question. The goals for this activity are for participants to learn more about each other and to practice basic interpersonal skills such as communicating clearly and listening effectively.

Motivating Participation

Your participants need to be tempted before they will feel motivated to join in and take the exercise seriously. Getting participants to buy into an activity is essential to the success of your planned exercise, especially if it involves risk or effort. Here are some ways to motivate participation:

1. ***Explain your objectives.*** Participants like to know what is going to happen and why. Don't assume that they know your objectives. Make sure they do.

> "Right now I'm going to ask you to take part in an activity called 'Making Connections.' This activity should help you to get to know other members of our group a bit more than you were able to during our brief introductions. In addition, this activity will allow you to practice clear communication and effective listening."

2. ***Sell the benefits.*** Tell participants what's in it for them. Explain what benefits they will derive back on the job as a result of the activity.

> "We often meet new people and introduce ourselves to each other. Usually, getting acquainted is somewhat anxiety-provoking. This exercise should help you to feel comfortable enough to really get to know someone."

3. ***Convey enthusiasm.*** If you sound motivated about seeing them engaged in an activity, participants will internalize some of your enthusiasm.

> "This activity is a good one; I think you are really going to enjoy some of the questions that I have planned for you to ask each other."

4. ***Connect the activity to previous activities.*** Explaining the relationship between activities helps participants to see the common thread in your program.

> "On the survey you just completed, many of you identified overcoming shyness as one of your goals. During our first exercise, you will get some immediate practice in conversation skills."

5. ***Share personal feelings with participants.*** Explain why you have found the activity (or one like it) valuable to you.

> "I know that I can be shy at times. It's nice to have a structured exercise designed to reduce the anxiety involved in meeting people."

6. ***Express confidence in participants.*** Tell participants that you think they'll do a good job with the activity or that they are now ready to tackle a new challenge.

> "Now that you've already met each other at least once, you should have no problem asking each other questions that are a bit more detailed. Let's go ahead and get started."

Directing Participants' Activities

Incomplete or unclear instructions can spell disaster for a structured activity. If you do not take the time to explain exactly how the exercise should be completed, participants may spend more time asking questions about what they were supposed to be doing than actually taking part in the activity. Although you need to be careful not to sound like a schoolteacher, don't be afraid of oversimplifying; there is always someone who needs clarification and repetition. Here are four tips for making sure that the group understands your directions.

1. ***Speak slowly.*** Processing instructions to a complex activity is harder than listening to a lecture. Slow down so that participants can follow you.

> "Before we begin the exercise, I'd like to take a few minutes to explain exactly how this activity will take place. Please let me know if I am speaking too quickly."

2. ***Use visual backup.*** If appropriate, write directions on a handout or flip chart and allow participants to refer to this visual information as you orally explain it.

> "As you can see from this handout, I will be asking you to discuss four separate questions with other members of the class."

3. ***Define important terms.*** Don't take for granted that every participant will understand the key words in your instructions the same way you do. Explain important directions in more than one way.

> "As you see, the first question is 'What are your strong points in communication?' In thinking about how you'll respond to this question, remember that communication has two parts, the speaking end and the listening end. So include your strong points in both of these areas."

> "We will be forming new trios whenever there is a new question to be discussed. When I ask you to rotate out of your trios, I am, in effect, asking your group of three people to split up and join other members of the class to form a new trio."

4. ***Demonstrate the activity.*** Sometimes it is important for participants to have a mental picture of what they are to do. Provide a brief sample of what the activity will look like. Use yourself and/or a few participants to illustrate the instructions.

> "Now that the first trio has been completed, we're ready to rotate. Each of you has been assigned a number—0, 1, or 2. The 0s will stay where they are but the 1s will advance one trio (clockwise) and the 2s will advance two trios (clockwise). Let's have a sample group try this out so that you understand what I mean. John, Kathleen, and Mary were together in a trio. Because he is a 0, John will stay where he is, while Kathleen will move one group over there [point] and Mary will move two groups over there [point]. Have I been clear? [Avoid saying, "Do you understand?"]

When a trainer's directions are ineffective, a few basic flaws are generally responsible, singly or in combination. Here are the flaws and their associated solutions:

Problem: It is not clear how the various parts of an exercise fit together.

Solution: Explain the big picture first, then describe each of the parts that form the whole activity.

Problem: Information is left out of either the oral or written directions.

Solution: Try out your instructions in advance on a colleague or friend. Ask the listener if anything seems unclear.

Problem: A confusing format makes written directions hard to find and decipher.

Solution: Redesign your handouts so that any written instructions are at the top of the page and are printed in bold type.

Problem: There is no mention of special requirements or obstacles in the activity (such as the importance of a group timekeeper or leader, the need for felt-tipped markers or paper, or pitfalls encountered by previous groups).

Solution: Take notes when facilitating an activity for the first time. Watch for any problems that come up and either alter the design or make the next group of participants aware of any pitfalls to be avoided or preparations to be made.

Problem: Separate parts of a complex activity are not clearly divided or differentiated.

Solution: Give the group detailed directions for one part at a time.

Clear, easily followed directions prepare your participants for the transition from trainer-led training to the independent learning that takes place in structured activities. Many trainers overlook the importance of verifying understanding before an activity begins, only to find that the participants are confused, frustrated, or misguided. A design that you have worked hard to perfect on paper is worth a few extra moments spent on clear directions up front.

Managing the Group Process

Most structured activities involve subgrouping. Small groups give participants an opportunity to discuss ideas and ask questions in greater detail than is possible in a large-group format. Group movement also accommodates the diverse personal learning styles of your participants, many of whom may feel more comfortable speaking in a small group than they do when all of the participants are together.

Managing this process of forming and monitoring subgroups is difficult because you cannot completely control how participants will behave in smaller units. Also, some participants may not be as comfortable, at least initially, in subgroups as they are when the full group is together. Here are some suggestions to maximize peer interaction and productive work.

1. *Form groups in a variety of ways.* In order to separate acquaintances or randomize group composition, assign numbers to participants after they have seated themselves and then form groups corresponding to those numbers. Or allow participants to choose their own partners when you want to encourage friends to work together. When you want to achieve a certain composition, form groups according to specific criteria (for example, by gender or department).

> Count the number of participants as soon as you believe that you have full attendance. Then determine how large your subgroups will be by finding a number that easily divides into your total number of participants. Twelve is the easiest number of participants to work with; a group of this size can be divided into subgroups of two, three, or four members without your having to join the last group to make it even.

2. *Mix teams and seat partners.* Mixing up groupings offers the participants the chance to get a broad range of opinions and adds interesting variety to their discussions. Keep teams and seat partners together for long periods only when you need continuity.

> Set place cards in new locations in the training room to change seating patterns and create new seat partners.

3. *Vary the number of people in any activity based upon that exercise's specific requirements.* The smaller the group, the more opportunities for each participant to contribute. Work with the number of participants in your course to create groups whose sizes fit your design's requirements. If possible, try to keep work groups to six people or fewer to maximize individual participation. Include yourself if subgroup adjustments have to be made.

> The "Making Connections" activity calls for trios, yet there are only eleven participants in the course. In this instance, the trainer can join with the participants as a contributor to form four groupings of three people each.

4. *Divide participants into teams before giving further directions.* Ask participants to move to their new locations first, and then describe the particulars of how to conduct the exercise. Many trainers have to repeat directions for an activity because the participants forget them by the time subgroups are formed.

Say, "Before I go over the directions for this exercise, I'd like you first to get settled in your project teams. So please go to your tables now."

5. ***Ask groups of five or more to elect a facilitator or timekeeper.*** Larger groups can be difficult to keep on track and on time. A facilitator for each group relieves you of that burden.

> Say, "I'm going to ask one person in each group to volunteer as a timekeeper. We need to keep each round of discussions to just five minutes in order to stay on schedule today."

6. ***Give groups instructions separately in a multipart activity.*** Subgroups may finish their assignments at different times. Instead of waiting for all groups to finish one section of a multipart activity, quietly give the next set of directions to each subgroup when it is ready to move on.

> Say, "I see that you have completed the first round of questions. For your next assignment, please complete this conversation skills rating that we will be discussing as a whole group when everyone else is finished."

7. ***Keep people busy.*** If one subgroup finishes all its work well in advance of the other groups, be ready with a "let's take this one step further" question. You are letting the members of the quick group know that they are going to be able to report their findings on the second question to other groups.

> Say, "Here is a follow-up question on delegating authority. Since you've finished the exercise, why don't you take a few minutes now to discuss your response. Perhaps you can tell the other groups about it."

8. ***Inform the subgroups how much time they have.*** State the time allotted for the entire activity and then announce periodically how much time remains. Visit subgroups to see how much they have accomplished. When you are about to stop a group activity, give the participants a warning.

> Say, "You'll have ten minutes to do this activity. Make sure each person gets a two-minute turn. . . . You should be about halfway around the group by now. . . . There are two minutes left. . . . Please wrap up your discussions now so that we can get back together as a full group."

A trainer who quietly and smoothly manages group process is rarely noticed; the chaotic atmosphere of the training course will give away one who does so clumsily. For example, an activity that calls for the participants to work together in pairs would be awkwardly set up by the instructions "Pair up with the person seated next to you" (on the left or the right?). Such pairing can be facilitated gracefully by pointing out two participants at a time and saying, "You two are a pair, and you two, and you two . . ." It is simple moves like these that give the participants a clear indication of what to do.

Keeping Participants Involved

Your job is not over once the participants have been organized into groups and begin working on a structured activity. You may find yourself redesigning an activity on the spot if it seems to be too long, short, simple, or complex for a particular situation. Altering a training design to fit the time of day and the mood of your participants helps to keep the energy level of your training group up and active. Redesigning also adds interest and fun. Go with what is happening in the classroom if it meets your training goals. If an activity or exercise yields an unexpected surprise or draws an unusual response from your participants, make a training moment happen by weaving that surprise response into what you are trying to achieve educationally. The ability to be flexible within the design of a planned activity adds energy to the exercise for both you and your participants. Here are some other guidelines for sustaining group energy.

1. ***Keep the activity moving.*** Don't slow things down by speaking very slowly, endlessly recording participants' contributions on flip charts, or letting a discussion drag on too long.

> Usually, more energy is generated when participants have to complete an activity within a specific time. Keep time frames short and move things along at a brisk pace.

2. ***Challenge the participants.*** There is more energy when activities create a moderate level of tension. If tasks are a snap, participants will get lethargic. Emphasize the importance of a challenging activity and encourage participants to really think about their answers or try out new behaviors.

> Say, "Now, I've got a tough role-playing situation for you. After trying it out here within your training group, you'll be prepared for anything that might happen back home."

3. ***Reinforce participants for their involvement in the activity.*** Show interest in the participants as they engage in the activity. Don't stand off or busy yourself with other things. Give the impression that you are really interested in how they are doing and praise success.

> Say, "I'm really impressed at the way you're going about this task. You're off to a great start!"

4. ***Build physical movement into the activity.*** Have participants move their chair, stand up, or use their entire body during the activity as a way to wake them up.

> Say, "Since you've been sitting for a long time, how about doing the next segment standing up? I'd like each trio to get up and find a spot in the room to discuss the next question."

5. *Let your enthusiasm show.* Genuine feelings of excitement and enjoyment about an activity will inspire like emotions in the participants. Your high energy level can lift up the energy level of the entire group.

> Say, "I can't wait to see how you'll do on the next part of this activity. I think that you're really going to like it."

Behaviors that energize participants can be easily woven into your facilitation style. Once your active training designs are joined with these behaviors, you'll become both effective and believable as you reinforce participant involvement. Using these behaviors in the classroom will help you to accomplish your educational objectives while maintaining high levels of energy and interest in your planned activities.

Processing the Activity

When an activity has concluded, it's quite important for participants to process it—that is, to discuss any feelings that the activity elicited and to share their final reflections and insights. Processing questions help to complete the learning cycle by collating information gathered by the participants during the activity and applying that information within the context of the subject of the training program. Here are some tips to help you facilitate the processing portion of an activity.

1. *Ask relevant questions.* Often, trainers think they are processing activities merely by asking participants questions such as "Did you like the activity?" or "Was it worthwhile?" Following are some examples of processing questions that encourage participants to go beyond simple answers and invite responses related to training goals. Be careful, however, not to ask too many processing questions at once. Usually one to three questions are all a group can handle at a time.

- How did you go about doing this activity?
- What were your concerns?
- On a scale from one to ten, how well did you think you did on this activity? What went well and what needs improvement?
- What helpful and not so helpful behaviors occurred in your group while you were doing this activity?
- Who else had the same experience? A different experience?
- What conclusions can you draw from this activity?
- How did this experience apply to your work situation?
- What struck you while doing this activity?
- What do you understand better about yourself or your group as a result of this exercise?

- What skills can you transfer from this activity to your own work or home environment?
- As a result of this activity, what would you like to change?

2. ***Carefully structure the first processing experiences.*** A high percentage of activities invite processing in an active training program. Knowing this, it makes sense to train your participants to process activities in the early phases of the program. The first time you process an activity with a group, ask only one or two simple questions and keep the discussion time brief. It is probably a good idea to direct the processing as well. For example, you might present a question and then go around the group, obtaining a short response from everyone. Later on, less direction will be necessary.

> One way to structure the processing of an activity is to use incomplete sentence stems. Say, "One thing I thought was worthwhile about this activity was . . . "

3. ***Observe how participants react during the processing.*** The most valuable and productive processing occurs when all participants feel comfortable expressing themselves. If participants begin to give responses that are personally critical of other members of the group, step in by modeling behaviorally specific information and deal with any personal confrontation in a positive manner. Through your own behavior, you can help the group to establish an open forum that promotes the expression of personal views without personal criticisms.

> Say, "I didn't perceive Mark as being as hostile in this role play as some of you are suggesting. What I heard was a loud voice and some pointed feedback to the employee. I imagine that you were very annoyed with his procrastination. Is that true, Mark?"

4. ***Assist a subgroup that is having trouble processing an activity.*** If you have asked subgroups to process an activity and one group finishes well before the time you have allotted expires, it's likely that they have experienced difficulty processing and have wrapped up their reactions too quickly, without probing below the surface. You can help them take a more in-depth look at the implications of an activity by asking them to share with you what they have discussed and then extending the discussion by probing further.

> Say, "I see that your group has finished. Would you mind if I join in for a while? Tell me what some of your thoughts were."

5. ***Keep your own reactions to yourself until after you've heard from the participants.*** Let the participants know that you respect them for their opinions. The processing time is primarily their opportunity to discover what can be learned from the activity. Your insights may be welcomed, but save them for the end.

> Say, "I noticed a number of interesting behaviors watching this project team at work. But before I mention them, let me hear your reactions."

TEAM LEARNING

It is one thing to place participants in groups for short, structured activities. It is another thing to place them in teams for longer periods of time. For example, you might decide to form permanent teams that last throughout the life of a training program. Or you might use teams extensively but change their membership a few times during the class. You might even form teams that have assignments beyond the boundaries of the training room.

Team learning has many benefits. Participants develop a bond with their learning teammates that may motivate the team to sustain collaborative learning activity through complex, challenging assignments. Further, participants in learning teams are willing to accept greater responsibility for their own development precisely because they have a sense of ownership and social support, which is often lacking in short-term groups. However, team learning also has its drawbacks. Chief among them is the fact that the trainer has less instructional control than when using short-term groups.

Have any of these things ever happened to you when you have been in learning teams and/or used them in your training?

- *Confusion:* Team members don't know what to do because they didn't understand or follow the directions.

- *Tangents:* Team members don't stick to the topic and get off task.

- *Unequal participation:* Some team members dominate; some remain quiet.

- *One-way communication:* Team members don't listen or respond to each other.

- *No division of labor:* Some team members don't pull their own weight, let the team down, and are not dependable.

- *Superficiality:* The team is done before you know it, breezing through the assignment in the fastest way possible and staying on the surface rather than digging below it.

Chances are you have experienced nearly all of these problems. When they happen, participants and trainers alike get turned off to team learning. What can be done?

Composing Learning Teams

The first consideration in promoting team learning is the size and composition of the teams. In my experience, teams can range from two to six members and be productive. Small teams work faster and can manage and coordinate their work with greater ease. Teams that are larger than six members have the advantage of greater knowledge, skill, and perspectives. They can cope with larger projects and can also cover for missing or slack members. But large teams often get bogged down in group process issues that prevent them from moving forward. They are difficult to organize and it can be especially difficult to pull the work of a large team together. If you decide to use large teams, realize that they need more structure, more formal meetings, and clearer roles for each member than small teams.

There are few hard-and-fast rules about composing learning teams. Any of the following can be considered:

- *Random assignment:* Form teams arbitrarily (for example, counting off or grouping by insignificant criteria such as birthday or first initial). This randomness often gives participants the sense that they are expected to work with everybody.

- *Diversity:* Form teams by deliberately varying the background, job function, gender, age, or style characteristics of its members. Diverse teams take longer to get started but often succeed in the long run because of the richness of their resources.

- *Homogeneity:* Form teams by assigning members with equivalent job experience, knowledge, or skill. Homogeneous teams organize themselves quickly and obtain immediate results.

- *Prior acquaintance:* Form teams by keeping together people who have worked with each other previously. Participants tend to be comfortable with each other and may have team skills that will transfer to the new situation.

Building Learning Teams

Once learning teams have been formed, it's probably a good idea to have them experience some initial team-building activities such as "Predictions" (see Figure 3–3), "TV Commercial" (see Figure 3–4), and "Group Résumé" (see Figure 3–5). Such activities help teams to get to know each other rapidly and build a degree of team cohesion early.

Since the teams will be working together for some time, the next order of business is to set expectations and ground rules. One way to begin this process is to ask the teams to write a brief vision statement that expresses their hopes for what the team learning experience will be like. You might want to start off by asking individual team members to list potential components of the vision statement using the format shown in Figure 14–1.

Next, ask team members to share their lists, combine ideas, and formulate a brief vision statement that will focus the learning team's efforts.

Besides asking teams to set their own expectations, you might want to set some trainer expectations as well. One of the best ways to do this is to demonstrate how an effective learning team functions. If you can, make a brief video

---

FIGURE 14–1. HOW I'D LIKE OUR TEAM TO BE

What do you hope your learning team experience will be like? Jot a few wishes down in the spaces below:

How I'd Like Our Team to Be . . .

_____

_____

_____

_____

_____

_____

---

that shows an effective learning team in action. Or invite a small group of participants to role-play an effective team. During their role-playing demonstration, either join the group and model successful facilitation behaviors or coach the group as they struggle to perform a team learning task.

Setting specific ground rules helps learning teams to concretize how they must function in order to reach their goals. You can ask teams to brainstorm potential ground rules or provide them with a checklist such as the one found in Figure 14–2.

FIGURE 14–2. OUR GROUND RULES

Below are ground rules that are helpful to learning teams. Check the four most important to you.

_____ Start on time with everyone present.

_____ Get to know members who are "different" from you.

_____ Let others finish without interrupting them.

_____ Be brief and to the point.

_____ Be sensitive to gender, race, and ethnicity.

_____ Be prepared.

_____ Give everyone a chance to speak.

_____ Share the workload.

_____ Rotate facilitating and other responsibilities.

_____ Reach decisions by consensus.

_____ Make sure that team meetings are "processed" from time to time.

If teams are going to be effective, some crucial jobs have to be done. If no one does them, the teams will drift aimlessly without achieving much. To make this point, you might want to share a well-circulated story:

> A team had four members called **Everybody, Somebody, Anybody,** and **Nobody.** There was an important job to be done. **Everybody** was sure that **Somebody** would do it. **Anybody** could have done it, but **Nobody** did it. **Somebody** got angry about that because it was **Everybody's** job. **Everybody** thought **Anybody** could do it but **Nobody** realized that **Everybody** wouldn't do it. It ended up that **Everybody** blamed **Somebody** when **Nobody** did what **Anybody** could have done.

Then ask teams to consider assigning themselves (preferably on a rotating basis) some of these important jobs:

- *Facilitator:* facilitates learning team sessions
- *Timekeeper:* allocates and monitors time needed and spent
- *Secretary or note taker:* keeps a record of ideas, conclusions, and achievements
- *Checker:* sees if all members are doing what they are supposed to
- *Investigator:* finds things out and brings information back to the team

Team building is not complete without promoting an awareness of group process from the beginning. Teams that go about their business without ever reflecting on how well they are doing eventually flounder. Ask learning teams to discuss their progress from the outset to build the kind of awareness that keeps the team from going off the deep end. Point out that all teams have problems and that if they are not brought to the surface, they won't go away.

Use any of the following processes:

- *Helpful versus unhelpful:* What behaviors have we used thus far that are helpful? What behaviors are unhelpful?
- *In hindsight:* If we had a chance to do that over again, what should we do?
- *What's going right or wrong?* What's going right in the team? What's going wrong?
- *Stop, start, continue:* What should we stop doing? Start doing? Continue doing?

Involving Participants in Team Learning

Whether your learning teams are small or large, it is crucial to structure team learning when it is first introduced into a training program. Use short, collaborative activities such as those suggested in Chapter Five:

- ***Study group:*** Give teams some learning material and ask them to explain it to one another.

- ***Information search:*** Give teams some questions and provide learning material that contains the answers. Have them find the answers.

- ***Group inquiry:*** Give teams learning material to study. Ask them to put a question mark next to or highlight anything they don't understand.

- ***Jigsaw learning:*** Give different learning material to different members. Ask them to study the material and teach it to one another.

- ***Learning tournament:*** Give teams material to master in preparation for interteam competition.

As learning teams become oriented to team learning and show signs of taking responsibility for their own learning, you can begin to give them tasks that are less structured. For example, you might provide a list of questions that teams investigate through reading, interviewing, and observing between training sessions. Here are some questions given to learning teams in a training program on team development:

1. Types of teams: What types of teams exist in the workplace? How are they structured?

2. Goal setting: How should teams set and clarify goals?

3. Tools: What group process tools exist for generating ideas, diagnosing problems, strategizing, planning projects, and making decisions?

4. Conflict management: What strategies exist for managing conflict in teams?

5. Role division: What roles are needed in teams? What leadership and facilitation skills are critical? How do teams share responsibility and promote individual accountability?

6. Team development: What stages do teams go through and what helps them move from stage to stage?

Or you might ask learning teams to do some collaborative problem solving, as in the following example.

EXAMPLE: In a course on process mapping, teams were given the following assignment:

As a group, figure out how to do a process map of the current ordering process in your organization. Then develop a new process and map it.

Consider giving learning teams the responsibility of preparing and teaching a training module.

EXAMPLE: In a course on creative thinking, individual teams were given the following training assignments:

1. Teach others four different kinds of brainstorming techniques.
2. Teach others about "reframing" and "perspective shifting."
3. Teach others how to use "mind mapping" to create novel solutions.

Finally, you might want to devise team self-study materials and form self-directed learning teams, mentioned in "The Delivery of Active Training" in Part One of this book. This represents a new way to deliver training that is convenient and cost-effective. The theory is that if organizations allow work teams to manage their own work, why not challenge trainers to have teams manage their own training. If you take up this challenge, keep the following in mind:

- It requires skill and commitment to learn in this mode. Train participants how to function in a self-directed learning team before putting them on their own.
- Do a trial run, directing the team at first and then relinquishing control.
- Have the team either elect a facilitator or decide to take turns.
- Serve as a "help desk" throughout the learning team's activities.
- Monitor and check what's happening so that you can provide any necessary support.

WORKSHEET

FACILITATING STRUCTURED ACTIVITIES AND PROMOTING TEAM LEARNING

Evaluate your effectiveness at facilitating a structured activity by responding to these questions the next time you are training. If you believe that the activity fell short of your expectations in any of the categories listed, work to improve those areas the next time you present the same exercise to another training group.

1. **Motivation**
   a. Did you give the participants an overview of the activity before starting?
   b. Did you explain why you were doing the activity?
   c. Did you show how the activity connects with the other activities that preceded it?

2. **Directions**
   a. Did you speak slowly and/or provide visual backup?
   b. Were the instructions understandable?
   c. If appropriate, was the activity demonstrated?

3. **Group Process**
   a. Did you divide participants into subgroups before giving further directions?
   b. Were changes in groupings managed smoothly?
   c. Did you keep idle groups busy?

4. **Energy**
   a. Did the design move at a good pace?
   b. Was there something challenging about the activity?
   c. Were participants reinforced for their involvement?

5. **Processing**
   a. Were the processing questions related to your training goals?
   b. Were participants' reactions discussed before your own?
   c. Was the activity tied into the overall learning goals for the course?

PROMOTING TEAM LEARNING

Evaluate your effectiveness at promoting team learning by responding to the following questions the next time you use this training approach.

1. **Composing Teams**
   a. Did you keep the teams as small as possible?
   b. How did you compose the teams?
      • Random assignment
      • Diversity
      • Homogeneity
      • Prior acquaintance

WORKSHEET continued

---

2. **Building Teams**

   a. Did you use initial team-building exercises to break the ice?

   b. Did you invite teams to build a vision statement?

   c. Did you clarify your own expectations, preferably by demonstration and coaching?

   d. Did you invite teams to create ground rules and job responsibilities?

   e. Did you promote awareness of group process issues early on?

3. **Involving Participants in Team Learning**

   a. Did you use short, collaborative activities to introduce team learning?

   b. Did you lessen structure as teams became more mature and give them greater control over their own learning?

◆　◆　◆

Chapter Fifteen

Concluding and Evaluating an Active Training Program

Some trainers teach until the last moments of a program and then conclude by passing out an evaluation sheet to be filled out by the participants. An active training program should not end in such an impersonal and noneducational manner. Don't settle for an ordinary conclusion; you can take many positive actions to bring your program to a meaningful close.

One of the many possible options is to leave plenty of time at the end of your program for reviewing *program content.* Another alternative is to invite participants to express any lingering *questions and concerns* about the course content. A third possibility is to engage them in some form of *self-assessment* of what they now know, what they now can do, and what attitudes they now hold. A fourth course of action is to focus the group on *back-on-the-job application.* A fifth approach is to provide an opportunity for participants to express their *sentiments* toward each other.

In this chapter, we will consider each of these steps. In addition, we will look at how you can build evaluation activities into the end of the program and also how you can obtain evaluative feedback during the program and several weeks after it.

REVIEWING PROGRAM CONTENT

Reviewing the program with participants can take many forms. On the simplest level, you can ask them to *recall* the information and ideas that have been covered. If the program contained several experiential activities, you could encourage the participants to *reminisce* about what they've been through together. You might also request that they *rehearse* one more time the skills they've learned. Finally, you could call upon them to *reconsider* their opinions about the training topic. Here are some tips on reviewing program content from these different angles.

1. **Recall.** Use games, exercises, quizzes, or tests that challenge participants to recall facts, concepts, and procedures they have learned. If you wish, use the format of a TV game show such as "Jeopardy," "College Bowl," or "Wheel of Fortune." You might allow a "study period" in which participants prepare for recall exercises individually or in groups. Utilize team competition to energize the review process.

   EXAMPLE: In advance of her final class, a trainer prepared a set of questions and their corresponding answers, putting each on a separate index card. The questions referred to previously covered material. After shuffling all the cards together, the trainer dealt one card to each person, then told the participants to walk around and match questions with answers. When the process was completed, the questions were read aloud, one at a time, for the group to answer. After each group response, the holder of the answer card would corroborate the answer or disagree with it.

2. **Reminisce.** Gather the group together to review memorable experiences that occurred in the training program. Ask them to share how these experiences affected them personally and professionally. Use an approach such as a fishbowl discussion or mental imagery exercise to add punch to the reminiscing.

   EXAMPLE: At the end of a five-day team-building program, participants were given a blank sheet of paper and told that it was time for their "final exam." The challenge was to write down, in order, the many activities they had experienced during the week. After each participant had finished, answers were compared until the correct list was jointly achieved. With the list in hand, participants were asked to reminisce about these experiences, recalling moments of fun, cooperation, and insight. The discussion was an intimate exchange that brought a wonderful, emotional closure to a special week.

3. **Rehearse.** Arrange an opportunity for participants to demonstrate all the skills they have learned in one final performance. Use methods such as role playing, simulations, written tasks, or projects as vehicles for rehearsing these skills.

   EXAMPLE: For a training program in family therapy techniques, four groups were each assigned a family type based on the model of family functioning taught by the trainer. Each group was given the task of role-playing a family of the type assigned to it coming to its first therapy session. The role play was to include a demonstration of techniques for beginning therapy with such a family. This assignment had the virtue of integrating all the cognitive and behavioral learning featured in the training program. The four therapy sessions created a powerful ending to the program.

4. ***Reconsider.*** At a program's conclusion, participants may have altered their views about many of the topics examined during the program. It can be useful, therefore, to allow time to discuss these shifts in perception. Use methods such as panel or case study discussions to allow participants to reconsider their opinions and attitudes.

EXAMPLE: At the beginning of a workshop on delegation skills, managers were asked to write down on index cards one of their fears about delegating responsibilities to their employees. The cards were then passed around the group. When participants read an item that was true for them, they were asked to make a checkmark in the upper right-hand corner of the card. After circulating, each card was returned to its originator. At the end of the workshop, the cards checked most frequently were read aloud. The participants were then asked to reconsider their fears in light of the workshop. A discussion was held using a "call-on-the-next-speaker" format to allow the group to exchange opinions without prompting by the trainer. It was an enlightening way for participants to conclude the workshop.

OBTAINING FINAL QUESTIONS AND CONCERNS

When a program is about to conclude, participants are often reluctant to raise final questions or concerns because they don't want to appear to be delaying the program's end. This is unfortunate, since identifying these questions and concerns is a valuable closing exercise *even if there is little time left*. Leaving with some unanswered questions and concerns invites further reflection by participants after the program is over. Here are some techniques for your consideration.

1. Prepare a list of questions you would like the participants to take away with them. Clarify each question and then, if there is time, ask participants to select a few they want discussed before the program ends.

EXAMPLE: At the end of a seminar on the Myers-Briggs Type Indicator, the trainer distributed a final handout asking participants in what ways each of the people in the following pairs might differ when interacting with the other:

Teacher	Learner
Salesperson	Buyer
Therapist	Client
Manager	Employee
Paid administrator	Board president

2. Hold a final question-and-answer period. Hand out blank index cards and request that each participant write down a question. Then answer as many of these questions as time permits.

EXAMPLE: Using this approach, a trainer received the following questions at the end of a train-the-trainer program:

- "How much should I charge for one day of training?"
- "How can I handle questions about how qualified I am to conduct the training?"
- "How do I get participants to be comfortable with active learning processes when they are only familiar with a passive approach?"
- "How can you give directions without sounding like a teacher or boss?"
- "What do I do when no one wants to volunteer for a role-playing activity?"
- "Is there any way to perk up a group that is extremely tired?"

3. Write the following on a flip chart: "One thing that still concerns me about [fill in the training topic] is . . ." Using a go-around format, ask each participant to complete the sentence. (Encourage participants to pass if they do not have something to share at that moment). Listen to the concerns without response.

EXAMPLE: At the end of a program on conflict management, participants supplied the following endings to the sentence stem "One thing that still concerns me is . . ."

How to handle a really aggressive person

Whether I can listen effectively in the heat of a conflict

What to do if there is a complete stalemate

How to communicate that my intentions are cooperative

Using role reversal techniques; they seem silly

How to pick the right time to confront someone

4. Break participants into small groups and ask each group to record on newsprint their final questions and concerns. Display the items and request a volunteer to edit them into a final class list. Send the list to participants after the program is over.

EXAMPLE: Secretaries attending a half-day automated purchasing program split into groups of four and came up with several remaining questions. The secretaries then edited their subgroup contributions into this final list of questions:

- Can I still order supplies if the automated system is down?

- Where can I find a list of the item numbers for both stock and nonstock supplies?

- Who else besides my manager can approve entries for my department's cost code?

- What if the warehouse sends me the wrong supplies? How do I make sure that my department isn't charged for orders that are filled incorrectly?

- What if I have problems when I try using the system for the first time? Is there someone I can call for help?

5. Hand out two index cards. Ask each participant to complete the following sentences:

Card 1: I still have a question about _____.

Card 2: I can answer a question about _____.

Create subgroups and have each subgroup select the most pertinent question and the most interesting answer from the cards of its group members. Then ask each subgroup to report the question it has selected. Determine if anyone in the full group can answer the question. If not, as the trainer, you should respond. Also, ask each subgroup to report the answer it has selected. Have the subgroup share it with the rest of the class.

EXAMPLE: Subgroups in a session on coping with change selected the following questions and answers:

Questions
I still have a question about . . .

- How to cope with my fears about all the new technology involved with my job

- What I can do to reduce the stress of adjusting to a new manager

- How to determine what I can control or influence and what I can't

Answers
I can answer a question about . . .

- The difference between limiting beliefs and empowering beliefs

- Why people resist change

- How to use change to your advantage

PROMOTING SELF-ASSESSMENT

If your program has been meaningful to participants, they have undergone some degree of affective behavioral and cognitive change. A fitting way to end a program is to engage participants in activities that allow them to evaluate their progress. The following suggestions may assist you in this process.

1. Ask participants to complete a questionnaire or test that provides feedback about their current functioning in areas related to the training.

   EXAMPLE: At both the beginning and the end of a bank platform training program, participants were given a self-scoring test on consumer lending products, business accounts, individual retirement accounts, and brokerage. Each participant was then asked to evaluate his or her results and assess areas of strength and weakness.

2. Design a way for fellow participants to give each other feedback and then ask them each to develop a personal profile based on the feedback they receive.

   EXAMPLE: In a team-building program, participants filled out an index card for each member of their work team describing their reactions toward this individual. Each participant was then given all the feedback cards commenting on her or his performance and asked to summarize the data and present the summary back to the team for clarification.

3. Create one or more statements that assess participant change. Examples might include the following:

   - I have changed my views about _____ as a result of this training session.
   - I have improved my skills in _____.
   - I have learned new information and concepts.

   Ask the participants to stand in the back of the training room, clearing away the chairs or desks by moving them to one side. Create a rating scale from 1 through 5 in the front of the room by using the blackboard or posting numbers on the wall. Explain that a statement will be read to the class and that after hearing each one, participants should stand in front of the rating number that best matches their self-assessment. Use the following scale:

   1 = strongly disagree

   2 = disagree

   3 = not sure

   4 = agree

   5 = strongly agree

As each statement is read, participants should move to the place in the room that best matches their self-assessment. Encourage participants to assess themselves realistically. Point out that several factors might create little or no change, such as previous knowledge or skill level and the need for more practice or time. After lines form in front of the various positions, invite some participants to share why they have chosen that rating. Underscore their honesty.

EXAMPLE: At the end of a session on telephone skills, the trainer prepared the following statements and showed them one at a time to the group:

- I have learned new information about how to deal with irate customers.
- I have changed my views about the importance of how I answer the telephone.
- I have improved my listening skills.
- I have learned better ways of phrasing negative statements.
- I understand that the telephone is not an interruption but an important part of my job.
- I know the appropriate procedure for transferring a call.

Participants were asked to assess themselves according to the instructions given previously.

4. Ask participants to write a short essay in response to the question, "How do you see yourself now as a result of this program?" Invite volunteers to read their essays or have participants exchange essays in small groups.

EXAMPLE: At the end of a workshop on parenting adolescents, one parent shared the following:

I am learning not to take my son's behavior so personally and not to blame myself for the unsettled nature of our relationship. He's going through a lot and so am I and that's to be expected. I think I'm now able to do a better job at sticking to the issue when we have conflicts and not getting sidetracked. I need to develop fewer but well-chosen rules with clear, enforceable consequences. Perhaps I need to give up control over little things and accept behaviors that don't make a big difference at this stage such as what he eats for breakfast. I think I can make sure that my firmness doesn't cause him to "lose face." Finally, I now can share my feelings and opinions with him without lecturing or sermonizing. Once I started doing that, it was easier for us to talk. I think I've come a long way.

5. At the beginning of a training session, ask participants to write down how they hope to be able to use the training on the job. Here are some ways to structure this exercise:

- Ask participants to list their own learning goals for the session.

- Ask participants to list recent successes and failures.

- Ask participants to list ongoing problems, assignments, or issues in their work.

Set aside some time periodically to allow participants to read their initial statement and consider what value the training has had for them thus far. At the end of the session, ask participants to assess whether their investment of time and effort in the training has been worthwhile in light of their initial comments. If you wish, also ask participants to assign a percentage that describes their return on investment (ROI) in the training. For example, a participant might indicate that he received a 75 percent ROI.

EXAMPLE: In a training program on presentation skills, participants were asked to list the things they would like to improve in their presentations. A combined list was displayed. Participants wanted to

- Be less "nervous" in the beginning

- Use presentation media more effectively

- Maintain better eye contact with the audience

- Rely less on notes

- Improve their pacing

- Begin with a "bang"

- Speak with less of a monotone

- Stimulate discussion and questions

- End with a strong conclusion

At the end of the program, participants were asked to assess the improvements they had made to determine their ROI.

FOCUSING ON BACK-ON-THE-JOB APPLICATION

In Chapter Nine, you were introduced to several activities—such as discussion of application obstacles, contracting, self-monitoring plans, and action planning—designed to support the transfer of training skills to real-life situations. These are excellent conclusions to a program because participants leave with an eye to the future. Unfortunately, participants are often weary near the end of a training program and are reluctant to participate in such activities. Anticipating this, a trainer can take some steps to get past the obstacle of fatigue.

1. If possible, ask participants to prepare application ideas in advance. This way, you can use the last moments of the program to share plans rather than to create them.

2. Keep these activities brief and move at a quick pace. Don't dwell on your advice to participants. Make your final remarks memorable but to the point.

3. Lend some drama, inspiration, or excitement to the activities by the way you conduct them: bring participants together into a tight group huddle, invite participants to stand up and announce their plans, encourage applause when appropriate, have participants address envelopes to themselves so that contracts can be sent to them later as reminders, or create a buddy system for later support and follow-up.

EXPRESSING FINAL SENTIMENTS

In many training programs, participants develop feelings of closeness for other group members. This is especially true if the participants have met for a long period of time and have taken part in extensive group work. They need to say goodbye to each other and express their appreciation for the support and encouragement they have received during the training program. There are many ways to help facilitate these final sentiments.

1. Assemble participants for a ***group photograph.*** As you are about to take their picture, express your own final sentiments. Then invite one participant at a time to take a final picture of the group. As this is happening, applaud the participant for his or her contributions. Later, send each participant his or her own photograph of the group.

2. Develop an ***artistic product*** that affirms the value of the group and each individual member. Make a group collage, design a group shield, or assemble a booklet with a page devoted to each participant.

3. Create a ***closing circle*** and invite participants to express their final sentiments and share what they learned in the program, the experiences they appreciated, and their future intentions. Encourage participants to comment as the spirit moves them.

4. Symbolically draw the training program to a close by forming a ***web of connections.*** Use a skein of yarn to literally and symbolically connect participants. Begin by asking everyone to stand and form a circle. Start the process by stating briefly what you have experienced as a result of facilitating the training program. Holding onto the end of the yarn, toss the skein to a participant on the other side of the circle. Ask that person to state briefly what she or he has experienced as a result of participating in

the training program. When that participant is finished, the skein is tossed to someone else. Have each participant take a turn at receiving the skein, sharing reflections, and tossing the yarn on, continuing to hold onto his or her piece. The resulting visual is a web of yarn connecting every member of the group.

5. End with a ***touch of humor.*** Have participants design humorous awards for each member or compose symbolic toasts or wills, or present real or imaginary gag gifts.

EVALUATING THE PROGRAM

Although you may want to end the program with one or more of the creative strategies we have just illustrated, it is still important for you to gather data for evaluative purposes. Ideally, you should conduct any evaluation several days after the end of the program. If it is more practical to do it at the last session, try to create a clear separation between the end of the program and the time set aside for filling out any evaluation forms.

Interim Feedback

Actually, evaluation should not wait till the end. You can design your active training program to obtain feedback and evaluation data on an ongoing basis so that you can make adjustments before it is too late. At the least, you should observe the behavior of the participants. Do they smile? Do they seem alert? Involved? Do they ask questions?

Behavioral cues are often good barometers; they can, however, give you incomplete feedback. You could fill in the gaps by guessing how the participants think and feel, but although these guesses might be accurate, it is more likely that they will be influenced by your fears (if you are anxious) or your ego (if you are too assured). Verifying your impressions is the only way to obtain accurate and detailed feedback.

There are two major ways other than observation to obtain ongoing group feedback: orally and in written reports. Obtaining oral feedback is a challenge. It can be time-consuming and threatening to both the participants and the trainer. Obtaining written feedback is usually quicker and less threatening. However, you will not be able to immediately clarify the information you receive if you want to probe further. Both oral and written feedback activities must be well designed. Here are some of the best techniques.

1. ***Postsession reaction surveys.*** Create brief questionnaires and give them to participants at an appropriate moment. Items can be presented in different formats:

Short Essay

Please respond in writing to the question "What would you suggest to improve the session?"

Checklist

Check the words that describe your reactions to today's session:

_____ Slow-moving

_____ Illuminating

_____ Overwhelming

_____ Fun

_____ Well organized

_____ Inappropriate sentence stems

Complete the sentence beginning "Something I still am confused about is . . ."

Ratings

Use the following scale to rate how valuable you found today's session.

(high)   5   4   3   2   1   *(low)*

Rankings

Rank each module by placing the letter A beside the one that was the most relevant to you, B beside the next most relevant, and C beside the least relevant.

___ module 1

___ module 2

___ module 3

2. **Anonymous remarks.** Write a question on a blank flip-chart sheet or a blackboard, and ask participants to respond to it—on the flip chart, on the board, or on blank index cards—during breaks. Here are some possible questions:

   "What one word best describes your reaction to today's session?"

   "What will you remember from today?"

   "What was the most important thing you learned today?"

3. **Oral survey.** Survey reactions by asking participants to share their feedback on the program out loud. Ask for volunteers to contribute or go around the group if you want to hear from everyone. Here is a good set of questions to pose:

   "What would you like more of tomorrow?"

   "What would you like less of?"

   "What would you like to continue?"

4. **Informal interview.** Casually solicit participant feedback at breaks and at lunch or schedule an evening rap session to discuss participants' feelings about the program in a relaxed manner. Ask questions such as these:

"Was the last segment helpful?"

"Am I relating this material enough to your situation?"

"Was anything unclear?"

"Are we ready to move on to new material?"

5. **Advisory group.** Meet with a small representative group to obtain reactions. If appropriate, ask group members to interview some participants and report their feedback. Use questions similar to those in the list.

Final Assessment

Most trainers subscribe to the model advanced by Donald Kirkpatrick (1994) that there are four levels of evaluation of a training program:

1. *Reaction:* how participants react to the training

2. *Learning:* the knowledge and skills participants obtain from the training

3. *Behavior:* how the training is applied on the job

4. *Results:* what impact the training has on the organization

EXAMPLE: A pharmaceutical company was evaluating the training it was giving to sales representatives. Here are some indicators the company used to evaluate participants' reactions to the training program:

• Participants were satisfied with the training facilities.

• Participants thought that the training program covered the promised objectives.

• Participants said that the trainer encouraged participation and questions.

• Participants wanted more opportunity to role-play during the training program.

Here are some indicators the company used to evaluate participant learning:

• Participants could state the features and benefits of the company's top-selling drugs.

• Participants were able to use clinical studies to reinforce benefits.

• Participants demonstrated how to quickly bridge from their opener to the main topics of the sales call.

• Participants knew the difference between fact questions and priority questions.

Here are some indicators the company used to evaluate on-the-job application:

- Participants described to physicians how the product met a specific, stated physician need.
- Participants established rapport with physicians in their sales calls.
- Participants planned their use of visuals in advance of their appointments.
- Participants used more open questions than closed questions in their sales calls.

Here are some indicators the company used to evaluate business results:

- Participants increased sales each week over a four-week period.
- Physicians reported increased satisfaction with the service received from representatives.
- Participants made more sales calls than in previous weeks.
- Participants' retention increased over the prior year.

A thorough evaluation of your training program might involve all four levels: ***reaction, learning, behavior,*** and ***results.*** Each level of evaluation has value in its own right, but it is the combination of evidence that truly assesses how effective the training has been.

Of course, the most common kind of training evaluation is that of level 1. It is easy, fast, and inexpensive when compared to evaluation efforts at other levels. When your program has ended, you will naturally want to find out if the training met the participants' expectations. Try to obtain a picture of participants' reactions to the training program as a whole as well as a sense of their response to the various parts.

Figure 15–1 presents the kind of form typically used to obtain these data quickly.

FIGURE 15–1. TRAINING EVALUATION QUESTIONNAIRE

Course Title: _____   Date: _____

1. Circle the number that best represents your reaction to the program.

   a. I feel that I will be able to use what I learned.

   (never)   1   2   3   4   5   (often)

   b. The program was presented in an interesting manner.

   (never)   1   2   3   4   5   (often)

   c. The training facilities met my needs.

   (never)   1   2   3   4   5   (often)

FIGURE 15–1. continued

---

    d. The program covered the promised objectives.

       (never)   1   2   3   4   5   (often)

    e. The trainer encouraged participation and questions.

       (never)   1   2   3   4   5   (often)

2. What did you find most useful in the program?

3. What did you find least useful in the program?

4. Is there anything in this program that could be improved?

A less standard way to obtain participants' reactions is to use a semiprojective technique. Provide a blank piece of paper with the following instructions on the top:

> "Imagine that a coworker (or friend) of yours was thinking about attending this program. He or she asked you, 'What has this program been like for you?' How would you respond? Please take the next ten minutes to write your response below."

The beauty of this technique is that you will usually obtain a deeper and more personal response than a questionnaire could elicit. The drawback, of course, is that it is much more difficult to quantify or summarize the results. The following is an example of one person's response to a program on counseling techniques:

> "This program provided me with a different look at what I had been doing. At first, I was bewildered. I was so much into crisis counseling—trying to solve

the problem by applying Band-Aids without too much thought as to how I could help make a difference down the road. I will be different in the future. Now, I have some powerful techniques that, with practice, will remove the rush, the uncertainty, and, yes, the sometimes wishy-washy techniques I have occasionally used. This program helped to refresh a weary soldier!"

Besides finding out how participants viewed the training program, you need to know what attitudes, knowledge, and skills they acquired. Testing whether learning and change have occurred should involve pre- and post-training measures. Be sure to go beyond testing factual recall. See if participants can state the information in their own words, give examples of it, and apply it in a variety of situations. Without this information, it is impossible to determine whether or not the training met its stated objectives.

Don't overlook the value of asking participants directly about what they have learned and how it will be applied. The simplest approach is to use a questionnaire or interview and ask participants such questions as these:

- What tools, skills, or ideas do you now have that you did not have at the beginning of this program?

- What have you learned that you can put to immediate use?

- What have you already practiced outside of class?

- What intentions or plans do you have as a result of the program?

- What do you want to learn next?

If possible, put these questions to participants not only at the end of a training program but also at a follow-up point a few months later. Ask them to report what they have done to implement the training they received. Don't forget to ask them what obstacles they have faced in their implementation efforts. A great idea is to summarize these reports and mail the results back to the participants.

In general, although the self-reports of participants may have value, there is every reason to confirm the changes that have been reported. Post-training performance should be evaluated by testing participants' skills, observing their actual performance back on the job, or obtaining feedback from supervisors or other key informants. A procedure that combines participant self-report and supervisory feedback can be utilized. You might do this by asking participants to fill out a follow-up form at the end of a program that contains statements about how they plan to implement the training (see Figure 15–2). In three to four weeks, send follow-up instructions (see Figure 15–3). Then, at each participant's option, the work statement and a supervisor's follow-up form (see Figure 15–4) can be sent to the participant's supervisor for evaluation.

FIGURE 15–2. WORK STATEMENT FOLLOW-UP FORM

Describe situations in which you plan to apply this material and tell when and *how* you plan to apply it. Be specific.

Course
Outline Implementation Goals (Do not write in this column)

I. _____ Situation:

_____

_____ My plan to apply: A _____

B _____

C _____

II. _____ Situation:

_____

_____ My plan to apply: A _____

B _____

C _____

III. _____ Situation:

_____

_____ My plan to apply: A _____

B _____

C _____

IV. _____ Situation:

_____

_____ My plan to apply: A _____

B _____

C _____

Please address the attached envelope to yourself; it will be returned to you in three to four weeks.

FIGURE 15–3. FOLLOW-UP INSTRUCTIONS

Please review the course content. Then review what you had planned to apply.

You may now place checkmarks in the third column of the work statement. If you were able to apply your plan successfully, check the "A" space. If you were partially able to apply your plan and are still working on the implementation, check "B." If you were not able to apply your plan successfully, check "C" and explain what obstacles stopped your application.

FIGURE 15–3. continued

Obstacles that stopped successful application:

Please feel free to make any additional comments about the workshop or yourself in the space provided below:

FIGURE 15–4. SUPERVISOR'S FOLLOW-UP FORM

[Name] was a participant in a workshop dealing with [subject]. During the last three to four weeks, s/he has attempted to implement the ideas or skills listed on the enclosed sheet labeled Work Statement. Please review what s/he has written. Did you observe any change? You should place checkmarks in the third column of the Work Statement. If you were able to note a change, any change, please check "A." If you were able to note some effort to change, check "B." If you were not able to note a change or an effort to change, check "C."

Were you able to offer your support to this person as s/he attempted to implement actions?

Please feel free to add any additional comments:

Assessing the ROI of training is the most difficult to do. Typically, level 4 evaluation requires surveys, focus groups, strategic interviews, and observation. However, many trainers overlook data that may already exist in the organization. Here are some examples:

- Employee satisfaction surveys

- Organizational and team morale scores

- Number of customer complaints

- Employee retention; lost time

- Sales revenue

- Work flow and efficiency data

- Awards from outside sources

- Operating costs

- Compliance versus violations

- Accuracy

- Consistency

- Product defects

Of course, evidence from these kinds of level 4 data doesn't constitute proof that the training was responsible for organizational results. Unless a carefully designed study is conducted, using experimental and control groups, the possibility exists that other factors could have contributed to the results.

As you consider at what level to evaluate your training program, don't make one-shot decisions. Establish an evaluation program. For example, Jack Phillips (1994) recommends evaluating 100 percent of all programs at level 1, 70 percent at level 2, 50 percent at level 3, and 10 percent at level 4.

As you can see, training evaluation requires the same careful design as the training program it assesses. Attention must be paid to three central decisions:

1. *Focus:* What elements are being evaluated? Data can be gathered concerning any of the following:

   - Participants' reactions

   - Participants' knowledge, skills, and attitudes

   - On-the-job application

   - Organizational results

2. ***Tools:*** What means are used to collect evaluative data? Any of the following can be utilized:

- Questionnaires
- Observation
- Tests
- Reports
- Interviews

3. ***Timing:*** When are data collected? Any of these times are possible:

- Pretraining
- During training
- End of training
- Follow-up period

Finally, it must be said that the evaluation of an active training program is not only about outcome but also about process. Evaluation efforts should address what is happening in a training program as much as whether it is making any difference. Why is process evaluation so important? Quite simply, ***without good records of what happened during a training program, it is not always clear what needs changing if the outcome evaluation is disappointing.*** Try to keep a log of the events in the program, how participants responded, and what your own reactions were as well. Or invite others to watch the proceedings and make observations about the program as it is being experienced. By doing so, you will be an active participant in your program.

WORKSHEET

CONCLUDING AND EVALUATING AN ACTIVE TRAINING PROGRAM

Jot down ideas for concluding your training program under the categories below.

Concluding the program (reviewing program content, obtaining final questions and concerns, promoting self-assessment, focusing on back-on-the-job application, and expressing final sentiments):

_____

_____

_____

_____

_____

_____

_____

_____

_____

_____

_____

Evaluating the program (obtaining ongoing feedback; determining the focus, tools, and timing of evaluation activity; and examining the process of the program):

_____

_____

_____

_____

_____

_____

_____

_____

_____

_____

_____

◆　◆　◆

References

Advanced Consulting Inc. "Boehringer Ingelheim Trains Sales Representatives with CD-ROM." *Advanced Solutions for Training and Education,* June 1997.

Arch, D. *Red Hot Handouts! Taking the Ho Hum Out of Handouts.* Eden Prairie, Minn.: Creative Training Techniques Press, 1996.

Blanchard, K. *Situational Leadership II.* Escondido, Calif.: Blanchard Training & Development, 1997.

Brislin, R. *Intercultural Interactions.* Thousand Oaks, Calif.: Sage, 1986.

Bruner, J. *Toward a Theory of Instruction.* Cambridge, Mass.: Harvard University Press, 1966.

Clark, R. *Developing Technical Training.* Reading, Mass.: Addison-Wesley, 1989.

Eikenberry, K. "Effective Listening: Better Relationships and Improved Results." In M. Silberman (ed.), *20 Active Training Programs.* Vol. 3. San Francisco: Jossey-Bass/Pfeiffer, 1997.

Gilbert, T. *Human Competence: Engineering Worthy Performance—ISPI Tribute Edition.* Washington, D.C.: International Society for Performance Improvement, 1996.

Grinder, M. *Riding the Information Conveyor Belt.* Portland, Oreg.: Metamorphous Press, 1991.

Gupta, K. *Conducting a Mini Needs Assessment.* Alexandria, Va.: American Society for Training and Development, 1996.

Hermann, N. *The Hermann Brain Dominance Inventory.* Lake Lure, N.C.: Hermann International, 1995.

Johnson, D., and Carnes, B. *Making Training Stick.* Eden Prairie, Minn.: Creative Training Techniques International, 1988.

Johnson, D. W., Johnson, R. T., and Smith, K. A. *Active Learning: Cooperation in the College Classroom.* Edina, Minn.: Interaction Book Company, 1991.

Kirkpatrick, D. *Evaluating Training Programs: The Four Levels,* San Francisco: Berrett-Koehler, 1994.

Knowles, M. *The Adult Learner: A Neglected Species.* Houston: Gulf, 1990.

Kruse, K. "Exploring the Internet: How to Understand and Benefit from the Information Super Highway." In M. Silberman (ed.), *20 Active Training Programs.* Vol. 3. San Francisco: Jossey-Bass/Pfeiffer, 1997.

MacKenzie, R. A. *The Time Trap.* New York: AMACOM, 1972.

Malouf, D. *How to Create and Deliver a Dynamic Presentation.* North Wollongong, Australia: Dougmal Training Systems, 1992.

Maslow, A. *Toward a Psychology of Being.* New York: Litton Educational Publishing, 1968.

Mayo, G., and DuBois, P. *The Complete Book of Training: Theory, Principles, and Techniques.* San Francisco: Jossey-Bass/Pfeiffer, 1987.

McKeachie, W. *Teaching Tips: A Guidebook for the Beginning College Instructor.* Lexington, Mass.: Heath, 1986.

Mosley, D. C., Megginson, L. C., and Pietri, P. H. Jr. *Supervisory Management.* Cincinnati: South-Western, 1985.

Mucciolo, T., and Mucciolo, R. *Purpose, Movement, Color: A Strategy for Effective Presentations.* New York: MediaNet, 1994.

Mundhenk, L. "Developing Career Resilience: New Career-Management Strategies for the Twenty-First Century." In M. Silberman (ed.), *20 Active Training Programs.* Vol. 3. Jossey-Bass/Pfeiffer, 1997.

Phillips, J. (ed.). *In Action: Measuring Return on Investment.* Alexandria, Va.: American Society for Training and Development, 1994.

Pike, R. *Creative Training Techniques Handbook.* Minneapolis, Minn.: Lakewood, 1994.

Piskurich, G. "Reconsidering the Promise of Satellites as a Distance Learning Technology." *Performance Improvement,* 1997, *36,* 19–23.

Pollio, H. R. *What Participants Think About and Do in College Lecture Classes.* Teaching-Learning Issues no. 53. Knoxville: Learning Research Center, University of Tennessee, 1984.

Rickard, H., Rogers, R., Ellis, N., and Beidleman, W. "Some Retention, but Not Enough." *Teaching of Psychology,* 1988, *15,* 151–152.

Ruhl, K., Hughes, C., and Schloss, P. "Using the Pause Procedure to Enhance Lecture Recall." *Instructor Education and Special Education,* 1987, *10*(1), 14–18.

Schroeder, C. "New Participants—New Learning Styles." *Change,* Sept.–Oct. 1993, pp. 21–26.

Silberman, M. "Force Field Analysis: A Suggested Training Design." In E. Stivers and S. Whelan (eds.), *Lewin's Legacy.* New York: Springer-Verlag, 1986.

Silberman, M. "Coaching and Counseling: Two Ways to Guide Employees." In M. Silberman (ed.), *20 Active Training Programs.* Vol. 1. San Francisco: Jossey-Bass/Pfeiffer, 1992a.

Silberman, M. "Negotiating to Win/Win: Conflict Resolution in Personal and Professional Relationships." In M. Silberman (ed.), *20 Active Training Programs.* Vol. 1. San Francisco: Jossey-Bass/Pfeiffer, 1992b.

Simmerman, S. "Square Wheels: A Powerful Discussion Tool on Organizational Change." In M. Silberman (ed.), *The 1998 Team and Organization Development Sourcebook.* New York: McGraw-Hill, 1998.

Simon, S., Howe, L. W., and Kirschenbaum, H. *Values Clarification.* New York: Dodd, Mead, 1978.

Steadham, S. V. "Learning to Select a Needs Assessment Strategy." *Training and Development Journal,* 1980, *30,* 56–61.

Stieber, W. "Proactive Project Management: How to Be in Charge from Beginning to End." In M. Silberman (ed.), *20 Active Training Programs.* Vol. 1. San Francisco: Jossey-Bass/Pfeiffer, 1992.

Thiagarajan, S. "Instant Analysis." *Training and Development Journal,* June 1989, pp. 14–16.

Training. "Industry Report 1997." October 1997, p. 56.

Trifiletti, D., and Alexandri, R. "Consultative Selling: How to Build Partnerships in Business Relationships." In M. Silberman (ed.), *20 Active Training Programs.* Vol. 2. San Francisco: Jossey-Bass/Pfeiffer, 1994.

University of Wisconsin. *Proceedings, 12th Annual Conference on Distance Teaching and Learning: Designing for Active Learning.* Madison: University of Wisconsin, 1996.

Vella, J. *Learning to Listen, Learning to Teach.* San Francisco: Jossey-Bass, 1994.

Zemke, R., and Zemke, S. "30 Things We Know for Sure About Adult Learning." *Training,* June 1981.

Index to Case Examples

Career Development

Change Management

Child Care

Coaching and Counseling Skills

Communication Skills

Computer Training

Conflict Management

Creative Thinking

Cultural Diversity

Customer Service

Disabilities

Family Education and Therapy

Measurement and Testing

Meeting Management

Motivation

Performance Appraisals

Presentation Skills

Problem Solving

Project Management

Purchasing

Real Estate

Sales

Sexual Harassment

Total Quality

Total Quality Tools, 85

Process Mapping, 279

Train-the-Trainer

Precourse Assignment, 33

Adult Learning Needs, 77

Ways to Obtain Participation Learning Tournament, 112

Problem Participants Exercise, 135

Peer Observation, 188

Participant Final Questions and Answers, 286

Index

About the Author

Dr. Mel Silberman is professor of adult and organizational development at Temple University. He received his A.B. degree in sociology from Brandeis University and his M.A. and Ph.D. degrees from the University of Chicago in educational psychology.

Silberman has an international reputation in the field of active learning. He is president of Active Training (26 Linden Lane, Princeton, New Jersey 08540), a provider of a wide range of services that develop instructional skills in any subject matter. He has conducted seminars in active training techniques for hundreds of corporate and governmental organizations throughout the world. A recent sample includes Bristol-Myers Squibb, Texas Instruments, ARCO Chemical, Merrill Lynch, Automated Data Processing, J.P. Morgan, Johnson & Johnson, the U.S. Army, the Naval Center for Acquisition Training, The World Bank, Hospital of the University of Pennsylvania, and Franklin Covey.

A popular presenter at training conferences, Silberman has appeared before audiences at the American Society for Training and Development, the International Society for Performance Improvement, the North American Simulation and Gaming Association, and *Training* magazine.

Silberman is the author or editor of eighteen books. The first edition of this book—*Active Training: A Handbook of Techniques, Designs, Case Examples, and Tips* (Lexington Books, 1990)—is one of the most widely read texts in the field of training and development. A field guide to accompany *Active Training* is entitled *101 Ways to Make Training Active* (Jossey-Bass/Pfeiffer, 1995). It is also a best-selling book. In addition, he is the editor of *20 Active Training Programs*, Volume 1 (Jossey-Bass/Pfeiffer, 1992), *20 Active Training Programs*, Volume 2 (Jossey-Bass/Pfeiffer, 1994), and *20 Active Training Programs*, Volume 3

(Jossey-Bass/Pfeiffer, 1997). These are collections of one-day workshops utilizing active training techniques.

Silberman can be contacted at 800–924–8157 or mel@activetraining.com. His Web site can be visited at www.activetraining.com.

Carol Auerbach assisted with *Active Training.* Auerbach is an independent training consultant as well as an adjunct faculty member at Baltimore County's Management Development Institute. She also consults for Technology Service Solutions, a subsidiary of IBM. She is a graduate of Duke University and Temple University.

Auerbach was formerly training and development specialist for Mellon Bank and CIGNA Corporation. She can be contacted at 609 Kingston Road, Baltimore, Maryland 21212, 410–377–9257, or at cauerbach@aol.com.